PRAISE FOR JOHN D. NESBITT

"Nesbitt is a true artist."

—*WESTERN AMERICAN LITERATURE*

"More books from this talented pen would be most welcome."

—*LIBRARY JOURNAL*

"Nesbitt demonstrates himself a skilled wrangler of detail and character."

—*PUBLISHERS WEEKLY*

"...certainly the genre can't ask for a better portent than a Western written by John Nesbitt."

—*ROUNDUP MAGAZINE*

"Nesbitt is always entertaining..."

—*BOOKLIST*

"John Nesbitt knows working cowboys and ranch life well enough for you to chew the dirt with his characters..."

—*TRUE WEST MAGAZINE*

BOY FROM THE COUNTRY

BOY FROM THE COUNTRY

JOHN D. NESBITT

WOLFPACK
PUBLISHING
— EST 2013 —

Boy from the Country
Kindle Edition
Copyright © 2024 by John D. Nesbitt

Wolfpack Publishing
1707 E. Diana Street
Tampa, FL 33610

www.wolfpackpublishing.com

This book is a work of fiction. References to historical events, real people, or real places are used fictitiously. Any similarity to real persons, living or dead, is purely coincidental and not intended by the author.

All brand names and product names used in this book are trademarks, registered trademarks, or trade names of their respective holders. Wolfpack Publishing is not associated with any product or vendor in this book.

Editing by My Brother's Editor

Paperback ISBN 979-8-89567-190-0
Ebook ISBN 979-8-89567-189-4
LCCN 2024948224

I present this work in appreciation for all of the fine educators I met along the way, with special mention of Mrs. Brose and Mr. Burchfield in Colusa, Mrs. McNolty in Gridley, Mr. Penner and Mrs. Walker in Orland, Mr. Beatty at Chico State, Mr. Anderson at UCLA, Mrs. Needham and Mr. Woodress at UC Davis, and Guido Smith at Eastern Wyoming College. There were many others, but these were the people who encouraged me and inspired me the most.

PREFACE

During the many years that I pondered this work, I came to call it a spiritual autobiography, a term I borrowed with some irony from an interpretation of *Moll Flanders* and *Robinson Crusoe*. What is now called a memoir is a selective autobiography, narrowing to some aspect of the author's experience. This story is about a boy who grows up poor in a difficult family situation, works in the fields, has a little trouble with the law, becomes educated, and goes on to have a career as an educator and as a writer. I could not tell my whole life story in one volume, for I have a pretty good memory and volumes of journals and notes. So I have focused on this aspect, which I hope is a tribute to the value of education in our country and to the aspiration of every individual who wishes to rise from difficult circumstances.

BOY FROM THE COUNTRY

BOY FROM THE COUNTRY

I heard my brother call my name. A sad, sick cry drifted on the autumn air, reaching me where I stood at the top of my ladder. It was the only sound I heard in the quiet orchard save the whisper and rattle of olives as I stripped them from the branches and into the picking bucket.

When Bob called to me again, I backed down the ladder, took off the bucket and harness, and went to the car at the edge of the orchard, where he had been sleeping.

His face was a mess, bruised and swollen from the fall he had taken in the gravel parking lot at the Silver Dollar Fairgrounds. The car still reeked from the night before, when Bob had vomited up the sloe gin. He would tell me later that the last thing he remembered was tipping up the bottle before we left the boarding house and went to the dance.

My brother Bob was a junior in high school; always anxious to grow up ahead of his age, he had been smoking and drinking for a couple of years. I was the cautious one, serious and sober, good in school, and young for my grade, enrolling in college at the age of seventeen. Bob, who was sixteen and didn't look any older, tried to prove he could fit in. That evening in the boarding house, he had jumped right into the festivities and had passed out early. I remember my room-mate's younger brothers coming to me inside the dance hall and telling me it looked as if Bob had been beat up. I went out to the parking lot, and after some belabored questions and mumbled answers, I gathered that the last big gulps of sloe gin had caught up with him. I left him in the car and went inside for a while longer. After the dance, broke and with my brother passed out drunk in the back seat, I drove to our home town.

Orland was twenty miles across the valley from the Silver Dollar Fairgrounds. It was a small town in farm country, where the main crops were alfalfa, apricots, prunes, almonds, walnuts, olives, and oranges. Being a highway town, it was now adjusting to the changes brought about by the new freeway.

When I arrived in Orland that night, I turned left at the only stoplight and drove south out of town on the old high-way. On a normal night we would have gone north, back to the house where Bob and our youngest brother, David, lived with our grandfather. David had lived with Grandpa for over ten years, and Bob and I had lived with the two of them, with or without our father and other brother, from time to time. At this point, in the fall of 1966, my father and my grandfather were on the outs, my older brother, Sandy, was in the Navy, and I was off at college and on my own. I did not have to answer to Grandpa (or anyone) for my comings and goings, but Bob did, so this weekend we had an alibi. We had said we would be working on the other side of the valley, in Gridley, fifty miles away. On another occasion, earlier that fall, we had gone to a place closer to home, where we knocked and raked almonds for a couple of days and slept in our car at the river. That excursion served as a model for our alibi this time.

I parked the car behind an all-night gas station and coffee shop, a place on the old highway called Greenwood Switch. Back then, just about any place in the valley was a safe place to sleep in the car, and this one was close to the orchard where we were to pick olives. The owner, Blevins, was easy to get along with. Because his olives went for oil, he was not in a hurry to get them picked. We could go in and pick a few boxes on the weekend, and he would pay us at the end of the day.

We needed the money, as always. We needed the money that day because we were broke. Being broke for us was not just a matter of being out of resources we could renew at home. It was all our problem, and only through our own effort could we do anything about it. The car was out of gas, and we had nothing to eat for breakfast or lunch. The last of our money had gone the night before—some of it for entry into the dance, and a larger part of it on the little party we had had in the room of the boarding house. As I did not yet smoke or drink, Bob had spent the last of our money on cigarettes and liquor. But that didn't matter, because we shared all of our earnings and all of our expenses. Our father had raised us that way, to share everything, and even though we had not lived with him for a couple of years, his teaching had become a habit of our life.

We always needed money because we were young and undisciplined and had never gotten a nickel ahead. We had been self-supporting since we had split from our father, and the little money that came in from the court, whose wards we were, did not pay for junker cars, gasoline, occasional new clothes, dates with girls, or the profligacies of tobacco and alcohol—not to mention the costs of going to school, even when I lived in the cheapest boarding house on the list. To make money, and to try to keep from stealing, we worked at field labor. It was what we knew.

We weren't going to make much money on this day because one of us was sick in the car and couldn't work. For a while, I felt smug and self-sacrificing, being the one who did not drink or smoke, and being the one who worked through the day without food because my brother had squandered our money. But when I heard him call me and I went to the cheap little Plymouth Valiant where he lay sick in the back seat, I didn't care very much about whose fault anything was. He was my brother, and he needed water.

I drove him over to the Greenwood station and café, where he was able to drink water and clean himself up. I found thirty-five cents and put a gallon of gasoline in the car. Then we went back to the orchard, where I worked a while longer as Bob stayed in the car, trying to recuperate.

Later that day, Blevins came by and paid me for the few boxes I had picked. He was a calm fellow, somewhere in his forties, with dark eyes, close-cut dark hair, and a clean-shaven face. He wore a ball cap and a dark-blue T-shirt, and he had muscular arms. He had known us when we came with our father to pick olives, and he told us then that he had grown up picking fruit himself. He understood the outlook of a field worker, so he did not seem troubled that we hadn't picked any more olives than we did.

He asked about my brother, who was sitting up in the back seat of the car.

I said he was all right but had a little too much to drink last night.

He expressed no dismay or disapproval, just wrote out the check on the hood of his pickup. As he did, he asked me about my father.

I said I hadn't seen much of him, but I guessed he was doing well.

Blevins said that if he wanted to come out and pick a few boxes, that would be all right.

I said I didn't know when I might see him, but if I did, I would tell him.

Blevins told me to come back again if we had more time before the end of the season. Having lived the fruit picker's life, he didn't pass any more comments. He had no doubt seen enough to understand two kids who weren't on top of the world but just needed to get paid. I appreciated that.

I have looked back on this episode and have thought how different our life was from that of people who grew up in normal homes and families—that is, in environments where the children lived with two parents, where the parents paid the living expenses, and where the parents oversaw the purchase of automobiles, enrollment at college, and management of money. Here we were, two underage boys trying to pay our own way, working in the fields, sleeping in the car, and squandering what little money we could get together. To us, it was a pattern we had been in for years, and the main features—lack of guidance and discipline but no lack of pride and self-reliance—would stay with us throughout our growing up.

There were four of us brothers, and we grew up as close and tight as brothers could. We had a code. Anything we had was assumed to be shared—our problems, our debts, our assets. There have been many moments with each and all of my brothers that still lie at the center of my life, but this one comes back to me time and again. The way of life I came from was destined to cause conflicts with my efforts at acquiring an education and pursuing a career, and much of my early life has lived on with me. The voice of my brother, as it came to me that afternoon in the olive orchard, has stayed with me not only as the voice of my one brother who needed me that day but also as the voice of something that united us all—a low-class upbringing and a code to try to overcome it. That voice has been in the air for me all the years of my life.

ONE

The world was cold and clear outside the open window of the truck. Inside, my mother held me up so I could see a man, my father, lifting a shovel of snow for me to observe. I remember my own sense of wonder as well as the feeling of good humor on the part of the two adults.

The incident took place in Oregon. We had moved there not long after my first birthday. My father and my grandfather, partners in the cattle business, had bought a ranch near Lakeview, in eastern Oregon. My father bought and sold cattle in a long string of towns from Klamath Falls to Los Angeles, and he ran up and down that whole length in his cattle truck.

Oregon and snow and frigid winters were new to us. I was born in Lompoc, California, in Santa Barbara County, as was my older brother, Sandy. My father was born in Solvang, not far from there. My mother was born in Los Angeles, and my sister Suzi, from my mother's first marriage, was born in Lancaster, out on the hot desert north and east of L.A. My younger brothers, Bob and David, were born in Oregon.

In my memory of this incident in the snow, I have only my father, my mother, and myself present. The others would have been around—perhaps in town with Grandpa and Grandma.

To many people, it would seem like a common incident—two parents taking a moment to share the wonder of life with a child. For me, it is a very rare one, not only because I do not remember any other definite scenes from the three years in Oregon but because it captures a moment in which we were happy together. My father and my mother had already found reasons to be unhappy with one another. By the time I was four, my father and my grandfather would have gone broke in the cattle business and lost the ranch in Oregon. The cattle business, with prosperity and some bits of happiness, would become the golden past, and the time in Oregon would become a part of that.

My father was wearing a winter cap instead of his usual black Stetson. I do not remember his exact words as he held up the shovel full of snow, but they were something like, "What do you think of that, Johnny?" Cheerful words on the cold, clear air.

———

Mama burned her finger on the Christmas tree. The event itself is vague as a memory, but I remember I was there. She burned her finger on a hot electrical cord or connection, and it caused a moment of excitement. It became a family memory in a game my brothers and I would play. One of us would start it by saying, "I remember something you don't." Like tossing the bat and grasping it hand over hand until the last grasp was an eagle's claw on the hilt of the bat, no one could reach higher or cover that most prestigious detail. It went back the furthest— so far that we remembered remembering it more than we remembered the incident itself. It became a soft, glowing memory of a time when we were all still together.

———

We lived in Orland for a while after my father and grandfather had gone broke. My father was trying to make a go of it buying and selling cattle around the Sacramento Valley, while my grandfather, having turned sixty-five, began to draw an Old Age Survivors pension, for people who predated or had not paid into Social Security.

We lived in a house near an irrigation canal. My brother Sandy and I went to the livestock auction with our father. An auctioneer named Tex Bullen gave us a puppy. My father still had the 1951 Hudson that he had bought new in December 1950, a few days after my second birthday. The fabled Christmas may have taken place in Orland.

Sandy began kindergarten in the fall of 1952. I was eager to go to school, and Sandy asked permission to bring me for a day. The teacher said it would be all right, so we went to school together, dressed alike, as was the custom in those days. As it turned out, Sandy had brought me to school for his own purpose. A larger boy had been bullying him. Sandy and I were both small, but we took off our belts and evened the score. The teacher sent home a note asking not to have Sandy bring me to school anymore. The story remained in the family as an example of how we brothers stuck together.

———

I was crouched behind the dashboard of a black car, my father's Hudson, I think. My father and my brother Sandy were also ducking. My mother was throwing white plaster-of-Paris figures, and they were smashing on the windshield divider, on the glass, and on the hood.

We were not living in the Sacramento Valley at the time. The stock of plaster-of-Paris items places the scene at a motel on the highway north of Escondido, in the northern part of San Diego County. My mother's parents had bought a piece of property there at about the time that Sandy and I were born or a little earlier, and, with the help of my Uncle Jimmy, had built

a motel with a gas station and small store. My grandfather
Schneider died in 1953, so my father and mother moved us to
Escondido so they could help with the business. My mother,
who played music and wrote songs and poems and stories,
also drew and painted. During our time at the motel, she
painted plaster-of-Paris objects in bright colors. She painted
The Last Supper, sleeping Mexicans with the tall sombrero and
loose peasant garb, chickens, and small cowboy boots that
could serve as flower vases. The dull, white, heavy casts of a
given image were always the same, but in the painted products, the disciples and the sleeping Mexicans wore garments of
different colors from one model to the next.

On this day, my mother was hurling her unpainted inventory along with a few imprecations. I do not remember the
words, just bursts of voice and the impact of those objects that
were small enough for her to throw with one hand.

————

I started kindergarten in two places. At that time, in 1953, a
child had to turn five years old by December 2 in order to enter
kindergarten that year. My birthday is December 14. I wanted
to go to school, and my parents did not see any reason for me
to wait a year. Sandy was doing well in school, and I took
interest in everything he brought home in the way of knowledge and subject matter. In later years, friends who were close
to the cutoff age would tell me that their mothers held them
back a year so that they would not be at a social disadvantage.
My parents, in contrast, saw that I was ready for the challenges
of education. Life was work and competition, and I might as
well get started. So they told the people at school that my
birthday was November 14. The school required a birth certificate. My mother said she would send for one. So they let
me in.

Not long after that, we moved from Escondido to Paradise,
back in the Sacramento Valley and near my father's parents.

The new school sent for my attendance record at the previous school, and my birth date was taken for granted. And so I was on my way, making teepees of clay and sleeping on my mat at nap time.

At home in the afternoons and evenings, we would hear Fibber McGee and Molly and Okie Paul Westmoreland on the radio. My favorite songs were "Bimbo" by Jim Reeves and "Pittsburgh, Pennsylvania," by Guy Mitchell. Life went on in its simple way.

I would not know my real birthday until I was in the second grade, and by then it was too late for the school to do anything. Up until then, I thought I was born on the same day as Prince Charles.

———

They had put my father in the back seat of the squad car, and I was standing by the door, screaming and crying. He was my daddy, and if they were going to take him, I wanted to go. For years, he would tell this story as an illustration of something to be valued—a child's loyalty. He had to have appreciated someone's loyalty that day, when his own father had brought the rim of a saucepan down on the ridge of his nose and had then thrown a hammer at him—this same father who, by my father's reckoning, had slept with my mother.

I am sure my father had his theory on the basis of more than one piece of evidence, but I had contributed at least a scrap when I told him I saw Grandpa and Mama taking a nap together. That incident was like the one with the shovelful of snow—an early isolated memory. My grandfather and my mother were sleeping on a bed, not under the covers. I was sitting in a doorway, leaning against the jamb and wishing they would wake up so we could go where we were supposed to go. The late afternoon sun was shining through the window.

I do not know if the house was in Oregon or California, but I do know that I became my mother's least favorite of five children for the rest of her short life, and I do know that I was no longer my grandfather's favorite grandson.

On the day that the police took my father to jail, we were living in Gridley, a small town across the valley from Orland and south of Paradise and Chico. Gridley had a cannery that processed peaches in the summer and pumpkins in the fall. My father worked in the cannery. I was in the first grade. I had a crush on a girl whose father was a policeman. At some point during the school year, our family began to live in separate houses.

Sandy and I lived with our father. Bob and David lived with our mother and Suzi. Sandy and I had dark hair like our father, while Bob and David had blond hair like our mother. The four of us were close together in age, from seven down to three. Suzi was twelve. She had brown hair and was starting to wear lipstick. She had been on my mother's side all along.

For a while, at least, it seemed as if we had taken sides. My father left Sandy and me at the other house on a Sunday afternoon. Bob and David told us about Uncle Floyd and Uncle Lloyd, who took them fishing. Later, Bob was inside the house, standing close to a screened window and taunting me as I stood outside. I took the ladder from a toy fire engine and hit at Bob through the screen. Bob received a cut above the eyebrow, and my mother had to doctor him. She scolded me over and over, telling me it was all my fault.

At Christmas, Sandy and I were in our little house with our father. We heard a noise outside, and we opened the door to see pots and pans of Christmas dinner on our doorstep. Our father would have none of it. We loaded up all the items, drove across town, and left them on my mother's doorstep. My father shouted something through the closed door. I do not remember his words, but I can guess at them.

I did not have much of a sense of money except that it was scarce. One day when Sandy and I were walking home from school, we stopped in the Funk Brothers grocery store to buy a jar of paste that I needed for a project in school. Sandy paid with the small amount of change our father had given us. Before we made it out of the store, I dropped the jar on the cement floor. The glass broke, and the paste spread out. I started crying and wailing. The storekeeper told us not to worry. He gave us another jar of paste and cleaned up the mess.

That evening, after we told our father of the incident, he took us to the store and offered to pay for the second jar of paste. Mr. Funk said it was all right. Things like that happened. My father thanked him more than once.

————

During this same period of time, a more singular event with money took place. It began with an argument between my father and my mother. He threw some money at her and shouted that she should take it. She threw it back and shouted that she did not want it. The argument went back and forth, and the money stayed on the floor. Each of them must have thought that the other took it, but when the argument broke up and we were about to go our separate ways, the money was still on the floor. Sandy and I took it.

The next day, we invited all of our friends at school to go with us for candy. I think we thought no one would know. That evening, I took part in a school program in which I was dressed in a cowboy outfit with a fringed vest and jingling spurs. The stage was crowded and noisy, and I was warm in my cowboy duds, but I was happy that my father and brother were watching.

On the way home, my father asked us where we got the money. He said Mr. Funk told him we had been buying candy for everyone and he knew we didn't have that kind of money.

Sandy and I tried to say we found it. Our father asked where. We said, along the road. He stopped the car. Where? Here? No, farther along. He stopped again. Here? Our story did not last long. We gave the rest of the money to him, and he prevailed upon our mother to take half of it.

_____

My father injured his hand at the cannery, and we were in for a hard winter. The temperature did not drop much below freezing in the Sacramento Valley, but the weather was damp and gloomy. Work was hard to find. My father found a job pruning trees in an orchard, and he talked the boss into letting Sandy and me pile brush for a small wage. When the job was over, the man paid my father but did not pay Sandy and me. Sandy was seven, and I was six. We had our first lesson about chiselers in the world of work, and we remembered the man's name.

_____

My parents became divorced. The living arrangements remained the same, as my father had custody of the two older boys, and my mother had custody of the two younger ones. My father, Sandy, and I moved to Live Oak, a few miles south of Gridley on the main highway. It was common at that time, and still legal, for children to go into a bar, so we would sit at the bar and enjoy the music and the decor of deer heads, steer horns, and stuffed birds. Other patrons would buy us soft drinks.

Sometimes our father left us in the car, which was also common. He told us to keep the window rolled down a little and the doors locked. We were not to open the door for anyone, least of all the old man he called Snoopy, who would peer in through the open space and make hissing and teasing sounds.

Our father drank but not very much at this time. One day we were in Marysville, a town that was larger than Gridley and had pawn shops, street women, and a small skid row. Sandy and I were left in the car for a while. We started out by drinking our orange soda pop—Nesbitt's Orange, I imagine—in the back seat of the car. It was a cool, overcast day, so we were not uncomfortable with the windows rolled up and the door locked.

We became bored. We took to spitting and pouring our soda pop into our father's toolbox, which was on the floorboard at our feet. We thought we might get in trouble for that, but we were restless, jumping around in the car, out in front of a bar in a strange town.

Black people walked by. We knew what people called them, so we did. A lady stopped.

"Hey, you old n-----," we yelled again.

She looked in at us, but she couldn't touch us. The windows were a sure defense.

"Yah, yah, you old n-----." We chanted on like that until she left.

Before long, she was back, with my father and a Black man, a very serious Black man looming over my worried-looking father. We opened the door and faced the music.

"What did you call this lady?"

"Nothin'…"

"What did you call her?"

"Nothin'…"

"*What did you call her?*"

"A n-n-n-----…"

"Did you learn that from me?"

We knew what to say at this point. "N-no-o."

"What did I always tell you?"

We blubbered, "That *they* were…just as good…as *we* were."

"Say it again."

"You always told us…that they were just as good…as *we* were."

"And not to forget it, didn't I?"

"Yes."

"Don't you think you owe this lady an apology?"

"I guess so."

"Then do it."

After we had stammered out our apologies, and the Black people assured us that no harm was done, and my father assured them ten times over that he had no idea where we picked up that kind of language, we were on our way.

We didn't get in trouble for spilling the soda pop in his toolbox, but we were yelled at plenty for hollering at the lady.

"You want to get me killed? That lady come in the bar and said, 'Those yo' two boys out in the car?'" As my father was the only white person in the bar, the lady had had an easy task finding him.

I knew my father liked these people, despite what he called them when they weren't around. I knew it because he went to their bars, joked with them, drank wine with them in the car, and invited them home. I remember one very cheerful lady, very dark in a turquoise dress, who woke us in the middle of the night in the house in Live Oak, pulling on the overhead light that hung bare from the ceiling, and asking us if we wanted her for our new mama. We knew enough to say yes.

The experience in Marysville put a scare into him for the moment, but it did not scare him away for good. He would go back.

———

While we were living in Live Oak, I discovered that my father's Stetson hat fit me—almost. I had a large head when I was a small child, and although I had grown into it, I still wore a larger-sized hat or cap than my older brother. I liked wearing the black Stetson. It linked me to earlier times and the black Hudson. When Sandy and I rode with our father out on the open road and we came up on a slower car, Sandy and I would say, "Pass him, Daddy. Pass him." And he would.

——————

My father found work with a large farming outfit in Colusa. It was a three-generation family operation, with big field tractors that my father knew how to operate. He also hoed beans and irrigated with ditch water and siphon tubes. One day when he was cutting alfalfa, Grandpa went out with him to ride on the tractor with a shotgun. Grandpa shot a gunny sack full of jackrabbits, which the two of them took home and cleaned for our consumption.

On another day, my father brought home a young fox from work. He and his coworker, the son of one of the owners, had caught two foxes in a hollow log at the edge of a field near the river. Grey foxes were common in the valley. Ours was a female. We called her Foxy, and she became a friendly pet. We kept her on a chain and fed her grasshoppers and locusts as well as table scraps.

My father was always on easy terms with butchers, as his father had had his own butcher shop before and during the Depression. At the local grocery store, my father asked the butcher for fox food. The butcher gave him the heads and tails of fish, often with an inch or two of meat attached. The butcher could see that we were not well off, and my father appreciated the small gesture. Later, we would recall when we lived on fox food.

My parents had not been divorced for long, perhaps six months, when my mother asked my father if he could take all four boys. The two younger ones were too much for her, along with Suzi, although Suzi had always been good at helping take care of all of us. I had no idea of how difficult it must have been for my mother. I did not know her well, and I was young when we went our separate ways. All I knew was that my other two brothers were coming to live with us, and I was happy.

We had a chicken pen made of lath strips, with a crop of chickens raised from chicks. One day it was time to kill them all for the freezer. My grandfather came over to assist. I did not enjoy catching the chickens and contributing to the frenzy, but I did my part. Bob enjoyed the excitement, I think, and at the end of the day his smiling face was speckled with blood. So I guess he was happy.

While we were still living in Live Oak, two other people came to live with us. A housekeeper named June arrived with her little daughter named Rosie. June was a dark-haired, heavy-set woman about my father's age, and Rosie was three or four—a little younger than Bob. A photo from this era has Sandy, me, Bob, Rosie, and the fox in the dirt yard in front of the house.

I began the second grade in the fall of 1955. Not far into the school year, we all moved to an old house in the country, ten miles south of Colusa, where my father had been working. The house belonged to the family farming company, and although it was rundown, it was rent-free. It sat on piers, as many houses did at that time. This old dwelling sat in a desolate place, on a bare spot with no trees, right off the highway, with dry fields of barley stubble all around. Three miles farther down the road, set up against the river like so many little towns in the valley, was a little hamlet named Grimes.

We moved to the house near Grimes in the dry, dusty time of year before the fall rains. Vast amounts of trash had accumulated under the house, so every day after school, when the sun was still warm in the hazy sky, Sandy, Bob, and I would change clothes and crawl under the house with rakes. June supervised from the back porch, and Rosie watched. For our reward, we drank Kool-Aid out of tall metal cups in the blue, purple, green, and yellow colors of the day.

Grandpa and Grandma Nesbitt moved to a house in town in Colusa, and David went to live with them. Years later,

Grandpa would tell me that they felt sorry for the little child, living in that cold house in the winter with that mean housekeeper. David turned four in October of 1955. He is not in the photo with Rosie and the fox, but he is in another photo on another day with Sandy, Bob, Rosie, and me in that same yard. I do not remember him moving with us to the house in the country, so he may have begun to stay with Grandpa and Grandma on shorter visits before the winter.

June was from Idaho, and she knew all about farm chores and home industry. She could milk the cow, pluck chickens, churn butter, and put up food. She put me to churning butter on the back porch, and the palm of my hand turned orange from the red wooden handle. We brought chickens from Live Oak, and we added other animals right away. When we butchered chickens, we salvaged and ate eggs that were at various stages of development inside some of the hens. The first winter in the country, my father and my grandfather killed a boar hog (after castrating it), and June rendered the lard in the house. The smell lingered for a long time. At Christmas, they cooked a small pig, whole, with an apple in its mouth. When we boys fed the animals in the morning and came in with frost-bitten hands, having no gloves, June made us run our hands under cold water first, then warm.

My father worked on the bean harvester and brought home a hundred-pound burlap bag of pink beans. June set Sandy, Bob, and me to sorting the huge piles on the long table my father had built. Beans from the field came with rocks, mud clods, shriveled beans, and worm-eaten beans. Sorting was endless drudgery.

Also from work, my father brought home fresh corn in burlap sacks, and we had a long siege of shucking corn, picking off the silk, cutting out the worms and bad spots, and cutting the kernels from the cobs. June cooked the corn in a hug pot, then packaged the creamed corn for the freezer. Spills on the linoleum floor melted into the surface and turned hard as rubber.

While we worked at these tasks in the hot summer, we listened to westerns such as *The Lone Ranger* and *Gunsmoke* on the radio. We also heard songs such as "This Ole House" and "Too Old to Cut the Mustard." Both of these songs were real to us, as we lived in an old rattling house and we were familiar with wild mustard. In the spring, June had cut an armful of the lush, green leaves and had fed them to the cow. The milk went sour for a few days. Another song that came to us at that time was Tennessee Ernie Ford's "Sixteen Tons." It was real, too, because it spoke of hard work and owing money at the grocery store.

June was ill-tempered most of the time. Her face and dark upper lip were wet with perspiration in the hot weather and the hot kitchen, and her heavy legs rubbed together and contracted a rash. I got along with her all right. She told me stories about kitchens where she had worked. One man picked his nose and didn't pay attention to where the product went. Another man went to the bathroom and did not wash his hands before he returned to handle food. She had to tell him about it. I could imagine it. She told me about a brother who had a good recipe for fudge and about a brother (perhaps the same one) who died from a blood clot in his leg. This was her amiable side. On her neutral side, she did not have any trouble or any comradery with Sandy. I imagine she sensed that he was my father's favorite and should be left alone. With my brother Bob, she was the opposite.

When we moved into the house in Grimes, we used a bucket on the back porch until my father repaired the bathroom. He put in a new bathtub, killed a snake with his hammer when it came up through the sewer (and told us not to tell anyone), and put in new sheetrock with the dark nails with wide heads that people used for sheetrock in those times. He also put in a new toilet.

Before the sheetrock was very old, someone took to smearing excrement on it. My brothers and I were sure that Rosie was the guilty party, as none of us had ever been known to practice that behavior. Sandy and I protested our innocence, and I think we were seen as being beyond that stage. Bob swore that he was innocent as well, and he went on to say that he had seen Rosie do it or had seen the fresh product when she came out of the bathroom.

June became furious. She slapped Bob around and shouted at him for putting the blame on Rosie when he was the one who had done it. This persecution went on for a while.

June also had the habit of reporting some bad behavior of Bob's almost every day when my father came home, which resulted in Bob receiving a whipping almost every day. Sandy and I could see the injustice, but there was not much we could do. My father worked long hours, twelve and often fourteen hours a day in the summertime, and if June was to be in charge, he had to let her have her authority. Also, of the three of us boys, Bob was my father's least favorite. My father always asserted that he had no favorites, and we had to agree on the surface. But deep down, we knew better, and I am sure June knew she was on easy ground when it came to picking on Bob.

The cruelest that I saw in June came out on one of the hottest days of the summer. We all had our chores, and Bob had neglected to water some animals—chickens or calves, I don't remember. To teach Bob a lesson, June staked Bob out on the hot, baked ground in the backyard. She tied a rope around his neck and made him stay in the blazing sun so that he would know how those animals felt. Bob had light-colored blond hair and never took the sun as well as Sandy and I did. His face turned red, and he sweated and drooped as he stood in the sunlight. June told us not to go near him. This was one of the most anguished days of my life, to see my brother suffering and not to be able to do anything about it. It may also have been a turning point in our relations with June, because even my father, who believed in slapping kids and giving whippings, would never have gone that far.

This was in the summer. Earlier in the year, not long after

Bob's birthday in April, June came home from the hospital with a baby. My brothers and I were still a year away from knowing where babies came from and how humans were like the farm animals that bred and reproduced. For the time being, as far as we knew, babies came from the hospital. This one was wrapped in a soft, pink blanket, and her name was Patricia. We called her Patty.

In the latter part of that same summer, in 1956, I was sitting on the front porch of the house in Grimes when a strange car pulled off the road and onto the packed dirt where vehicles parked. My father was at work. Sandy might have gone with him that day, as my father had the custom of taking one of us to work with him every day—to keep him company and to lessen the chance of the three of us getting into trouble.

I could not see who was sitting in the shadows of the passenger seat. The woman driving had red hair and bright red lipstick, and I did not recognize her as she got out of the car. Bob did. He jumped off the front porch and went running out toward her, calling, "Mama! Mama!"

I was not excited to see her, but I made my way out to say hello. Suzi had gotten out on the passenger side. My mother said she was going away for a little while and she had dropped by to say goodbye to us.

I do not remember much of the visit, which lasted but a short while on a bright summer day. I believe Suzi and our mother came to visit with us in the shade of the porch for a few minutes. Years later, Suzi would tell me on more than one occasion that a surly woman came to the door. A baby cried inside, and my mother said, "Your baby is crying. You should go see what it needs." The woman, June, said, "There's no baby here."

My mother said it would be a while until she came back to see us again. She and Suzi got into the car and drove away.

———

Because we lived ten miles out of town, we were the first ones to board the school bus in the morning and the last ones off in the afternoon. One day after school, we missed the bus, and we did not know what to do. We did not have a telephone at home, and we thought we might have to wait until our father came home and then came into town to fetch us. The teacher on bus duty suggested that we wait, so we did.

The bus driver returned after he had left off all the other passengers, and he made a second trip to take us home. June came out of the house to meet us. She heard the story and thanked the bus driver with great effusion. When he was gone, she chewed us out for missing the bus and told us over and over again that we should be thankful to the bus driver.

———

One day we came home on the bus, climbed down, and went into the house to find no one there. June was gone, along with Rosie and Patty. All of their things were gone. My brothers and I thought that was pretty good.

———

At some time of the year when the days were not long and the weather was dry but not hot or cold, I went to spend the day with a friend from school. His name was Terry, and he lived in a house facing the school grounds. Between the two of us, we arranged for me to visit on a Saturday. My father dropped me off early on his way to work and drove away.

I went up the steps and knocked on the door, and nobody answered. After I knocked several times, I imagined that the family had left for the day and had no way of letting me know.

I did not know what to do, but I knew what not to do, and that was not to wander very far. So I spent what was for me a very long day moping around the school grounds. It was a day of concrete and asphalt. I watched other kids play, but I did not know them, and they did not pay me any attention. I did not feel lost or bewildered, just sad and alone—and, before long, hungry.

As the day wore on, the sad, hollow feeling persisted. I thought about food. I remembered seeing a program on television in which the people ate their spoons and forks and dishes after they ate the food. The utensils were made of a crunchy substance, and the people described for the audience what the material tasted like. All afternoon, I thought about how much I would like to eat a spoon or a saucer or a bowl like those happy people were doing.

I do not know if this experience took place in the spring of my second-grade year or in the fall of the third grade, but it was early in our stay in Colusa. My grandparents lived in town, but I did not know how to get there. My father had taught us not to talk to strangers, and no one spoke to me or seemed to take notice. So I wandered, sad and alone and hungry, until my father picked me up in the evening.

————

Deeper into the fall of 1956, after June and Rosie and the baby had left, the weather turned wet and gloomy. One morning before the school bus arrived, my father called Sandy and Bob and me together in the kitchen. He sat on a stool as he told us our mother had died. He had gone for the mail the day before, and he had received a copy of the Lompoc *Record*, his hometown newspaper from which he had cut out a photo of his high school class's twenty-year reunion earlier that year. He had also received a letter from someone from my mother's family, none of whom would have communicated with him except in the direst circumstances; but with my mother's obituary in the Lompoc paper, they could not avoid it. He had read the news in both places, and now he was sharing it with us. It was somber news, without ceremony or lamentation or discussion. None of us talked about her very much anyway. Sandy and I had not lived with her for a couple of years, and I had not recognized her the last time I saw her. Bob was closer to her, but even he had not seen her for a while.

My father did not say anything comforting that I recall. He did not say, "I know this is a hard thing for you boys to hear," or "Your mother and I didn't get along, but she was your mother." He conveyed the information to us, and he told us we should tell our teachers. It was the kind of thing they should know about.

TWO

M rs. Brose was my third-grade teacher at Colusa Elementary School. She was neither young nor old —perhaps my mother's age, which was thirty-three. She was of average build, with medium-length brown hair, and she wore glasses and lipstick. Mrs. Brose was not vivacious in that sense, but she was affectionate and caring as well as enthusiastic in all subjects. We, her students, remembered her best for reading to us and encouraging us to read and write. We loved to hear her read "The Pirate Don Dirk of Dowdee" and "Paul Revere's Ride" as well as stories such as "The Fisherman and His Wife" and "Rikki-Tikki-Tavi," Rudyard Kipling's story about a mongoose.

Life at the time was a two-strand rope for me—subsistence and anger at home, alternating with harmony and happiness at school. On the first day of third grade, I was full of joy at being back in school. As the others and I sat in class, about to begin a wonderful year with Mrs. Brose, we heard a crying, screaming child coming down the hallway. His exclamations were uneven, and we could hear kicking and scuffing. He did not want to go to school. At last his mother and a school employee dragged him into the classroom, where he stood red-faced and sulky with tears in his eyes. We all knew him. His name was Eric. I was astounded to know that someone did not want to go to school. It was a sanctuary to me. Now in late November or early December, I sat through class until school let out. I lingered, waiting to talk to Mrs. Brose alone, but other children were hanging around as well. I did not want to miss the bus, so I had to tell her, with a couple of others not far away, that my father had told me to tell her my mother had died.

She said she was sorry, and I said that was all right. I walked outside, and a girl came hurrying after me. A boy who had not been inside stood by to pay attention. The girl said, "John, did your mother die?"

"Yes," I said. But I didn't want to talk about it. I wouldn't have known how, and I didn't understand it myself. I tugged on my jacket, which I had draped over my shoulder, and I said, "This is a good old jacket." I walked away to catch the bus.

My eighth birthday came around. A bit of suspense had built up with the appearance of a long, narrow package. We boys had always done housework, and now with June gone, we did more. Sandy did a great deal of the cooking, and I did some. I also washed dishes, which I enjoyed, and I had begun to iron clothes. I thought my gift was going to be an ironing board.

I was pleased at the idea. Gifts were always practical in our family. New clothes at Christmas came just in time to replace the clothes from the beginning of the school year. For a birthday, one of us could expect one gift from the rest of the family. An ironing board seemed prestigious to me. When I said out loud what I thought was in the package, my brothers and my father went along with the illusion and congratulated me.

On the day of my birthday, I opened the package and found something I had not dreamed of. It was a B-B gun, new, with a polished stock and a shiny barrel. The surprise over-whelmed me. I cried. For once in that isolated place in the country, I was more than a person who did chores and tried to stay out of trouble. For once, we showed each other that we cared. No one ever said, "I love you" to another family member, and we did not speak of that emotion. But I had a sense of it out in that rundown house where a couple of weeks earlier we had heard the news of our mother and where, in the winter to come, my father would be laid off and we would know not to ask for anything.

———

At some time when my father was working during that school year, I did ask for something. A couple of Scout leaders came to school and gave a presentation to interested boys. I very much liked the color of the Cub Scout uniform, and the activities sounded like fun, so I took a card. When I found the time to be alone with my father, I asked him about it.

He said it would be too hard for me to go to the meetings because of the hours he worked. That was something mothers did—take their kids to meetings and other activities—and since I didn't have a mother, I didn't have the opportunities that other boys did. He did not mention that it would cost money as well. He did not have to. One reason was enough, and he had succeeded in making me feel sorry for myself. And in an indirect way that may not have been conscious to him, he succeeded in blaming my mother.

———

Christmas was a day of bleak sunlight that year. Early in the day, two men came out to our place in the country. They were from some group or organization, not the school, and they brought charity—a box of groceries such as flour and canned goods, and a box of toys. The two men left the items without much comment or expression of holiday cheer.

The toys were second-hand and not wrapped up. They consisted of dull-colored, mismatched soldiers, trucks, and other military pieces. The soldiers were pale yellow and dull green, holding rifles with bayonets or poised for crawling or fighting. My father, born in 1919 and part of the World War II generation, was patriotic, but he had not served in the military, and he did not glorify war. We boys did not care to watch war movies on television or to read war stories in the comic strips or in comic books, so we were not excited by the jumbled toys in the open box. We discovered that one of the cannons had a lever and spring that propelled straight pins, and we took to shooting at the little soldiers. My father was not a pacifist, and he was not delicate in his language, but he did not allow us to use the word "hate," and he did not like us to repeat lines we heard on television such as "I'm going to kill you." Our glee at shooting pins with the little toy cannon touched off his anger. He sprang from his chair, seized the metal object, and twisted it with his hands. We went back to playing with our cowboys and Indians, horses and cattle, and homemade ranch wagons.

Our father took us to spend the night in town with Grandpa and Grandma Nesbitt. We were rambunctious from living in the country, and they were old and settled in their ways. Grandpa was almost seventy. He had been heavy with a big belly since his forties, when he developed diabetes. He spent periods of time sitting in his chair, smoking King Edward cigars or Prince Albert pipe tobacco. Grandma was thirteen to fifteen years older than he was, and she was eccentric. She wore a knitted cap all the time, and she went around the house at night with a flashlight. She would check the knobs on the gas stove and nod as she said, "Off, off, off, off." In a family story I heard later, one of her brothers, blind, had died in a gas explosion when he came in from a night at the pub and lit a smoke.

As soon as we were in the house, we started teasing David.

"Leave the baby alone!" Grandma cried. When David started fussing, she said, "Oh, the dear, the dear, the dear."

Grandpa and Grandma were from Ireland—Northern Ireland, land of Presbyterians and Episcopalians. My grandfather was gruff and would dismiss small topics with "Ach!"

Grandma was more of a busy talker. "Your father's the best man in the world," she told me.

I nodded.

"He's the best man in the world."

"Well, he hasn't been to jail or anything." I must have forgotten the incident in Gridley.

"Oh, don't say such a thing! Of course he hasn't."

Grandpa cooked dinner, a thin, tough steak like round steak in gravy, with a serving of spuds as always.

Grandma crowded next to each of us and cut up our meat with a pair of scissors.

In the night, my grandmother came to the back room where we slept on the floor. She had her flashlight and a coffee can. She woke up each of us and had us "shed a tear" in the can so we would not wet the bed.

Her name was Elenor, and he called her Nell, as in "Come to bed, Nell," when she wandered around the house at night. She was kind to us and full of worry for my father.

———

When Mrs. Brose discovered that I had never been to a rodeo, she told me she would take me to one. The details were never worked out, though, and I don't think my father liked the idea of one child having a privilege over the others or of someone providing something that he couldn't.

Mrs. Brose also offered to adopt me. My father said it was very nice of her, but he couldn't let the boys be broken up like that. I did not want to leave my family, but if I had ever had to, I do not think I could have done better than Mrs. Brose.

———

Out at our place in the country, we continued to acquire animals. In addition to the milk cow, we had calves, goats, pigs, geese, ducks, chickens, and guinea hens. My father built chicken coops, livestock pens, calf sheds, and a feed shed. All of this was home industry. We boys kept a separate account of the calves we bought and sold and what it cost to feed them. We bottle-fed calves and buried the ones that died.

Our first fox disappeared when we were in Live Oak, so after we moved to the country, my father found another fox in the Sacramento newspaper. It ate grasshoppers as the previous one did. My father did not like cats, so we did not have them. Indoors, we had flying squirrels for a while, and later we had parakeets.

One pet we had for almost a year was a raccoon. I think my father brought him home as he did the first fox. He brought home other animals as well, like young jackrabbits, which almost always died in captivity, and pheasants, which would work their way out of the chicken wire. Once, he caught a gopher, which I took to school in a wooden box with a wire top. We did not keep the raccoon in a pen. We had him in the house to begin with, and when he grew, he lived outside. When the weather turned cold, he tried coming into the house through the squirrel-cage swamp cooler, and he got stuck. When someone tried to pull him out, he became combative, and in the end, I was the only one he would let extract him. He and I were good friends after that. I would carry him around or sit with him in my lap. He fell into disfavor, however, when he took to hanging on the underside of the chicken pens and chewing their toes off. My father took him for a ride, only in the literal sense, and he came back. The next time, my father took him across the river and let him off, and we did not see him again.

Inside the house, on the wall above the table where we ate, hung a large, colorful calendar illustration of a roundup camp. A meal was cooking on the fire, a man in an apron was ringing the triangle, and riders were on the way in. One rider was swinging down from the saddle, another was close in, and a few more were on the way. My brothers and I projected our family members into the figures in the picture. The cook was Grandpa. One of the riders was our father, and the others corresponded according to faint resemblance.

We had heard many stories about the cattle business. My father and my grandfather had had a diversified farming and ranching operation, so we heard about raising beans, flax, mustard, and market tomatoes. But my father's passion was buying and selling cattle, and when the two of them decided to specialize in cattle, they gave up their long-time lease with Union Oil in Santa Barbara County and bought the ranch in Oregon.

What remained, in addition to the calendar, was a stately mule deer head (much larger than the coastal deer in California), a separate rack of antlers on a varnished rectangular plywood plaque, two sets of deer hooves mounted to serve as gun racks, and a leather briefcase containing A. Nesbitt and Son stationery, a few flyers for past livestock sales, and other assorted papers.

At the table, or when we went somewhere in the car, we heard the plan. We were going to get back into the cattle business together. Sandy would by the buyer and the business genius. Johnny would be the bookkeeper. Bobby would be the mechanic to keep all the trucks and other equipment running. Our father would teach Sandy the business. We would all work together and pool our money to put me through college for an accounting degree. Bob would go to a trade school.

Our father was so insistent with this plan that none of us disagreed or raised doubts. He had our aptitudes well matched with our roles, and none of us, as far as I knew, had yet formed an idea of some other career. Our father registered a brand for us, the numeral 4 in a circle, and he had a small brand made. We burned it into the flat end of a baseball bat handle.

Sandy was also going to learn to auctioneer. My father could do a little of it, and he would practice it when we were in the car. He would sell things we saw along the way, and the three of us would bid on them.

My father ordered a set of lessons on a 78 rpm record. The lessons started out slow, with "Bid-a-one, go-one, bid-a-one, go-one," and picked up. From time to time, they would break into a flurry of the real thing, to keep up interest.

As for me, I was on my way to any line of work that required learning. Sandy and I were good in all subjects at school, and I learned things from him a year ahead of time, such as how to borrow and carry in arithmetic.

Our father pushed us to do well in school. We never missed a day. He kept track of when we had tests, and he would ask how we did, who got the best grade. Sandy and I often did. Bob did all right in school, but Sandy and I were the stars.

My father would sometimes say, "I got a high school diploma, and it never did me any good." He meant that it was never required for a job and it never made him any money. But he did not belittle education itself. He was proud to see us excel in a small world where we had so few advantages. We did not dress well, we often needed a haircut, we did not have dental care, and we did not have a mother to do all the things that other children took for granted.

On the other hand, we had each other. We lived by ourselves with no neighbors for miles. We did not go to other people's houses, and they did not come to ours. My father's Negro friend and pal from work, Robert, would visit for a few drinks. Otherwise, it was us, and in some ways, it was us against the world.

Along with telling us of his days of prosperity, when a

person would ask him for a dime and he would give him ten dollars, my father had a wounded sense of going broke. "When you're down, they kick you," he would say. There was some truth to the saying. Public assistance was very hard to get, for a man in that time and place, and for a man who did farm work, being laid off in the winter was inevitable.

One method of survival was to stick together. Our father drilled that idea into us, over and over. "You boys stick together," or "Stick up for your brother." I do not remember when I first heard him express that philosophy. It might have been before he went broke, or before I went to school with Sandy for a day. It might have been at the time when Sandy and I worked with him in the orchard and were stiffed for our wages. Now it included Bob, and, although David lived in town with Grandpa and Grandma, it included him as well. The brand on the hilt of the bat handle was a four.

———

As we raised our calves and goats and pigs, our father looked for other ways of building up. We tried chickens, but the margin was poor. The chicks were cute and fluffy when they came in flats in the mail, but of those that grew up and put on feathers, any number might turn up dead in the morning, each with two holes in its neck, the mark of a weasel. My father looked into raising chinchillas, and then we settled on rabbits.

He and Sandy went to meetings of a rabbit growers' association. I went to at least one meeting and watched the films. I read a book entitled *Domestic Rabbit Production*, which my father also read. We built up our breeding stock and kept records in a ledger. The does all had numbers, and the bucks had letters. If we bred #27 to D, the information went in a ledger. We kept track of how many babies a doe had and how many she raised. Seven or eight was a good average. Does that fell too far short of that became dinner for our table.

My father built pens and next boxes. He and my grandfather built a shed with upright railroad ties and a roof that kept a straight ridge line. Sandy was allowed to work up off the ground with them. I handed things on a device like a hod, which hod carriers used to carry bricks and mortar. Mine consisted of two short boards fastened at a right angle, attached to a two-by-two for a handle. I handed up nails and small tools and, on at least one occasion, cold beer.

Raising rabbits was a good enterprise. The animals were clean and docile, and the production was efficient. The does were in gestation for a month, the babies were weaned after a month, and the fryers were ready in another month or so. My father asked my grandfather to teach Sandy how to butcher rabbits. My father was a good teacher, but my grandfather was not. He killed and cleaned one rabbit, then another, but he did not explain anything. Sandy learned, and he taught Bob and me.

We had rabbits to take to the market, alive or dressed. People came to the house to buy them. If they wanted them cleaned, Sandy would do it in a jiffy. He could process a rabbit from beginning to end in one minute.

One man who came to buy rabbits was a retired barber. His name was Lyon. He was pale and slender, and his wife was the same, with thinning red hair. In exchange for the rabbits, he would cut our hair at the rate of a dollar per head. My father sat in. Like many barbers, Lyon could talk the whole time.

We peppered the pelts, stretched them, and pegged them with clothespins on wire racks my father made. We sold red worms from the manure beds. We sold rabbit feet at school, having peppered the raw end and let the foot to dry before we tied a string to it.

We were not prosperous, but we were working together out on our hardscrabble place. I knew that we owed money at the little store in Grimes and at the feed store in Colusa. My brothers knew it, too. We kept track of how much we made on our own enterprises like raising calves, and when the money went toward living expenses, we kept a running total of how much we would have coming to us some day.

————

School was a sanctuary because it was a place where a person like me or any of my brothers could have worth. We were not valued or judged on the basis of who our family was or what we could afford. In the classroom, we had equal opportunity, and we were recognized according to our achievement. One could say that we were rewarded according to our ability, but it was not quite so. I knew more than one person growing up who was told, early on, that he had a high IQ and great ability, and the person seemed to think that having the ability was good enough. It wasn't. A person had to work and learn, study and memorize, and apply knowledge from one area to another.

From early on, I felt that school, or public education, was a place of true equality. Later in life, I would understand that I had advantages nevertheless. I was aware of some of them at the time—that I lived in one of the best states in the country for economy, agricultural production, and natural beauty; that we had one of the best educational systems in the country; and that I was a male. Later I would understand that I also had the advantage of being white. In all the towns we lived in and in all the schools we went to, there was a small ethnic mix, with Mexican Americans, Native Americans, Asians, and some-times a Black family. I imagine that some of these students felt a disadvantage, but I was not aware of it—perhaps because my family was poor, but also because in small-town life in California at that time, there was less prejudice than in later years, when many of those same people became older and responded to change in society. Many of the children my age were grand-children of immigrants. My father's parents came from Ireland, and my mother's parents came from Hungary. In my father's generation, in rural California, the Portuguese married

Portuguese, the Italians married Italians, and so forth. At the same time, there was a big push to be American, which meant to set aside or suppress differences. Still, there may have been some prejudice, although I did not feel much of it.

I also came to understand later in life that even if education seemed egalitarian or democratic, not everyone felt that way. It was evident all along that not everybody liked school, but it was not until I was in my profession, more or less on top of my early problems in adjustment, that I learned from my own students that school made them feel stupid, inferior, and sometimes unwanted. Rather late in my career, I heard a vice president of student services express the idea that the most important feeling for a student was that he or she belonged. That helped me understand why education had such a good influence on me. Not only did I feel valued for who I was and what I could achieve, but I felt that I belonged there. I always knew that education provided, for me, what many people received at home and in their families. Education was open to everyone. We all had the same books, the same classes, and the same libraries. My great fortune was that I felt that I belonged. One person who helped me feel that way was Mrs. Brose, and another was Mr. Burchfield.

Colusa was just a small town in the middle of the Sacramento Valley. It was not on either of the two main highways, as Orland and Gridley were. It was built right along the Sacramento River, where the weather was sweltering in the summer and the mosquitoes were terrible. The water had a bad taste all year round. But in those days, very good educators ended up in many out-of-the-way places. Mr. Burchfield was principal of Colusa Elementary School, and he was a benevolent figure for all of his students. He might have been the person who helped drag Eric down the hallway on the first day of school; I do not remember. But I do remember that his presence was felt.

I can see him still, standing in the doorway of Mrs. Brose's classroom, looking at the students, smiling, and rubbing his hands together in an up-and-down motion. He was tall and silver-haired, always immaculate in a shirt and tie, always cordial with a pleasant voice. I am sure he knew every student, and every student knew him. By the fourth grade, we were moving into that age where we would make fun of our teachers by referring to them by their first names or distorting their names. I do not remember anybody ever referring to him as anything but Mr. Burchfield. And I do not remember anyone being afraid of him.

When I was in the fourth grade, a Hispanic boy named Jesse wore a pair of shoes that had the soles coming apart. I knew him as a friend, his brother Nicolas played marbles with my brother Bob, and his father came to buy rabbits. I had worn shoes with floppy soles as well, so I knew how he felt.

One day, our teacher, Mrs. Montgomery, told the class that Jesse had not come to school for the last few days because somebody had made fun of him for his shoes. She said she hoped that whoever did it would know better.

The next day, Jesse came back to school. He smiled as he showed us his new shoes, and he had a cheerful tone as he said that Mr. Burchfield had bought them for him.

I came to understand how it worked when, later on, I was called to Mr. Burchfield's office, and he took me downtown and had me fitted out with a pair of shoes—good, durable shoes for someone who lived in the country.

My father went to talk to Mr. Burchfield, to express his gratitude and to protest that the principal did not have to do something like that. My father said he did not feel right accepting that kind of charity. Mr. Burchfield told him not to feel bad about it, because he had a group of people, businessmen and other citizens who could afford it, who contributed to a fund to buy shoes for students who needed them. My father felt better after talking to Mr. Burchfield. Later on, my two brothers each received a pair as well.

There were no lunch programs for needy students in those days, but Mr. Burchfield had a discreet plan for some assistance in that area. For a period of time—not the whole school year, but, I imagine, as long as the funds lasted—Mr. Burchfield arranged for my brothers and me to eat in the cafeteria and not be charged. None of the other children asked questions or made comments, and we were not made to feel patronized.

If there was ever a person whose actions refuted the saying that when you're down they kick you, it was Mr. Burchfield. I was not surprised, when I was looking things up more than forty years later, to learn that a newer elementary school carried his name. Several years after that, I came across an alumni newsletter online. People had great praise for Mrs. Brose and referred to her as Pat, but the principal was still Mr. Burchfield.

———

I continued to enjoy all aspects of school. Once in a while, we had programs in an auditorium with a large crowd. One program that brought us great delight was "The Bremen Town Musicians." For me, it offered an early example of the magic of the theater. I would remember the speaking donkey forever. A more realistic, more practical program came our way with Nehi, a fluffy little dog. Nehi was the name of a soft drink at the time, but the dog's name came from its stature. Nehi's mission was to teach us safety. Two young men conducted the show. In one skit, one of the fellows brought out a bicycle and called to his friend, "Hey, Duffy, you wanna ride double?" Duffy said, "Sure do," and as he was preparing to sit up on the handlebars, Nehi came running and barking to prevent such dangerous behavior.

During this time, Sandy was reading books about Freddy the Pig. The stories took place on the farm of Mr. Bean. All the animals could talk, and they had names. Sandy introduced the stories to me, of course, and before long, I was reading them along with him. I began by reading *Freddy the Detective*, went on to such volumes as *Freddy the Cowboy* and

Freddy Rides Again, and progressed to *Freddy and the Space Ship.*

————

At the end of the school year in mid-June, we had a picnic on the large front lawn, in the shade of spreading elm trees. The whole school sat on the ground together, with hot dogs, potato salad, cake, and ice cream. Mr. Burchfield went among us, wishing us a good summer vacation. All children looked forward to vacation, but I was also sad to be away from school.

On the last day of school in 1957, we took a different bus and got off at a field where my father was irrigating. We floated on a straw bale in the irrigation ditch and tried to catch small, hopping frogs.

At home on our place in the country, the summer turned into monotony. The weather was already hot in mid-June. The weeds had dried. The barley was harvested at about that time. We had a few small heaps of bulging burlap sacks to play on, and then they were gone, leaving dry stubble all around us. The gnats were a plague. We had our hair cut short for the summer, but we had to soak our heads several times a day to try to keep the gnats off. Still, they raised red bumps on our scalps. My father wore a turban beneath his cap, and when he ate lunch in the field, he had to walk back and forth to keep the gnats from settling. If one of us went with him for the day, we did the same.

At home, we did our chores. We tried making a swimming or bathing pool by digging a hole and filling it with water, but it was too muddy to enjoy. In the heat of the day, we hid in the house. We soaked in cold water in the bathtub.

We were careful with fire. The year before, Bob had started a fire in the barley stubble, and June deployed us with burlap sacks soaked in the washtub. This summer, we were by ourselves all day long. We had to be careful about everything.

One day, two young fellows were driving around in the

barley field in a Jeep. Any people were a novelty, and those two were racing around. We knew one of them. Sandy and I climbed up onto the barbed-wire fence to wave at them as they came speeding past us. They laughed and beeped as they roared by. The commotion caused me to lose my grasp, and I fell backward. A barb went through my pants leg and cut a slice in the calf of my left leg.

Sandy took me to the house and bandaged my leg with blue freezer tape. When my father came home, he looked at it and said it was about as good as anyone could have done. The cut healed into a wide scar, but it never gave me any trouble.

———

In the fourth grade with Mrs. Montgomery, I did well in all subjects. In those days, it was common for a teacher handing back tests to announce who had the highest score or who had a hundred percent. I would feel the suspense, and whenever I was named, which was often, I felt the euphoria. Spelling tests were the most frequent, and I did very well on them.

We had standardized tests that year, and I scored high. For a while, there was talk about passing me on into the fifth grade. At that point in social history, some students skipped grades, while others were held back. While these talks were going on between the school personnel and my father, it came out that I was already young for my grade, so I stayed where I was. I was not bored, though. I did my work and found plenty to read.

———

In one incident that occurred during this time, the world of school did not raise me up from the feeling I had of being an inferior boy with dirt caked on his jeans. About a year or so after my unsuccessful request to join the Cub Scouts, I had the opportunity to participate in music. My father did not have much aptitude for music and did not express much appreciation for the other arts, either. He said our mother could hear a tune somewhere and come home and play it on the piano. He seemed to admire the talent, but he may have been jealous as well. When it came to one of us wanting to undertake music, he would say that was for our mother. Nevertheless, I was allowed to try an instrument. The band teacher had a trumpet to lend me, so there was no expense to present itself.

I took the trumpet home and practiced it outside, away from the house and other people. I practiced it until my lips became numb and swollen. Moisture ran out of the instrument. I blared away, crooking my finger on the hook and depressing some of the valves just to hear the different sounds.

When I finished my practice session, I could not get the mouthpiece to come out. I twisted and pulled but could not move it. In a bad moment, I tried a pair of pliers, but all I succeeded at doing was to flatten the tube of the mouthpiece.

If it had been something else that I felt less private about, I might have asked for help. Someone might have told me to let the band teacher solve the problem of taking out the mouthpiece, or even when I had done the damage, someone might have told me how to apologize to the band teacher. Instead, I suffered in silence and shame. I put the trumpet in its case with the mouthpiece sticking out the end. I hid it at home, and I covered it with a jacket when I took it on the bus the next morning. Still early, I took it to the band room and left it.

Nothing came of my error. No one asked me questions, held me to account, or offered to make things better. I lived with my guilt, and I did not feel that I belonged in that smaller world of band and music.

———

My father went one whole year without drinking while we lived in the house near Grimes. I do not remember which year it was, and I do not remember a time when things were better for it. Drunk or sober, my father had a short temper and was given to rant about the same old things.

"I work my ass off for you kids, twelve, fourteen hours a day, seven days a week, and no one appreciates it. What did your mother ever do for you? She ran off and left you, that's what. Left me to raise all four of you."

It was hard to listen to, but we were used to the routine and bore with it. It was hard to be told how to feel. And it was hard for us, at a young age, to appreciate how difficult my father had it. He had to work long hours because the boss expected it and because he had to work all the hours he could in good weather. When winter came, income went down to zero. One time, my father showed the boss all the repairs he had done to the house, at his own expense. The boss said, "I gave you a dime raise last year." It brought him up to $1.30 an hour, when he worked.

He was proud that we never missed a meal, and he never begrudged us for how much we ate or for our basic needs. But he would revert to his complaint.

"A lot of guys wouldn't do what I did. They would have left you at an orphanage. I've had 'em ask me why I didn't, but I just couldn't."

It was difficult for me to feel thankful that he did not leave us at an orphanage, because it did not seem as if it was an option for him. As he himself said, he didn't have it in him. Also, I thought he was doing what he was supposed to do anyway. Furthermore, I did not know how many men would leave their children at an institution. Later in life I would come to know that some men did give up their children. I would also learn that many more of them just took off and left the mother to bear the brunt of the abandonment. Our case was an unusual exception, something like the reverse. I do not remember being bitter about it. It was just the way things were.

———

One Sunday afternoon, a man and a boy came to visit. The boy, Greg, was a friend of mine from school. He played outside with us while our fathers sat inside and talked. Greg told us that his father was going to ask if Greg could stay with us for a while. When they left, we asked our father what the outcome was. He confirmed that Greg's father was looking for a place to leave the boy for a while, but my father already had as much as he could handle.

It did not occur to me that my father had had even more to pay for when June and Rosie and then the baby lived with us, before the ten-cent raise. Things did not seem to change. One day, in a typical somber moment, I said to Bob, "We're poor." He agreed.

———

I ran around in circles on the clover lawn my father had planted, emptying one water jug and then the other. The moon was out on a clear summer night, just right for me cackling like a witch as the water gurgled out. My father was inside, taking his supper and trying to rest for another long day. He kept two of these jugs—one-gallon wine bottles he had wrapped with burlap and had sewn snug with the needles he used for sewing sacks in the bean or grain harvest. When I had the jugs emptied, I filled them with fresh water, careful not to chip the glass mouth on the faucet. I soaked the burlap and put the jugs in place in their wooden box. I was careful with the jugs. I remembered when one came home broken from being cracked against the steel track on the Caterpillar tractor. The sagging burlap held a mass of broken glass. My father had to rig up another one with a jug he acquired from the sheepherders. I remembered them, too. They lived in a trailer in a sheep camp out by the Sutter Buttes. My father told my grandfather he couldn't believe how clean they were, for sheepherders.

———

With Sandy in the lead, we sneaked out of the house in the dark, each with a club in hand. At the feed shed, Sandy opened the door and turned on the light in an instant, and the three of us began clubbing rats. They squealed and scrambled, and we banged on the steel feed barrels as much as we did on them.

Rats grew in great number in that climate, and they came in from the bare fields. We trapped them and poisoned them, and there were still so many that we had to kill them by hand. One Sunday morning, Sandy got up early and killed nine by himself. He laid them out to show Bob and me. Most of the time, we killed them at night, after a television program ended. We made our raid, disposed of the dead, and went into the kitchen to have a drink of Kool-Aid. Holding up our glasses, we said, "To the rats."

THREE

For a while, we had a pretty housekeeper named Dixie. She was blond and smiling, quite the contrast with June. She came in response to an ad my father put in the Sacramento paper. She was from somewhere around Sacramento, and she was hoping to get her kids back. I was very fond of her, and she was nice to us, but she moved on.

When Dixie was gone, another woman answered my father's ad. Her name was Donna. She was tall and slender with brown hair and prominent yellow teeth. She wore lipstick and held her cigarette between the ends of her first two fingers. She wore a dark bandanna around her head and undertook the housework, but not quite like the woman on the Old Dutch Cleanser can. She paused to smoke a cigarette or have a drink. Before long, we learned that her name was Donna Dunlap and she had worked in Sacramento for a Filipino man named Max who had four or five children.

One day she went to Sacramento to fetch the rest of her belongings or to tend to some other aspect of business. As I recall, she spent the night. When she was coming back on the river road, she rolled her car off the levee. As she would tell us many times, the sun was in her eyes.

From the hospital, she wrote letters to my father with lipstick kisses and "SWAK" on the back of the envelope. We went to visit her in the hospital on a sunny day. In the parking lot, we drank down half of two bottles of Nesbitt's Orange, and my father filled them with vodka and re-capped them. In the hospital room, he put the rest of the half-pint of vodka inside the back of Donna's radio. We had a nice visit at the hospital, although we could not all be in her room at once.

When she came home from the hospital, she was in a wheelchair. My brothers and I waited on her, bringing her coffee or vodka or wine as well as doing the cooking and the other housework. I learned that her family name was Christensen and her father was tall. I understood from my father that she had been married four times, the most recent man being Dunlap and the first one being a man named Sommers, the father of her son, who lived with her parents in Santa Cruz.

As with June, I got along well with her. She told me her son was in the same grade as I was. His name was Fred.

My father and Donna drank and argued. Sometimes they were lovey-dovey. One day we went on a drive, the two of them in the front seat and the three of us boys in the back seat. My father took to wooing her, and she demurred. He brought us into it, prompting us to tell her we wanted her to be our new mother.

———

That summer, the rabbits began to die. At first we thought it was the heat, so we became more diligent about sprinkling the roof and the manure beds. My father also experimented with a misting system. But the rabbits kept dying, several per day. We opened up a few and did not see any evidence of a liver disease that sometimes took one. The fur came off in patches on some of the rabbits. We wondered if they had caught a disease from the mosquitoes. My father took a few down to the university in Davis, which had a famed agricultural school, and he called back several times, but he did not learn anything from there.

Before the mortality began, we had more than a hundred does and as many as twenty bucks. We had gone through the alphabet once. We had more than a thousand rabbits in all, including a line of checkered rabbits that I thought of as my own. We had them in many pretty colors, and they died the same in great numbers. Every day, my brothers and I had to dig in the hard, dry ground to bury another ten or twenty.

In the latter part of the summer, my father had a business trip to make. His Aunt Jenny, his mother's sister, was selling her house in Santa Barbara and going into a rest home. I knew who Aunt Jenny was, for I had written and addressed letters to her on a street called West Canon Perdido, at my father's dictation, along with letters to an aunt who lived in Ozone Park, Long Island, and an aunt who lived in Moose Jaw, Saskatchewan. (Later I would learn that Canon was Cañón and that Cañón Perdido meant Lost Canyon.)

The trip must have been serious for my father to have to take time off from work in the summer. He set off with Donna and Sandy for company. Bob and I stayed at home to take care of the animals and garden and to bury rabbits. Grandpa came out to look after us, and we spent some nights in town.

A small pinpoint in history occurred at this time. For the first time in many years, the price of postage went up, from two cents to three. It would have little consequence for a boy living out in the country, except that I had seen a contest on a kids' program on television, and I wanted to send in my entry. On a trip to town, under the guise of going to the park, I slipped off to the post office and mailed my envelope. The next day, I learned that postage was going up, and I was left to wonder forever whether my entry arrived.

Sandy came home full of stories from the trip. The biggest news was that our father and Donna had gotten married in Tijuana. I knew that people went to Tijuana as well as to Reno and Las Vegas to get married because it was easier than in California, where people had to wait three days for a blood test. The test was said to serve the purpose of detecting genetic incompatibilities and inadvertent incest, but I later learned that its primary purpose was to detect syphilis. I also learned, later, that Donna had not been in the habit of obtaining divorces except from her first husband. People could marry in Tijuana with no questions asked, and, although I do not think it was anyone's intention on this occasion, people could later regard a marriage in Tijuana as not being worth the paper it was written on. It was not on record anywhere in the U.S.

Sandy also told me they had picked up Fred on the way. Sandy did not speak well of him, as Fred had been grabby when the four of them were sorting out Aunt Jenny's effects in the house on West Canon Perdido, and he had been obnoxious in other ways. Fred and Sandy had attended the happy event in Tijuana, and Fred was going to come live with us later on. For the present, we had someone we now had to call Mom, and we were to do whatever she said.

———

Fred came to stay with us in the fall. My brothers and I were small for our ages, and he was big. He and I were both in the fifth grade, so it fell to me to share a room with him, while Sandy and Bob shared another room. Fred's father had been in the Army, so Fred wore a military jacket with his father's medals, and he had toy soldiers. He and I agreed that he could have his toys on one half of the dresser top and I could have mine on the other half. But Fred was an only child, spoiled by Grandma Christensen, and he had not learned to share as we had. I came into the room and saw soldiers and tanks where I was supposed to be able to put my cowboys and horses.

I took a paper bag and began clearing his things off of my area on the dresser, and he smacked me on the temple with his fist. I might have called him something like a fat slob, and he hit me again. I went down, and when I came up, I was dizzy. I still had to share the room with him.

I also had to introduce him to my friends at school. He embarrassed me by talking so much, but at least one girl was impressed by his father's medals.

———

Fred had to do his share of the housework, and he did not like it. When it became evident that he and I would be on schedule to wash dishes at Thanksgiving, he whined for days and begged his mother to use paper plates. We laughed at him for being afraid of work.

He said he wanted a job that would pay him money.

My father came home one day and said, "I found you a job in town."

"Really? Doing what?"

"It's at the jeweler's. Shoveling shit out of cuckoo clocks."

On another day, my father said, "I found you a job in town."

Fred fell for it again and asked what the work was.

"It's at the Ford agency. Shoveling shit out of the show-room to make room for the new models."

"You sure want me to shovel shit."

My brothers and I looked at each other. We spoke that way to one another, but not in front of our father.

———

I turned ten in December, and thanks to Donna, I had a birthday party. It was the only birthday party I had when I was growing up, and it was an extraordinary event. My friends, boys and girls, came from town to our house, and we had cake and ice cream. It was not the time of year to have sack races outside, but we played games like Pin the Tail on the Donkey inside. When the party was over and the children were gone, I wandered among the paper cups and plates and thought about what a special event it had been.

———

My father had missed my birthday party because my grandmother was sick, and he and my grandfather had to take her to the hospital.

On the day after my birthday, in the middle of the week, Donna gathered us in my grandparents' house and told us our grandmother had died. She was very old, about eighty-five (no one knew for sure), and she had had an abscess on her lower abdomen. Our father was broken up, and he and my grandfather were making funeral arrangements.

My three brothers and I were pallbearers. To fill out the group of six, Fred and a friend of Sandy's joined us. My father bought matching shirts all the way down from Fred to David. The services in the funeral chapel were austere, and my father choked up when he assured the funeral director he would pay him for it.

———

I did not get along with Fred, but he could knock me down any time he wanted. He was not so lucky with Sandy. Fred thought he should have more authority, being the biggest, but Sandy was used to being the oldest and in charge. He was also good with his fists and was used to defending himself against bigger kids.

Donna called Sandy "Mac," after Sandy MacTavish, a cartoon character in advertising. A car dealer in Sacramento also used the name.

One day Bob and I were in the back yard, while Sandy and Fred were having a dispute inside the house. As the commotion grew louder, Bob and I crawled underneath the house to listen and to stay out of the way. Scuffling traveled across the floor above us as Fred cried out, "Stop! Don't hit me!" and Donna called, "Hit him, Mac, hit him!"

The fight had started in the living room, had carried through the dining room and kitchen, and now thumped on the back porch right above us. In a few more seconds, they were in the backyard, where Fred was holding up his hands and Sandy was stepping into him and punching him left, right, left. Fred fell back onto a bench by the clothesline and scattered a basket of clothespins.

Bob and I came out and heard the story. Sandy and Fred had been arguing in the living room, and when Sandy turned to leave, Fred threw a pair of pinking shears at him, which struck with the tips between Sandy's shoulder blades. That was not a fair fight as we knew it, using a weapon when the other person's back was turned. Even though Donna did not adore Sandy, she said Fred got what he deserved.

My brothers and I were not sad when Fred went back to live with Grandpa and Grandma Christensen.

———

Our father and Donna drank and argued, so in a way, life was like it was in the earlier days. But Donna was crude and sarcastic. She went around the house in her undergarments, and in cold weather, she would turn her back to the heater, raise her dress, and rub her buttocks. She complained that my father thought Sandy was "the little Lord Jesus," and she called my father "Kroo-cheff," a grave insult taking the name of Nikita Khrushchev, leader of the Soviet Union. She stuck out her tongue and called, "Russian!"

My father hollered back, "Don't call me a Communist!"

"Kroo-cheff! You're just a dictator."

She went from name-calling to more dreadful accusations, which may have been true. "You tore my clothes off me while I was in the wheelchair."

"No, I didn't."

"Liar!"

One night, the argument went up to a notch we were not familiar with. Sandy and I were in bed, and he nudged me. Our father's voice was coming through the wall.

"If that baby has slant eyes, I'll kill you. If I look through that window and see that baby with slant eyes, I'll take my .22 to the hospital, and I'll shoot you right between the eyes. I'll scatter your brains all over the floor. Do you hear me? Right between the eyes."

I knew the scene was real, because Sandy and I repeated it to each other the next day. As with many things my father said when he was drunk, nothing came of it.

Years later, my father told me he had been suspicious of why Donna had gone to see Max on the trip when she wrecked her car. He badgered her and badgered her, and on one cold, rainy day in the car, she confessed that she had had sex with Max on that trip. "But he only went in this far," she said, showing a span of two inches between thumb and forefinger. The encounter had happened months before the marriage in Tijuana and Donna's subsequent pregnancy, but my father could not let anything rest.

———

In school, things went on in a normal way. I did well in all subjects, and the teachers encouraged us to read. I read a great many books about frontier and western heroes, such as Daniel Boone, Davy Crockett, Sam Houston, Big Foot Wallace, Kit Carson, Buffalo Bill, Wild Bill Hickok, and others. In fourth grade we had California history, and in fifth grade we had U.S. History. All of it held great interest for me, as did geography. I read books on the school bus, which with its many stops took about an hour each way.

An older boy on the bus was reading *The Deerslayer* by James Fenimore Cooper, and he recommended it to me. I found the vocabulary and the elaborate sentences difficult and uninteresting. Either the teacher or the librarian recommended *Oliver Twist* by Charles Dickens, and I had a similar experience of feeling that the writing was too dense and slow for me. However, I did make it as far as the part in which Oliver requests more gruel, and I thought I would come back and try the book again when I was older.

My father turned forty on February 3, 1959. Many years later, I would learn that on that day, Ritchie Valens, Buddy Holly, and The Big Bopper died in a plane crash. We had no awareness of such an event out where we lived. We did understand that turning forty was an important moment in the lives of grownups.

Grandpa and David came out to live in a house trailer that was parked in the muddy yard of winter. Donna had someone to appeal to when she and my father argued, but I do not think my grandfather cared much for her.

During this time, a while after my father's birthday, we learned that a change was under way. Donna, whose family lived in Santa Cruz and San Mateo Counties, south of San Francisco, persuaded my father to look for better-paying work in those areas. He found a job on a cattle ranch in the mountains east of San Mateo. Like other traditional ranch jobs, it provided a house, meat, and a vehicle so my father would not have to use his own for work. He told me that when he went for the interview, the furniture in the ranch house had calfskin upholstery, and the house had plenty of woodwork. It was the type of thing he liked.

We boys thought it sounded good. We thought it might

fulfill a promise we had lived with, that some day we would have a horse.

The job did not start until later in the year, however, and my father was still out of work for the winter. He decided to find a job in the San Mateo area in the meanwhile, and he succeeded. He found work in Half Moon Bay, on the coast, with a greenhouse nursery company from Daly City, in the San Francisco area, that was setting up a new location in the small town about thirty miles south of The City.

I was chosen to go with Donna and our father, while Sandy and Bob would stay with Grandpa and David. We would take the trailer, and the four of them would stay in the house.

With about three months remaining in the school year, I went with my father to say goodbye to Mr. Burchfield. After our short visit in his office, he stood up and shook my hand. He said, "Goodbye, John. I want to hear from you in ten years. From Stanford." With blinking eyes and a tightness in my throat, I left the school in Colusa that had been so good to me.

I awoke in the trailer in an unfamiliar atmosphere. My father and Donna were still asleep, so I went outside. Fog hung thick on the hillside where we were parked. The air was different, the plants were different, and the soil was different. I saw snails. I found an empty waxed milk carton and began to collect snails. They crawled up out of the carton with a method of movement I had not seen before.

My father came out and asked me what the hell I was doing that for. I told him I was interested in my discovery, and he scowled. Those slimy things? He had seen millions of them in Santa Barbara County.

I enrolled in my new fifth-grade class. My teacher was a portly woman with brown hair and beady eyes. She made fun of me for my long hair and the substance I applied to keep it in place. The boys called me Shaggy, in reference to a new Disney movie named *The Shaggy Dog*.

The classroom work was casual, and I did not have much competition in becoming the top student in my class. But I did not feel welcome with either the teacher or the students. I did not feel well, and for a week or so, I kept company with my stepmother.

We went here and there, to the local drugstore for medicine for me, and "over the hill" to San Mateo, where the big supermarkets were located. In the parking lot of one store, she pointed out a new car with some well-dressed people in it.

"R.B.'s," she said.

"What's that?"

"Rich bitches."

One of the well-off individuals was a male. I wondered about my stepmother's vocabulary, and I was surprised at her sentiment. We had been poor for as long as I remembered, but I had not known anyone who resented others for having more.

Inside a supermarket, she slipped a pack of cigarettes into the pocket of her long coat. When I showed her a candy par I would like to have, she said, "Just put it in your pocket." She seemed so calm about it that I was not afraid when I did what she told me to do.

On the soft side, she avoided running over a paper bag in the street. There was always a chance there was a cat inside, she said.

When I returned to school, my teacher upbraided me. "Where have you been? Why have you been gone so long? People said they've seen you everywhere."

———

My father, Donna, and I went over the hill to go shopping. We were in a big supermarket, close to closing time. My father was shopping for bargains, as always, and he bought in quantities such as cases of canned goods. We had two carts of groceries at the checkout, and the clerk was calling out the prices as he hit the keys on the cash register. When he came to the two large cans of coffee, he said there was a limit of one per customer because the item was on sale.

My father asked him what he meant, and the man repeated his statement. My father said they couldn't do that, it wasn't fair, and there was no sign or notice announcing it where the coffee was on display. The argument continued, and the store manager came into the discussion. He said the same thing, that there was a limit of one per customer. My father argued more, and the manager did not budge.

My father had already raised his voice, and now he shouted. "Well, shove it in your ass! All of it! Just shove it in your ass! We won't buy a god-damned thing!"

We left the two carts of groceries where they were, as customers and employees stared.

We went back to Half Moon Bay empty-handed. As was his habit, my father said the same thing over and over. "F--- the son of a bitch. Was I right? Huh? F--- him!"

———

My father did well at his new job. The owners were building new greenhouses for cultivating flowers like chrysanthemums, azaleas, and African violets. My father was skilled at carpentry but was also handy with a shovel and wheelbarrow, so the owners treated him well. He started at $1.35, and within a few months, he was making $2.00 an hour. The work was steady and would continue past the construction into year-round employment. The cattle ranch in the mountains disappeared from the family conversation, and my father and Donna made plans to move the whole family to Half Moon Bay.

On the last day of school, one girl had a camera. I did not know her very well because she had been absent quite a bit. She took a picture of the rest of us holding up our report cards to show that we had passed into the sixth grade. Word went around that she was the only who had not passed. She did not seem to worry about it. She smiled as she took our picture, and we all smiled as we held up our report cards.

We made it back to Colusa in time for my sister, Jackie Lee, to be born there on June 10, 1959. The house in the country seemed desolate. The weather was hot already, and all the weeds were dry. My brothers needed haircuts, their clothes were worn, and their underwear hung in tatters. I felt guilty for having had it so well, such as it was.

We were riding in my father's pale yellow Dodge convertible, towing a trailer load of rabbit cages from Grimes to Half Moon Bay. Slim was driving. He was a friend of my father's a Black man. Slim's girlfriend, Bernice, also Black, sat in the middle of the front seat. My father, who had had something to drink, was on the passenger's side. Sandy and I were in the back.

A police car pulled us over after we crossed the Bay Bridge. The officer said he stopped us because the woman was lolling her head around. He asked Slim for his license, and Slim said he didn't have one. The officer reprimanded my father for letting someone drive his car without a license. My father said to Slim, "I didn't know you didn't have a license." Slim said he had not said anything, but that was the case.

My father took the wheel, and we went on. Bernice said over and over, "I told you so, Slim."

They had all had something to drink, and that was why my father had let Slim drive.

———

The move to the coast was arduous. Although we sold off all of our animals, including my two Chinese geese for five dollars, we had to make more than one trip to move tools, feed barrels, water troughs, and rabbit cages.

We moved into an old house on an irregular lot off the coast highway north of Half Moon Bay, near a community named Miramar. The house had two stories, the bottom one being a ground-level basement with a dirt floor. We parked the small house trailer in the dirt yard for a while, but there was room in the house for all of us, including Grandpa and David, so the trailer went away. The house rent was thirty dollars a month.

Fred came and stayed with us for a little while and went back to Santa Cruz, which was about sixty miles down the coast. My brothers and I had a dog. We had a baby sister, which I learned to take care of, as Donna was given to be gone for periods of time. She had me take the empty gin bottles from beneath her car seat and throw them in the trash barrel. My father often had a whiskey bottle beneath his car seat, so that was not unusual. He did not have empty bottles in the closet, however. She did.

Our father worked with a variety of men. One was an old Irishman, a friend of the owners' family. They were all Northern Irish, like my father's family. Another worker was a middle-aged Anglo man who, according to my father, looked as if he was trying to stay sober. Another was a Portuguese man named Joe who spoke little English but communicated with my father, who knew a little Spanish.

One worker was a Mexican lad, who rode back and forth to work with my father. Rather than exchange money, they agreed for the young man to come to our place on the weekend and hoe weeds. Bob and I sat with him outside when he ate lunch, and he taught us a few words in Spanish, including the word for our dog. *Perro.* The way he pronounced the word, it sounded like "payroll," which we knew from the stagecoach holdups in the movies. We already knew a few words in Spanish and liked to chant off the numbers, so this was a nice addition.

Our father told us to be careful about one man named Rudy. He was a darker man who lived by himself. When we saw him driving his car, alone, my father said, "That's Rudy. Don't get in the car with him if he offers you a ride. I heard he's been in trouble for doing things with little kids."

The house we lived in was old and wobbly. My father and grandfather had to dig a new pit and put in a new septic tank. They built it of redwood and dug a leach field.

Grandpa and David stayed in a bedroom that had been built onto one end of the house. On one occasion, Donna was off somewhere, perhaps at her parents' house, and my father did not come home. As we waited, a highway patrolman showed up and told us my father had been taken in for drunk driving. The patrolman asked my grandfather if he was going to bail him out, and my grandfather said it might do him some good to sit and soak.

At some point, my grandfather must have gotten fed up with my father or Donna or both. He and David moved to another community named El Granada, a couple of miles farther north along the coast highway. They lived in a one-room log cabin in the backyard of a chatty old woman named Mrs. Wolfe, who had an eccentric middle-aged son named Chester who still lived at home. The cabin did not have plumbing. The bathroom was inside the back door of Mrs. Wolfe's house. Grandpa and David got along fine there.

———

Sandy, Bob, and I were riding with our father in the Dodge convertible. Our father handed Sandy a brown bag with an empty wine bottle in it. Our father did not litter, with the exception of empty liquor bottles, which he did not want to have on hand if a cop stopped him. Sandy stood up, drew back his left arm, and hurled the bottle at a billboard. With the speed of the car, however, the bottle in its bag sailed over the billboard and landed on the roof of a house, where it rolled up the pitch of the roof, over the ridge, and down the other slope. We turned and watched as we cruised by, and the timing worked out for us to see the bottle, now out of its bag, land in someone's front yard.

My father was furious. That was a good way to get turned in. All he wanted Sandy to do was toss the bottle into the roadside ditch. What the hell made him throw it like that?

For us boys, it was a moment of unity in a small, humorous way. We kept our mouths shut as we knew how.

———

When I went back to school in the fall and entered sixth grade, I was in class with many of the same students as the year before. Bob was in the fourth grade in the same school, and Sandy was in seventh grade, across the highway at the junior high. I should have felt more at home in the school, but I still felt like an outsider. The boys still called me Shaggy, and my teacher was not much more cordial than the one I had the year before.

The six grade was not hard. I finished all of my work in short order when it was assigned, and I did all of the work for another boy, Jimmy. I think I did it in an effort to have someone like me. I also did a great deal of the teacher's grading for her, and I still had time to read works such as *Robinson Crusoe* and *Evangeline*. In addition to all this, I was a hallway traffic officer at the other end of the school, where my brother Bob attended class. I had a yellow cap and a white diagonal belt.

Little by little, I became friends with some of the other boys, and I learned of their interests. They bragged about shoplifting, stealing money from their parents, smoking, and knowing dirty things from their older brothers. Jimmy was as bad as any of them. One of his suspensions from school came from his lewd comments he made to a girl as he was peeling a banana.

Half Moon Bay should have been a polite, civil community like the ones I knew in the valley, as there were dairies and small farms, where people grew cabbage, Brussels sprouts, artichokes, peas, and other row crops. Residents also worked in fishing and related businesses, such as places that sold fresh fish, cooked crabs, or clam chowder and broth. Half or more of the students had Anglo-American last names. Many of them had familiar-sounding Portuguese and Italian names. Several came from Filipino families, which for a generation or two had abounded in those areas where there was work to be found in the carrot, onion, garlic, and asparagus fields. There were a few students of Mexican origin and one Black student in Sandy's grade. My classmates spoke of an Indian or Native American student who had lived there a while. His name was Digger, and they referred to him as "Digger the ------," even in class.

I do not know where the general incivility came from, but the boys in my grade and in the next one aspired to a kind of hoodlum culture. Some of it might have come from the movies, and some of it might have come from television. Movies showing juvenile delinquency, such as *Hot Car Girl* and *King Creole*, were popular. I saw them both in the show house in Half Moon Bay. There were plenty of old gangster movies on television, and my classmates knew of Al Capone and Alcatraz. Even if the stories had moralistic endings, there was plenty of vicarious illegal experience for young boys to revel in and repeat.

I do not think they got it from books, as I do not recall any of them reading or talking about what they read. This atmosphere or collective attitude may have derived in part from being close to San Francisco, which everyone referred to, with near reverence, as The City.

————

Donna had a cat named Snowball. My father had never liked cats, so we were not used to them. This one was not a good introduction. He walked the length of the table, lifting his tail and showing his anus. If someone left a butter dish on the table, the cat found it and licked the cube into a small mound.

We did not have bicycles earlier because my father had known them to be dangerous to the point of people being killed on them, and he was not around to supervise us. Donna did not supervise much, either, but she lobbied with our father for us to have bicycles. Sandy was the first. He was acquiring a newspaper route, so a bicycle was almost indispensable. Sandy bought his bicycle for three dollars, exacted a bill of sale as he was instructed, and was in business.

Another modern touch that Donna brought was having a telephone. We had not had one before because of the cost and, I believe, because of my father's bad credit. Now we had one.

It might have seemed as if we were a normal family, and perhaps we were, by some standards. My father and Donna became friends with a couple named Lupe and Agnes Aguilera, who were serious drinkers. Lupe had been in the mental hospital at Agnews, and he was not cured. Agnes, or Aggie, could sit around and drink wine with Donna all day, pausing to light her cigarette on the gas stove ("This is my Ronson."). On one afternoon, they chatted on with me within earshot, taking care of the baby. Aggie whined in nasal tones, "I've had my cherry pushed back so far by men." I had already heard Donna, once in the night, tell my father, "You men and your hard-ons make me sick," so the conversation did not shock me.

On another occasion, Aggie vomited a stream of wine onto the floor.

My brothers and I made the acquaintance of Lupe and Aggie's two daughters, who were about our age. The five of us stood outside, downstairs in the dark, talking about how unpleasant it was to live with drunkenness. Meanwhile, our parents sat in the living room and drank away the evening.

Christmas came around. My brothers and I had learned not to expect great things for Christmas, but this year held something different. We were going to spend Christmas in Santa Cruz with Donna's parents. I had been there much earlier when we first came to Half Moon Bay and lived in the trailer. I had gotten along very well with Grandma Christensen and had ingratiated myself with her by washing dishes (at my father's direction). She had told a touching story from the Depression, when in a moment of inattention she had thrown the month's grocery allowance, a twenty-dollar bill, into the wood-burning kitchen stove. She couldn't bear to tell her husband. She borrowed the money from a friend and scrimped for the next year to pay it back. She was a kind, gentle woman who had raised eight children and was now raising Fred and the young daughter of one of Donna's wayward sisters.

When it came time to leave for Santa Cruz, we packed the presents and the baby in the car. Our father and Donna had been drinking and arguing, and now he threw a fit and said he wouldn't go. The argument went on, and he said, in a great huff, that we should all go without him. We piled into the car, and as Donna was pulling out of the yard, he leaned out the window and hollered down at us.

"If you leave me, I'll never talk to any of you again."

We waited for him to get dressed, put together a few things, and come down. We drove to Santa Cruz and made it to Christmas dinner before our father and Donna began to argue. They had brought along their liquor and were drinking it on the sly, not fooling anyone, I imagine, and now things got bad enough for us to hurry through dinner and leave early.

My father sat in a sulk on the driver's side while Grandma Christensen spoke soft words to Donna. "Blessed are the peacemakers, for they will be called children of God."

We left the house on Bethany Curve and drove home in the night. At some level, I knew that this was the type of thing that some people did at Christmas and on other events. I had seen it before. I also knew to keep my mouth shut and wait it out with my brothers.

————

My father held down his job. According to standard household roles, Donna would have been in charge of the house and looking after the kids. But she had her own car, an old grey Dodge, and she was prone to be gone without explanation. On one occasion, she was supposed to pick us up in town, and we had to wait for hours, wondering if we should tell someone.

My brothers and I did not expect a Norman Rockwell dinner scene, or wholesome family meals such as we saw on television programs like *Father Knows Best* or *Leave It to Beaver*, but my father did insist that we all eat together at the table. We had home-cooked meals, even if the meat was the cheapest in the supermarket. We boys had helped buy the groceries, and we had been preparing food and washing dishes for years. We were not prepared for Donna, who, when our father was at work, would throw food on the table and say, "There. Go ahead and eat. Fill your bellies."

————

Although the sixth grade was not challenging for me in the Half Moon Bay system, I had an enhancement once again with the learning that Sandy brought home. He had a good teacher

in the seventh grade, and he had an interesting course in ento-
mology. He began an insect collection. My father built him
wooden display boxes with glass tops—glass from the nursery.
Sandy was meticulous as he learned to kill, pin, mount, and
label his specimens. He taught me those skills along with the
common orders of the class Insecta—Coleoptera, Diptera,
Hymenoptera, Lepidoptera, Orthoptera, and many others. I
had my own collection, which I kept in King Edward cigar
boxes. Even my father carried a small killing jar in his pocket
and brought home an unusual green fly or silver earwig.

On my own school grounds, among my juvenile delinquent
friends, I fell into a diversion one day of filling glass soda pop
bottles with sand and hurling them in an arc to see the sand
spiral out. I was hauled into the principal's office and was left
to sit in the waiting area, where the serious face of President
Dwight D. Eisenhower looked down at me from its frame.

The principal was a stern woman named Fannie Alford.
Boys made fun of her first name, but there was no humor in
her office. She told me that what I had done was dangerous
and inconsiderate and that I should know better. She said she
knew I was trying to break into some kind of a gang, and of
course I denied it. She notified my father, I made my excuses at
home, and life went on.

At the far edge of the playground sat a mound of dirt for some
unfinished project. It and another heap or two were out of
bounds, so of course some boys dared to hide there when the
teacher on playground duty turned away. I ended up there
with Jimmy, whose schoolwork I did, and a boy named Ralph.

I did not know Ralph very well. I had gone on escapades
with Jimmy and four or five other boys, sneaking off the

playground at noontime to smoke cigarettes at the creek or at Jimmy's house. Ralph, by comparison, was a hardened criminal. He had one or more older brothers and knew of older things. He was freckle-faced with yellow teeth, a sharp nose, jug ears, and red hair slicked back in hoodlum fashion. He wore his short sleeves folded up, and he had wiry arms that he dangled on the meat-hanger handlebars on his bicycle. Although he held himself aloof of lesser punks, he was a friend of Jimmy's. And so the three of us met beyond the edge of the playground, to smoke cigarettes with brazen courage.

The smoke rose above the mound, however, and a teacher in a long coat began to walk our way. We stuck our cigarettes into the dirt at the base of the mound and ran to another dirt pile farther away, and another.

That afternoon, I found myself again beneath the serious gaze of President Eisenhower. This time, in the inner office, I faced the Superintendent of Schools, Mr. Beacock. Boys made fun of his name as well, but as with Fannie Alford, there was no humor with him. He had two crumpled cigarette butts as evidence as he interrogated me. I prevaricated and equivocated and tried to keep Jimmy and me in the clear.

Mr. Beacock said, "John, you've split a very fine hair. Do you know what that means?"

I said that I did not.

He explained that to split a hair was to bring things down to very narrow terms and then to make a narrow distinction. He did not think mine was very probable.

I held out, though, and he said he would talk to my parents.

He spoke with my father on the phone, and my father tried to get a reasonable story out of me, but I did not yield and tell the true story. So the case remained in suspension.

At school the next day, I heard that Ralph was holding out with great contempt. He had not squealed on anyone, and he was not going to. If it was determined that he was guilty, he would be sent to reform school. If I squealed on him, he would kill me. That was the word that came to me.

After a couple of more evenings of interrogation at home, I softened. I admitted that, yes, someone had smoked behind the dirt pile, that I had gone along and taken a puff or two, and that Ralph had the strongest influence.

I was told not to associate with Jimmy at school, and I was not to go anywhere near him out of school. My father now knew who Jimmy's father was, and although the man had a nice house and made enough money to send his older son to a Catholic school in San Mateo, he had a reputation for being crooked and making money through illegal gambling.

I did not see much more of Ralph. His family might have moved away, or he might have found another school to attend. I did not hear of him going to reform school, but I would not have been surprised at any time in later years with news of larger deeds.

———

I became friends with a boy named Dude. He was in my grade but not in the same classroom. His parents were divorced. His father had a grocery store in Miramar, and his mother and her second husband had a similar store in Princeton by the Sea, a community north of Miramar and across the highway from El Granada. His father gave my father good deals on canned goods and on items in the meat case, such as large sticks of bologna that had developed mold. At home, we cut off the mold, ran the bologna through a manual meat grinder, mixed it with sandwich spread consisting of mayonnaise and relish, and made our sandwiches for school.

One day at school, Dude told me an intriguing story. He said he had been on the beach and had seen a couple go into their tent to make out. They left a purse outside, so he sneaked up in the dusk, opened the purse, and took about forty dollars in bills. That was a great deal of money in a world where a pint of milk in the milk machine at school cost a nickel and where candy bars cost a nickel or a dime. Dude shared some of the money by buying candy and soda pop for me.

———

The end of the school year came. Jimmy was held back to spend another year in the sixth grade. I passed with no trouble, but my teacher wrote on my report card that I did not work up to my potential. She wrote, "He has his mind on other things."

FOUR

cross the road from the old house we lived in, set back among trees and other growth, sat a house that must have been a rental, as it was unoccupied for a while and had different occupants over a period of a year. One summer day when I was out wandering around, I saw a group of three or four young men gathered beside a couple of vehicles. They were talking and laughing, and a dog was barking and snarling. I thought they might be dangling a cat from a tree limb, as we had read about such an incident in the newspaper the year before. A group of young men in town, in a service station after hours, had suspended a cat for a couple of large guard dogs to lunge at and bite. I thought these young men might be up to something similar, but when I reported the incident to my stepmother, I wasn't sure, and I did not want to be imagining some illegal activity based on a story from before. So the incident remained inconclusive.

Less than a month later, I was poking along the creek in back of that house, among trees and vines. I looked up and saw an open garage on the lower level of the house. Inside, a deer was hanging with its head downward. I had a sense of hunting season being in the fall and of legal deer having antlers, which this deer did not have. I told my stepmother, and she did not seem certain about whether to report it. I went back later that same day, and the deer was gone. The door was still open, and the floor was scrubbed clean.

———

My father and Donna got into one of their usual arguments at night. We boys went into our room to try to ignore it, but after a while, Donna began shouting for help. She said my father was going to hit her. We had already heard him tell her not to call the cops. She told me to go to the neighbors to call. I was stuck. Our father had told us many times to do what she told us, even if it didn't agree with what he told us. Now she insisted with me, and I went out into the night, down the road to some neighbors I knew, and asked them to call.

The police came, determined that nothing serious enough had happened to justify an arrest, and left. When they were gone, my father began to harangue at me. Here I was, turning on him, when I had once been so loyal that I wanted to go to jail with him. This incident became one that he would throw in my face, to use his term, for years to come.

In the days of prosperity, in Lompoc, when my father was on the road buying and selling cattle, he had two pinto horses that would get out of the pasture. My grandfather would have to gather them up and put them back in. One time, rather than take care of the horses, my grandfather sold them to a neighbor who had been wanting to buy them. Through all the years of our growing up, when my father would go on a rant with my grandfather, he would bring it up. "Just like the time you sold my two pinto horses."

"Ach, shut up!"

Now he had one for me. "Just like the time you called the cops on me!"

———

By now, Bob and I had bicycles. Sometimes Sandy and Bob would do things on their own, and I would ride my bike across the highway to Miramar and meet up with my friend Dude.

He and I were riding our bicycles on a sunny summer day when he suggested that we take a look at a place that belonged to a person he called the Chinaman, a common mode of reference at the time. The property had a house with an enclosed yard, shrouded with trees and shrubs with a sense of privacy. I understood that it was a kind of second home to some Chinese people who lived in the city—Los Angeles, I think, which was nearly five hundred miles away. Dude said they had pheasants in some cages, which caught my interest and helped him persuade me to trespass.

I do not remember devoting much attention to the cages, and I think they were empty. I do remember that before long, we had crawled through a window and into the dark, silent house.

At the time I had a fascination for knives, and the Chinese people had an impressive collection of artifacts with colored handles of Oriental design, long sinister blades, and elaborate sheaths and scabbards. I was parading around the house with a large machete and belt, the belt cinched to the last hole but still loose, and the machete almost the length of my legs. Dude was decked out in similar fashion. As we were enjoying our escapade, we heard sirens, coming closer and getting louder.

I was terror-stricken. My heart was pounding, and my head seemed as if it would burst, as I ran from the house with the machete banging on my leg and the belt trying to slip down and trip me.

We made it to a hideout in the creek, where, as things quieted down, we realized that the sirens had been fire engines going past the house. It had been a false alarm for us. We decided to go back to the house to tidy up, perhaps to do some more looking around, and to retrieve our bicycles.

On the way back, we met Mr. Gilles, the old German storekeeper. We told him the Chinaman had given us our regalia. He said he didn't believe us and we should return what we had taken.

Inside the house again, with the clumsy items removed, we snooped around a little more. Dude found a closet that was locked. He went to the kitchen, found a cleaver, and hacked his way into the closet. He brought out a rifle, cold and shiny, which scared me.

"I just knew there was a gun in there," he said. At this point, I realized that Dude had not been telling me everything that was on his mind.

He wanted to take the rifle, but I was able to talk him out of it.

By now we had satisfied our curiosity about the treasures of the Chinaman's house, so, taking some smaller knives that we could hide on our persons, we left. As the Chinese people were known to visit the place only once a month, we were hopeful that Mr. Gilles would forget about us by the time the people came back. We returned to our hideout in the creek, where we played with the knives and left them hidden in an old log.

The next day, when the police car pulled into our driveway, I knew I was in for trouble. I was dismayed to learn that the Chinese people had made their monthly visit, had seen the evidence, and had called the police, who in turn went across the road to ask the old German storekeeper if he had seen anything suspicious. It was an easy case for the police.

The Chinese people surprised me by being agreeable when we were hauled into their house to face them. They seemed to understand and forgive our adolescent impulses, and they just wanted their property back—the knives, and the money.

The money?

The Chinese man was adamant that he had had a stash of money, about three hundred dollars, as I recall, and it was gone. I knew nothing about it, and I said as much. The old man, still friendly, poked his face into mine and brandished a ten-dollar bill.

"I give you ten dollars. You go buy candy. You tell me where you put munnee."

I told him I didn't know anything about it, and we went through this routine several times, with the Chinese man making his curious offer to each of us. At last he gave up, and I was convinced he was mistaken in thinking he had lost any money at all.

After our confrontation with the Chinese, the police took us to the creek and sent us after our booty. We left two knives in the log and brought back a few others. After again declining the Chinese man's reward, we were taken back to our fathers.

They agreed to pay for damages—Dude's father to pay for the closet, and the two of them to share the other minor restitutions. Both fathers were thankful that the Chinese people did not seek any further damages or justice. The police, in turn, laughed it off as a minor incident, saying they hoped the rest of their shift would be as easy.

A month later, I was able to slink off by myself to check on my knife. It was gone. When I asked Dude about it, he said he had gone there and the knives were missing. I didn't believe him, but I still considered him my friend.

————

One day during this summer, my father and my stepmother called Bob into the house by himself for a conference. When he came out, Donna and our father told Sandy and me that they had told Bob that he was not my father's son. He was not theirs. But they were going to let him live with us anyway.

This was a strange turn, even in the small, often confusing world in which grownups said and did twisted things. My father had always been given to hold grudges and to make spiteful declarations, but this was more poisonous than ever. One cannot imagine these adults thinking about what good could come of it. My father was capable of this lowness by himself, but he had not gone that far before. Rather than help him combat his impulse, Donna abetted it—two adults with a bottle of wine on a day off.

———

David and Grandpa had been living in the cabin at Mrs. Wolfe's for a while when my father decided to take David to live with us. I do not remember the provocation, but it may have been something my grandfather said to Donna. I was happy that David was going to be living with us, but when he got out of the car, he was sobbing and crying. There had been a confrontation, and my father had asserted his parental authority, as my grandfather had never had custody of David.

Things changed when my grandfather arrived in his 1949 Ford, with his shotgun. David and his box of belongings went back to El Granada, and there was never another discussion about David staying with Grandpa.

———

Sandy, Bob, and I each spent a week in Lompoc that summer. Our father's boss hauled truckloads of nursery plants to Los Angeles, and Santa Maria was right on Highway 101, so the transportation was free. We each stayed with the family of an old friend of my father's, a cattleman and horseman and bosom drinking pal. He and his wife had two boys and a girl our ages.

I stayed at their little ranch in the country. We played with the neighbor kids, children of another old friend, and talked about where babies came from. I went camping with the two boys, caught poison oak, and was confined for a couple of days. The girl helped tend to me, and she kissed me once.

Afterwards, my brothers and I argued about who had the most fun there. Since the early days in Grimes, our family talked about moving back to Lompoc. My father was reluctant to return after having moved elsewhere and having gone broke, but the idea came up from time to time. My father's friend knew of work. We could have a horse. My father would teach us to shoot a rifle.

My father's friends two boys were going to come stay with us, perhaps the next summer, when there would be time. It would not have occurred to me then, but it was just as well that they did not visit. Life was much more wholesome where they lived, out in the country, where only one of the parents drank.

———

Dude called me on the phone. We were not allowed to hang around together, but sometimes he called. That was how we compared notes on what happened to the knives we stashed. On this day, his voice was low and secretive.

"I found a dead man."

"You did what?"

"I found a dead man. I was riding my bike on the road that goes along the beach here in Princeton, and I saw a car parked. He had a hose running from his exhaust pipe to his window, and some of it was covered up with paintings and stuff. He killed himself. I went and told my mom, and she called the cops."

I kept my eye out for the story in the newspaper, and I found it. The article was entitled "Paintings, Peanuts, and Death." It told of a truck driver from the San Mateo area who was "despondent" about his wife leaving him. He had covered the hose with paintings and other objects as Dude told me, and he drank whiskey and ate peanuts as he waited for his death. The article ended with a sentence about Dude finding the body as he rode by on his bicycle.

———

I was used to reading the newspaper at home. Nikita Khrushchev's tantrums were familiar. A famous U.S. spy flight was shot down in May of 1960, and the Soviet leader went on to threaten war. Perhaps the most memorable headline was the one announcing the execution of Caryl Chessman, whose case had been in the news for years until his appeals ran out.

———

We moved to a house across the highway in Miramar, not far from Mr. Gilles's grocery store. We had rabbit cages in the shade of trees along the creek, the same creek where Dude and I hid the knives and where I had seen the deer in the neighbor's garage. The house was better than the previous one. It cost seventy-five dollars a month. The owner was a sometimes surly sort of fellow who frequented a bar where we sold newspapers.

Sandy had started with a delivery route of thirty-five customers. When the opportunity came up for me to acquire a route in El Granada with sixty customers, I took it. Sandy became the business manager. The San Mateo *Times*, our newspaper, had a rewards system for new subscriptions. We went to a skating rink in San Mateo, to the boardwalk in Santa Cruz, to a theater in San Francisco for a showing of *Ben-Hur*, and to Disneyland. The amusement park in Santa Cruz was our favorite, and we went a few times. Sandy and I worked hard for new subscriptions, and we carried a few ghost customers so we had newspapers to sell on the street. He and I drew up a large, colored map of El Granada and Miramar, with every house and business. We kept track of every residence where we had a subscription. He knew my route, and I knew his. We folded our newspapers next to the post office in El Granada, near the El Granada Market. Sandy hired other boys to fold papers and to deliver to some of the out-of-the-way customers. He bought the soda pop and candy. As we folded papers and talked about things that adolescent boys talked about, a donkey across the gully brayed.

My paper route helped bring me back into responsible behavior. My predecessor had been casual. He walked the route and folded the papers as he went. After I took the route, I heard that he sometimes did not deliver all the papers and that he would stop and play baseball with his friends. He lost subscriptions. Sandy and I built them back up, so I had a full route on unpaved streets in a hilly community. In the short days of the year, I saw the moon rise as I pushed my bike up a hill.

On another stretch, my route took me downhill through shadowy trees. I was memorizing "Paul Revere's Ride" for school, and when I came to that place, I would recite

Beneath, in the churchyard, lay the dead,
In their night-encampment on the hill
Wrapped in silence so deep and still
That he could hear, like a sentinel's tread,
The watchful night-wind, as it went
Creeping along from tent to tent,
And seeming to whisper, "All is well!"

My father was glad to see us working. We practiced responsibility, got into less trouble than we would have otherwise, learned about business, and brought home money. We did not squander it. Our soda pop and candy money came from our tips and from the extra copies we sold for a dime each in the evening. Our regular income, one third of each monthly subscription of $1.50, went for serious purposes. We bought clothes. We contributed to living expenses. When Bob acquired a route in Moss Beach, north of El Granada, the three of us were earning enough to pay the rent, although sometimes the money went for groceries or gasoline.

I was in the seventh grade and attending the junior high school with Sandy when I memorized "Paul Revere's Ride." Donna was living with us in the second house in Miramar when news came that my sister Suzi had gotten married.

Donna said, "Maybe she had to."

I asked why a person would have to get married, and she explained.

On another day, news came that one of her sisters had to go to the women's prison in Corona. Donna cried. The sister had been in trouble a few times for writing bad checks or forging checks, and now she had to serve a sentence. I thought that if she kept breaking the law in the same way, she could expect to face the consequences. But I had not cared much for the sister, and I did not know her very well. She was one of twins. The other one was married and had an ice cream business in San Leandro. Her family was fun to visit. The incarcerated sister was the mother of a girl, Fred's cousin, who also lived with Grandma Christensen.

Donna and the baby left for a while, and my father arranged for a high-school girl to cook our evening meals, as we boys were delivering newspapers. The girl was the older sister of one of Sandy's friends. Her name was Liz. She was Hispanic and very pretty as well as well-mannered. We stayed on good behavior around her.

Donna came back. She was there at the time of the general election. It was a big year, with Nixon and Kennedy debating on television. My father was what was called "a good Republican." Donna said she was a Democrat. She told my father she voted for Nixon, and then she complained when he did not thank her.

We had trouble with the sewer in the house we rented. When my father went to talk to the landlord where he could be found in the bar, the man said, "Don't bug me, or I'll knock you off your stool." The word "bug" was Beatnik slang, which my father didn't care for. It gave us a line to repeat and make fun of.

At the end of the year, we moved to another house. It was in Princeton by the Sea, where Dude's mother had her grocery store. The rent was ninety dollars a month. We were now in a different school district, but we continued to go to school in Half Moon Bay.

We watched the Kennedy inauguration at school. We heard the new president's speech, watched as an aged Robert Frost read a poem, and were entertained when a fire broke out in an electric heater in the outdoor seating. Years later, I read in a book about social and class behavior that everybody remembered the least substantial part of the day—the fire breaking out. He was right, but I also remembered seeing the great poet Robert Frost.

———

Sandy and I were doing well in school, but we did not resist the temptation of being smart-alecks and not following rules. The junior high took a harder line than the elementary school did, and detention slips were serious. If a student received nine, he would be suspended for three days.

When Sandy reached nine, my father put him to building rabbit cages for three days. After a couple of more slips, my father transferred him to a school in Montara, the next community up the highway past Moss Beach. Sandy came back with stories about what a primitive school it was, but he did his work and fit in.

When I reached eight detention slips, my father did not want me to have suspension on my record, so he moved me to the Farallone View School with Sandy. We lived in that district anyway, and we caught the school bus near our house. Before long, Bob made the change as well.

The Farallone View School was located on a hill, and the weather was colder and windier than in Half Moon Bay or Princeton, which was gloomy enough in comparison with the warm, sunny climate we remembered from the valley. The school took its name from the Farallon Islands, which are a place of interest off the coast south of San Francisco. The discrepancy in spelling still exists.

At that time, in 1961, the school was run by a retired Air Force officer who went by Major Richards or just Major. At his outpost, he ran things his way. If two boys had a dispute, they were welcome to Put on the Gloves, two pair of boxing gloves. If a boy did something bad enough, Major gave him The Strap. He called the parents first. After I had been there for a while and weakened to a dare one day and spit in a girl's desk, Major called my father and asked for approval to use The Strap. My father said, "If you don't, I will." Major had me bend over and touch the table while he gave me ten swats. I pretended that it hurt, but it was mild compared to my father's whippings. Still, it helped me be ashamed of myself for my crass behavior and for yielding to peer pressure.

When I arrived at Farallone View, two students tried to enlist my friendship. They were in the seventh grade, also, but they were fifteen going on sixteen years old. I was twelve. They had been good friends, had run away from home together, had stolen a car, and had been picked up for taking a corner on two wheels. Back from juvenile hall, they were now enemies.

"I can take anyone in this school," Bernie told me, when he had me alone. "But Steve's an A. I can take him in one minute."

Steve secured permission for the two of us to go down to the wood shop. He took out cigarettes for us and lit them with a soldering gun. He told me he could kick Bernie's ass, simple.

Bernie's and Steve's campaigning and bad-mouthing went around the whole little school in a short while, and the edict came out that it was time to Put on the Gloves. The school was built on terraces, and the whole population climbed to the big, wide playground on top. Our seventh-grade teacher, Mr. Manginello, served as referee.

The fight went on for a while. It was not spectacular, and it was not brutal. Steve was tall with dark, slicked hair, and he leaned into the fight. Bernie was good-sized, but he had a heavy build, and Steve had the reach on him. Steve wore him out, and Bernie conceded.

After the fight, down on the classroom level, Bernie still tried to keep me, the new kid, on his side. He pointed at his lace-up boots. "See these boots? These are heavy. By the time I got up top, they tired me out. And then I had to move around for all that time. He wouldn't fight me. If I was wearing tennis shoes, I could beat him."

The schoolwork was not difficult. For geography, the students traced maps out of the textbooks. For science, they copied articles out of the encyclopedia. There was some genuine textbook material as well. When it came time to memorize "Paul Revere's Ride," I was quick to announce that I already knew it. I was given the task to listen to other students as they practiced their memorization.

When we had less than a fourth of the school year left, a new student joined our class. I knew him from Half Moon Bay. He was of the delinquent population, but he had not been among my group of friends. He had been expelled from school there, so he was finishing out the school year in another district. Soon enough, everyone knew why he had changed schools, and I was associated, on the surface at least, as being his friend. He was also dark, of Filipino origin, and the students of Farallone View, although they came from medium to low socio-economic levels, were all white.

One day, as part of our geography interest, a mild-mannered girl brought a piece of rock from a famous place in the Mediterranean—the Acropolis in Athens, I think, but it may have been the Colosseum in Rome. It was about two inches high and an inch wide at the base. She passed the rock around, and each of us held it and looked at it.

A little while later, Mr. Manginello announced that the girl was very upset because someone had broken off part of her rock. He held it up, and we could see that it was smaller. Mr.

Manginello asked for the guilty party to confess. No one did. He asked again and waited. Still, no one spoke.

He had us all sit around a pair of end-to-end tables where we did work like cutting and pasting and tracing. He asked each of us in turn, "Did you take it?"

Each of us answered, "No, I did not take it."

We went around a second time and a third time. At last, the boy from Half Moon Bay reached into his shirt pocket and said, "Yes, I took it." He produced a piece of rock that we could all recognize.

It was a memorable experience to sit through. I had a clear conscience all the way, and I appreciated Mr. Manginello's management. I was sorry that the other boy, now an outcast, had confirmed the view that people already had of him. To him, I was his only friend at this school. He told me how discouraged he was and how he had fallen into the temptation of stealing a piece of the rock. He knew the older brother of a girl we both knew in Half Moon Bay—a very well-mannered Filipino girl, as it happened. The brother had an interest in such things, and my tenuous friend was sure the brother would have paid money for the piece of rock.

———

Donna packed up the baby and their things and left. This time she said she was leaving for good, and it seemed as if she meant it.

My father met a woman named Paulina. She lived in a small apartment in San Francisco and was a native of Tampico, a coastal city in Mexico. She had a little boy about two years old. We taught him swear words just for the fun of hearing him say them, but he repeated them in front of the grownups, so we had to give up that entertainment. We called him Pancho, and Paulina went on a long tirade about what an insult that was. How would we like it if she called us the name of someone who was a terrible criminal, someone we hated?

The subject was so sensitive, or her reaction was so volatile, that it took us a great deal of apology and roundabout questioning to find out why our thoughtless nickname was so offensive. We learned that to some people, Pancho Villa was a cutthroat and a desperado, and there was no room for humor.

We spent a few desolate weekend afternoons on a concrete playground in a dull neighborhood in San Francisco while our father spent time with Paulina in her apartment. We went up a couple of times in the old elevator cage, an experience that came back to me many years later when I read the noir-ish mysteries of Dashiell Hammett and Raymond Chandler, set in California in the 1930s and 1940s.

Paulina spent time at our house in Princeton. When summer came and my father had two weeks' vacation, she talked him into going to Watsonville, down below Santa Cruz, to pick strawberries. Sandy was deemed to be old enough for that kind of work as well, so he went with them.

———

Grandpa and David came to stay at the house. Bob and I did our newspaper routes and covered Sandy's. Sandy and I had worked for a while at a mink farm, cleaning cages and feeding ground-up fish paste to the vile, sharp-toothed minks, but that work had ended.

We lived near the beach, so on indolent days we went there, where the long ropes of washed-up seaweed rotted. One of my newspaper customers named Woody had fallen asleep on the beach and drowned. He was about my father's age, and, as I would become aware in later years, the age of other men (like Woodrow Wilson Guthrie) who were born in the time of President Wilson. My late customer was a casual sort, a few months behind on his subscription. According to gossip, he had been drinking. The tide came in and carried him out, and the crabs had nibbled at his ears and lips.

Bob liked to fish, and he learned how to make a crab trap.

He lowered it from the pier, but being close to shore, he caught only rock crabs. We boiled them in the backyard and picked out the meager meat.

A year or more had passed since Dude and I had committed our offense at the Chinese people's property, so we were allowed to associate again. His mother's little supermarket was not far away. She and her husband lived in quarters adjacent to the store, and Dude and his brother stayed with them part of the time. Dude invited me to stay over so we could get up early to go deep-sea fishing the next day.

Charter boats were common and not very expensive for some excursions. Bob and Sandy and I had gone out, paying with our newspaper earnings, and we had caught enough ling cod and rock cod to make it worthwhile. This time, Dude was going to pay. By then he had told me that he had not taken money from the couple in the tent on the beach. He had stolen it from his father, who had ready cash from his store. He also stole from his mother. I regret to say that at that time, I did not have a good sense of why such behavior was wrong and why I should stay away from it. We didn't steal from our father; to the contrary, we helped with living expenses. If other people did—and I had heard from Jimmy that he took money from his father's wallet—that was up to them.

I spent the night in a room with Dude and his brother. Their mother and her husband slept in another room in the built-on area in back of the store. In the early morning, Dude told me he had not gotten the money yet. He made me follow him to the area where his mother and stepfather slept. The cash drawer from the store sat on a low dresser, and a set of curtains separated it from the sleeping area itself. Dude stuck his head through the curtains, held them tight, and joked with his mother as I, almost paralyzed with fear, lifted and pulled two twenty-dollar bills from beneath the roller in the cash drawer.

Dude cut dry salami from the meat department and made dry sandwiches for our lunch. He was still in charge. He neglected to take along something to drink, however, and the motion of the boat that day made me seasick. It was a long, miserable day, with an undercurrent of guilt I felt at having been made an accomplice.

————

I did not know how much money Dude stole or why his parents were not more attentive, but he made another gesture of generosity with me. He bought two beagle puppies and gave one to me. My grandfather said it was too good a puppy to have for free and my father would not want me to keep it anyway.

————

Sandy came back with our father and Paulina. He had several entertaining stories about picking strawberries with the bracero crew. Our father was pleased with the amount of money they had made together.

Meanwhile, he had become disenchanted with his work at the nursery, and for all I knew, his boss may have had similar feelings. My father made me call on the phone to say that he would not be going back to work there.

The plan, we learned, was that he was going to work in the cannery in Gridley. We had an eviction notice tacked on the front door, so our time was limited in the house in Princeton. My father chewed me out for not taking down the notice, but I did not know if I had such authority, and we did not use the front door, anyway, so we had ignored it.

Sandy went with our father to the valley. When they came back, Sandy told us they picked prunes during the day when my father worked night shift in the cannery. They stayed in Live Oak, and Sandy had gotten heat stroke riding his bicycle to Gridley.

Sandy and I changed places, and I went to the valley with

my father. Paulina stayed with us for a few days. My father was working day shift, so I was left to loaf around the cabin court where we stayed. The shared bathrooms were in the middle. One day, I found a five-dollar bill on the floor by the toilet. I reported it to my father and asked what I should do with it. He said that people kept money that they found like that, so we used it for groceries.

———

We moved to Gridley in time to enroll in school in the second or third week in September. This time, we sold the rabbit cages as well as the rabbits. Grandpa and David stayed in their cabin at Mrs. Wolfe's, and David, almost ten, was going to keep up the smallest and easiest newspaper route.

Bob and Sandy and I were glad to be going back to the Sacramento Valley. In the two and a half years we had lived on the coast, we had never cared for the climate. We had to wear jackets in the summer. Scrapes and sores did not heal fast. We had found plenty of things to keep us busy, but the general atmosphere or way of life seemed to belong to someone else. We did not adopt the idea that San Francisco was The City, the only city that mattered. We didn't care that much for any city. If we couldn't live in Lompoc, we would be happy going back to live in the valley.

Our time on the coast was a closed chapter. It would give me plenty to remember and think about as time went by. I could track some of my later problems back to influences I had there. Many years later, I would wonder if Ralph or any of the others went to prison. It also occurred to me that Dude might have found some money in the Chinese people's house and that he might have checked to see if there was any money on the dead man.

FIVE

We moved into an old two-story farmhouse set back from the small highway that ran east out of Gridley toward the Feather River. Our house was on the north side of the road, with peach orchards on two sides and a pumpkin field in back. A grocery store large enough to be called a market sat on the other side of the highway another half-mile from town. Beyond it, close to the river, we saw rows of low-quality government housing that others referred to as the labor camp. People used the term "labor camp" to refer to housing for seasonal workers, but when school was under way, we saw that year-round students at our economic level lived there.

Sandy began high school, having graduated from Farallone View. I was in the eighth grade, and Bob was in the sixth. We attended Sycamore School, a clean and orderly institution. One of my first impressions was that Gridley was a friendly place. My classmates around me laughed. They knew each other and welcomed me. This upbeat atmosphere struck me as a contrast with the depressed classroom atmosphere I had known on the coast.

For the first week or so after school, we joined our father in the prune orchard. Picking prunes entailed picking up the fruit from the ground where it had fallen. The grower used a mechanical shaker, a modern development. His wife was very cheerful as she wrote out the paycheck. She told our father we worked like little troopers. At another moment, with equal cheer, she said we worked like little n------. She was as nice as anyone I had met in Sunday school, and we soon learned that the grower's family was a prominent one in the community.

When prune harvest was finished, we picked up English walnuts. Some of the walnuts still had the solid, light green hulls that enclosed them when they grew, but on many of them, the hulls had split and had begun to turn soft and brown. Our palms and fingers absorbed a brown stain that did not wash away. At school, one could see who picked walnuts. Basketball was popular, and when a boy made a shot, his palms and fingers showed.

We had not been living in Gridley for long when news came from Half Moon Bay that Grandpa and David had been in an accident. My father left and within a few days came back with the two of them. We heard the story. Grandpa was driving David on his paper route and pulled out on the Coast Highway. The other car looked like it was a mile away. The 1949 Ford was totaled. Grandpa was not injured, but he had a subdued air about him. David had black eyes and a goose egg on his forehead. The two of them were now living with us again, and David enrolled in fifth grade at Sycamore School.

My teacher in the eighth grade was Mrs. McNolty. She was bright and healthy-looking and outgoing. One day when I could not find my pencil, I said, in the manner I had acquired, that someone stole my pencil. Mrs. McNolty smiled and said, in her positive way, "People don't steal things here, John."

We went to other rooms and other teachers for subjects such as math and English. The English or language arts class consisted of grammar and sentence diagramming, which I enjoyed. With Mrs. McNolty, we studied science, health, U.S. history, world events, and reading. She encouraged us in all subjects, but her greatest inspiration was in reading and in writing poetry. We received extra points for imaginative written and oral book reports, and we wrote poems that we put together as a mimeographed collection at the end of the year.

In the second half of the year, when we all knew each other well, she told us one day that students wanted to know three things about their teacher—what her name was, how old she was, and how much she earned. We already knew she came from Canada. She told us that her first name was Lillian and she was fifty-two years old. She said we did not need to know how much she made. One self-assured boy, whose father was president of the school board, said, in the good-natured tone of that class of people who ran things in a small town, that he could find out. I did not hear anyone ask him.

In class, we read stories like Washington Irving's "The Legend of Sleepy Hollow" and Guy de Maupassant's "The Necklace," as well as Charles Lamb's "A Dissertation Upon Roast Pig" and an excerpt from Jesse Stuart's *The Thread That Runs So True.*

Out of class, I read a great many books and enjoyed creating original book reports. Among the works I read were Jack London's *The Call of the Wild* and *White Fang.* The most memorable was *Of Mice and Men*, by John Steinbeck. I continued reading about historical figures, and I became interested in reading murder mysteries. Sandy introduced me to Erle Stanley Gardner and a couple of his pseudonyms, and we could explain why the book was better than the episode on television. Some of the books I read had alliteration in the title, such as *The Case of the Fiery Fingers*, *The Case of the Dangerous Dowager*, and so forth. When I read *The Case of the Negligent Nymph*, I asked my father what a nymph was, as the current context did not correspond with dragonfly nymphs in the order Odonata. He said it was a woman who stayed in bed all day. He did not object to what we read, and he was willing to buy inexpensive books for us at second-hand stores, where a hardcover might cost a quarter and three mysteries might go for the same price. He also subscribed to a book club with works about U.S. History and presidents. These books were compatible with a television program called *Biography*, which presented documentaries with old black-and-white footage about figures such as Babe Ruth, Winston Churchill, and Fiorello La Guardia.

One day Sandy showed me a magazine article about Jerry Lewis, the actor. He brought my attention to a passage that told about Lewis's habit of throwing out new socks after he had worn them for a few hours. I had been stuck with wearing a girl's shirt my father had bought by mistake at a second-hand store one day, and this celebrity's extravagance was a long ways away from our experience.

———

Sandy had a very good Spanish teacher at the high school, a Mr. Garcia. The textbook was *El Camino Real*. We knew the phrase from California history, as it was the name of the King's Highway that linked the California missions in colonial times. Spanish words and Spanish place names were part of our heritage, and language was another subject to enjoy. Sandy brought the textbook home and taught me all the material, including vocabulary, masculine and feminine nouns and adjectives, and verb conjugation. It was all a great adventure. I studied the textbook with its boldface vocabulary words and verb forms, and I conjugated verbs with Sandy as my tutor.

———

Paulina had come to the house in Gridley a couple of times, but she was gone by the time I was practicing Spanish. So was a metal cashbox my father kept under his bed. It had a couple of gold watches as well as gold coins worth one, five, ten, and twenty dollars. The twenty-dollar coin carried the date of 1910, the year our grandfather came to this country. My father had pawned or sold his deer rifles, his shotgun, later his .22, and a ruby ring, but no one would have thought of touching these heirlooms, these precious pieces that served as a last link to our faded past—no one inside the family, that is.

———

In the corner of the dining room where I studied Spanish, we had a stack of pumpkins that helped get us through the winter. We got tired of them along with other cheap food like instant potatoes, powdered milk, and ground bologna.

More as a matter of conversation than an actual complaint, I told my father one day that I got tired of eating breast of lamb. He bought it in quantity, often at nineteen cents a pound and sometimes at nine. It consisted of bone, thick layers of dense fat, and thin layers of tough meat. We cooked it in the oven with tomato sauce on top, so when the melted fat cooled, the grease was orange. Separating the meat from the fat and bone was messy work, and the meat was greasy.

"I get tired of it, too," my father said. "I'd like to eat T-bone steak every day, but this is what we can afford."

His answer surprised me. I had known forever not to

complain about food, to eat what was on my plate, and to clean my plate. My father liked things that almost made me gag, like boiled summer squash, fried eggplant, and Brussels sprouts. I thought he liked breast of lamb as well.

————

Bob and David and I walked down the lane after getting off the school bus on an overcast day. Sandy had ridden home on his bicycle. As we went around the corner of the house, we came upon a scene with my father and my grandfather, a galvanized washtub, and a few lumpy burlap sacks. Steam was rising from the tub. My father turned around, and from his relaxed face and half-open mouth, I could tell he was drunk. My grandfather's cloudy demeanor suggested that he had had something to drink as well.

"Get your clothes changed," my father said. "We've got work to do."

We knew the routine and took our places. My grandfather cut the chickens' throats and let them flap until they expired. Bob and I soaked the dead chickens in hot water and plucked the wet, smelly feathers. Sandy rinsed and soaked the carcasses in cold water in the kitchen sink as my grandfather cut them open and cleaned them. David pulled pin feathers and hairlike strands. My father wrapped the chickens for the freezer. The kitchen smelled of opened carcasses and of guts piling up in a five-gallon bucket.

When the feathers were dry or close to it, my grandfather burned them and stood by with a rake. The pungent smell hung in the winter air.

————

At the market down the highway from the house where we lived, our father arranged for Sandy and me to work. We were too young to work in the store, but we could sort bottles out back. When we showed up on Saturday morning, frost covered the sea of empty soda pop bottles. Sandy and I went into the store to ask for two pairs of gloves on credit. With our hands protected, we went outside again and began sorting two or three months' accumulation of glass bottles and putting them into wooden crates. Customers returned the empties for the three-cent deposit, and the store employees put the bottles out back in uneven piles so that the surface looked like waves on the ocean. The sun rose in the sky, and the frost melted. Sandy and I performed a job for which we had a natural talent —putting things in order.

By noon, we had the job done, much to the satisfaction of the store manager. He deducted the cost of the gloves from our wages, and we applied the money to our grocery account.

We did this job three times that winter.

In January of 1962, my father had to make a trip to Santa Barbara. Perhaps because Sandy's curriculum was deemed to be more important, I was elected to go on the trip. My father, full of caution ingrained from his many years on the road, gave me two twenty-dollar bills and told me to hide one in each shoe, or better, in each sock.

We must have slept the first night in the car, for it was a long trip, with a stopover to see an old and now dying friend of my father who had been his mentor in the early days of the cattle business, and I did not take off my shoes and socks until we rented a hotel room in Santa Barbara. I was dismayed to see that my feet had sweated and the bills had fallen apart.

We took the remnants to a bank, where a teller gave us two bills in exchange. She said that the serial numbers were still intact, so we were fortunate.

Our room was in an old hotel. My father had already

schooled me on not talking to strangers, not going into a man's hotel room if he invited me, and not sitting on his bed. That evening, a man on the same floor struck up a friendship with my father and invited us to his room to visit. Each of them had a bottle in a brown bag. My father sat on the only chair, the man sat on the bed, and I stood by.

The man patted the mattress and said, "Sit here."

I stood firm.

"Sit here."

I did not move.

My father said, "Go ahead and sit there."

I took a seat and kept my distance.

Later, I told my father why I did not want to sit on the bed.

"Oh, hell," he said. "I was right there. He wasn't going to put the make on you."

—

We visited Aunt Jenny at the nursing home. She was white-haired and drawn but not feeble. She was happy to see her nephew Dunville and to meet me. I was named after her father, whose first name was John and whose middle name was Dunville. After we visited with her, my father spoke with somebody about the inheritance, and we drove past the address on West Canon Perdido, where the old house had been replaced by a common-looking four-unit apartment house.

While we were in the southern part of the state, my father called someone on my mother's side to find out where Suzi was. He talked to her on the phone and invited her to go back with us. She took the bus to Santa Barbara and met us.

She was no longer married and had no children, so Donna's suspicion that she had to get married was invalid. She was not yet twenty, and she was clean, with a well-kept appearance of tight pedal pushers, a white blouse, and lipstick.

She told me about finding our mother dead. They had been

staying in Carmel, as I knew. Suzi was fourteen at the time and had gone somewhere, perhaps to buy cigarettes, with a fellow who was eighteen or nineteen. When they returned to the motel, they found our mother unconscious. They put a mirror next to her mouth and saw no breath, so they called the police. To add to the trauma, Suzi was put in jail until the cause of death was determined.

I had been given to understand, all along, that my mother drank herself to death. My interpretation of that phrase had an image of a person sitting up with an elbow on the table. Suzi's account made the cause seem more general. My mother had been drinking, but it was part of a pattern of negligent living in the time after we saw them that last day in Grimes, as they stayed in one place and another and did not eat on a regular basis.

Suzi went back to Gridley with us. She had a cordial reunion with my grandfather, and she was delighted to see all the boys she had taken care of in the earlier years. She played basketball with us and visited with her friend Patsy from 1956 and before, when Suzi had lived with our mother in Gridley. After a week or so, Suzi took the bus south, and life went on in the all-male Nesbitt household.

———

My father wrote for and received information on the auctioneer school in Billings, Montana. The plan to get back into the cattle business had never died, but it had quieted down when we lived on the coast and Donna was with us. Now it was back. My father rehearsed it at the dinner table. Sandy would do the buying and selling and auctioneering, I would be the bookkeeper, Bob would be the mechanic, and we would see what David would be suited for.

My grandfather said, "What if one of 'em doesn't turn out the way you want? What if John runs off with all the money?"

"What do you have against Johnny? You never liked him."

"I don't have anything against John. I'm just sayin' you can't count on everyone."

"Well, it's a good plan. We all work together."

———

In the dirt yard behind the house, facing the plowed-up pumpkin field, I stood as if in the batter's box. Sandy was pitching. Bob was catching. Sandy had formed an ambition to become a professional baseball player. In Half Moon Bay, he aspired to be better than a classmate who already had a reputation for being a good pitcher and later went on to play and coach in the minor leagues. Sandy, being left-handed, was determined to excel, and he knew he needed practice. He could throw hard, but he was not accurate. Bob was better than I was at catching because he didn't mind chasing wild pitches and digging others out of the dirt. Therefore, I did more than half the batting, and I was hit by pitches so many times that I was ruined for ever playing in organized baseball like Little League or Babe Ruth.

In the dirt field in front of the house, Sandy obliged us to help set up four posts and a rope enclosure for a boxing and wrestling ring. We watched the phony wrestling matches and the credible boxing matches on television. Sandy remarked on a conspicuous boxer named Cassius Clay. In our own ring, Sandy had no real competition with Bob or me, but we had to Put on the Gloves to give him practice. Bob and I were obliged to pummel one another. For wrestling, Bob and I faced off. We were also a tag team against Sandy and David.

I took refuge when I could in the rooms upstairs, where I read mysteries. Bob played with tiny airplane motors and small electric circuits. He helped me prepare a science demonstration with a battery, a small light bulb, and a strip of aluminum to show that aluminum conducted electricity. Mrs. McNolty said it was nice that my brother helped me.

We all drew, but Sandy and David were the best. Sandy

drew a realistic sketch of a man being pulled over a cliff by a whiskey bottle tied to his lower body.

Marysville was a place where my father went to pawn or redeem his toolbox. It was the town where Sandy and I had taunted the Black woman. One day my father came home with a strange, troubled air about him. He said he had been on the street in Marysville, and two Black men engaged him in conversation. One of them made a joking remark, and the other "clipped" him from behind. He went off his feet. The next thing he remembered, he was halfway home, driving fast. He had lost his wallet.

I went to Marysville by myself on a Saturday. I bought a bus ticket and took a traveling bag with me. At a pet shop, I bought some white, brown, and grey-and-brown mice for a science project. At home, I did not conduct experiments on the mice; rather, I kept track of what I fed them and made notes of their appearance. On another Saturday, I bought guinea pigs.

We lived about two miles out of town, so it was common for us to walk home if we had something to do in town. On a sunny day, I waited on the side of the road as Bob came home on foot. I heard him from a distance. He had a drum slung in front of him, and he was practicing with a pair of drumsticks. *Dum-da-dum-dum-dum, dum-da-dum-dum-dum* all the way. Bob's face had an open expression, full of happiness.

My father found work in Colusa, driving tractor. It was time to work the ground for spring planting. He drove back and forth, and I went with him on a Saturday. We left in the early morning, in the dark, and I listened to the farm radio program on the way. The sun was coming up when we reached the farm headquarters. I heard a strange, haunting call and realized it came from peacocks. A couple of them were perched on the peak of a tractor shed, with their long tails reaching almost to the eaves. We took a farm pickup out to the field. Another tractor driver named Dude went with us. My father referred to him as the Indian boy, and I had an image of someone like Little Beaver in the Red Ryder Comics, but when he appeared, he was full-grown and wore a western hat. It was a long drive to the field, and he did not speak the whole way.

———

My father rented a room in Colusa, and I went for the weekend when it was my turn. He had a list of errands for me on Saturday. One task was to pick up a shirt at the cleaners. When I went there, the man showed me a shirt that my father had left when we lived in Colusa and Grimes. The shirt was vermilion, with double pockets, the style that my father used for carrying two packs of cigarettes. When I saw it, it seemed to step right out of the past. It had hung there for three years— a long time for me at that age.

———

My father had to give up his room in Colusa when he fell asleep smoking in bed. I went with him to pick up his things, and I saw the burned-out bed springs in the alley.

———

One day I left school at lunchtime to go to the house of a boy I had become friends with. His name was Dan, and he had brothers the age of Bob and David. His family came from Oklahoma or some similar place, but they were not Okies in the sense of working at migrant labor or staying in labor camps. His father worked at Beale Air Force, near Marysville, and they lived in an average house in town.

At their house, he showed me items his father took from work—useful things like flashlights, but also objects like safety vests and helmets that no one used in daily activities. He showed me a separate room by the alley where he and his brothers sometimes slept. The bed covers were of burlap, which I think also came from the Air Force base. I felt sorry for him and said, to myself, "The poor boy." Then I learned that he and his brothers slept there for fun, like camping out.

Back in the house, we ate peanut-butter-and-honey sandwiches. The honey came from a gallon jar with five long-handled iced-tea spoons standing inside where the level of honey was down to an inch or so. I fancied that there was a spoon for each family member. My friend told me that his father took the honey from work, also.

———————

I do not know if my realization that some people in Gridley did steal, after all, helped revive some of my earlier influences. I do not think my behavior came from reading murder mysteries, in which people were always caught and there was no glamour or adventure associated with the murderer. Not long after we moved to Gridley, Sandy and a friend from high school were caught trying to steal salami at lunchtime. The store manager took them in back and told them he wasn't going to report them. When Sandy told me the story, he said he wasn't going to do any of that stuff anymore. I think I heeded his lesson and pushed those impulses underground foı a while, until my relaxed sense of consequences combined with a chronic lack of money.

Whatever the cause, I reverted to earlier habits, stealing candy or beef jerky in the grocery store and taking an occasional Perry Mason mystery from the drugstore. I might have lifted one or more toy airplane motors for Bob. I discovered the pocketknife case at the variety store, and I availed myself of a model I liked. Then, wanting to impress someone or wanting someone to like me, I stole one for a friend at school. When I went back to take another one, the manager went into the back room and made it easy for me. He caught up with me before I made it out of the store, and he took me by the arm. He said we were going to the police station.

I begged with him not to do it. I promised I would never go to his store again and would never steal again. He marched me down the sidewalk. If I had been a real criminal, I would have broken away and run for my freedom. But I submitted to authority.

Two boys were coming our way. I continued pleading, and I saw the startled faces of my brothers Bob and David as we passed.

Later, David told me that he and Bob asked Grandpa where I was, and Grandpa said, in a voice that came straight from the old country, "John's gone to jail."

I was kept at the police station until my father came home from work and went into town. The policeman told him that in cases like this, they released the child to his parents, or, as in this instance, one parent.

He passed a remark about my coming from a broken home, and my father said, "That doesn't have anything to do with it."

Quick with apology, the policeman said, "I know."

All the way home and into the night, my father railed at me. "What the hell's wrong with you? How stupid can you be? Do you want to spend the rest of your life in jail?"

Teachers, principals, and police had been asking me a

similar question. "You know the difference between right and wrong, don't you?"

I always said yes. What I meant was that I knew what a person was supposed to do and not supposed to do. A person was not supposed to do certain things, like lying or stealing or intruding on other people's property, because a person could be punished. That was the meaning I interpreted from my father and saw reinforced at school and in town.

In retrospect, it would seem that I understood what was wrong but that I did not have a clear understanding of why it was wrong. Perhaps someone had told me and I had deflected it, thinking that that was for people who were better off and had it easier in life. For the most part, however, I believe that I had not heard a consistent message of why. I was a bright boy, and I was not malicious. I was at an age, thirteen, when it might have done some good if someone had said, "Look, John. These things are wrong, and here is why." But I do not remember having things presented to me in that way. Later I would learn that some people developed a moral sense later in life than others. At that point, when I was thirteen, the concept of a moral sense was unknown to me.

———

I got back on track with good behavior. I do not think many people at school, if any, knew I had gotten into trouble. I wanted to do well in school, and I enjoyed the recognition I received for doing imaginative book reports, writing poetry, having an almost perfect year in spelling, and doing well in all subjects. At the beginning of the school year, a fellow student asked me what I wanted to be, and the only trade I knew of was my grandfather's, so I said a butcher. By the end of the year, when we stated our goals in anticipation of graduation, I wrote that I wanted to be a successful businessman.

As we prepared for graduation, we received encouragement that I had not known since my years in Colusa. Mrs.

McNolty impressed upon us that we were on the threshold of a large new phase in life. Our teacher who drilled us in sentence diagramming and in using the comma, Mrs. Mitchell, took the time to tell us that of all the graduations she had gone through, eighth grade was still special and memorable to her.

———

My father took me to more than one store to buy my shoes for graduation. In each place, he said, "They're just for one night. He's graduating."

"Oh," said the clerk each time. "Do your kids go barefoot in the summer?"

"No." He had never let us go barefoot. That was for people he had known since the Depression, people from Oklahoma, Texas, Arkansas, and Missouri. We had known them everywhere we had lived, including Gridley. Bob told of a boy in his grade named Moochie, who did not comb his hair and who had his shirt tail sticking out below his coat as he clomped around. My father's "No" had a trace of indignation. He went on to say, "They're goin' to work all summer."

———

I wore my new shoes and a white shirt. When Mrs. McNolty said all the boys should wear white shirts, one of my friends joked, "John doesn't have a white shirt."

"Yes, I do," I said. I just saved it for special occasions and did not want to ruin it.

Graduation took place outside on a warm evening. A boy who acted like a sissy but had beat me up during the school year sang. A girl of Filipino origin gave a speech about why she was proud to be an American. Being the shortest boy, I was matched with the shortest girl to lead the group in and out. On the way out, I began to walk fast as I felt the emotion welling up. Bob was playing in the band and forgot his drumming when he saw me speed up.

At the dance, we were all happy. I did not dance because I did not know how. But some of the boys got to kiss some of the girls, and I was not excluded.

We said our happy goodbyes as the dance ended and the gathering broke up. Outside, Sandy and Bob were waiting with my father in the old Ford station wagon. We had packed it earlier in the day and were leaving that night.

One of my friends asked me if we were going fishing.

I said, no, we were going to work in the fields.

SIX

We crawled out of the station wagon in the early morning with fog all around. I pumped up the Coleman stove to heat water for instant coffee. In a few minutes, the blue flame was shining in the darkness. Sandy set out bowls and spoons for cereal.

We were camped at the edge of the berry field, where we took turns in our sleeping arrangements. One of us slept on the front seat of the station wagon, and the other two slept in back with our father. We set out some of our kitchen items on a stack of wooden posts and some of them on the tailgate. For the first week, we had eaten cold food for all three meals, so that our dinners consisted of canned macaroni, canned spaghetti, and canned pork and beans. Now we had a stove.

After breakfast, we put the food and utensils in their cardboard boxes and stored them in the station wagon. As usual, we were the first ones in the field.

I went to my row where I had stopped the day before, and I began picking blackberries. The fruit was soft, and the work was quiet. It was not hard work. Most of the time, I was standing up, although I had to crouch and kneel for the lower fruit. A person learned to pick with both hands, or he would make even less. We tried to average a dollar an hour, but sometimes the picking was not that good. I had a wooden stand such as some workmen used for tools. It had two slanted legs on each end, joining at the peak in an "A" frame, with a horizontal dowel for a handle attached to each peak. A cardboard tray, which would end up in a supermarket, sat in the stand. When I filled the tray, I took it out to the end of the row, where the owners worked in a roofed area, arranging the berries in the trays. One of them punched my ticket.

The owner's mother told me that her son would like the trays rounded. I supposed so. She and whoever else was working under the shade could take the extra berries and put them in another tray, so at the end of the day, they would have more trays of market berries than they paid to have picked.

When the fruit was very ripe and in excess of what the owners needed for market, we picked freezer berries. For this purpose, we picked into larger, wooden crates with a sheet of brown waxed paper in the bottom of each. Everything went into the crate—imperfect or uneven in color, misshapen, bird-pecked, overripe, moldy. We were assured that it would all be cooked very well. We swore we would never buy a jar of jam in a store. Later, in other crops such as apricots and peaches, when we learned that the soft and spoiled fruit went for baby food, we became more cynical.

In addition to the work being light, the weather was mild. I worked alone, walled off from the others by rows of berry vines. No machinery disturbed the calmness. Voices carried as people chatted back and forth from within the rows, and one person's transistor radio determined what everyone else would hear. "I Left My Heart in San Francisco" played a few times per day. So did a song entitled "At the Point of No Return," which did not wear as well.

After work, we went to our camp. We fixed dinner on the Coleman stove, ate, and washed dishes. In the light of evening, we played catch with our mitts and a baseball. When the ball went into the trees and undergrowth at the edge of the berry patch, I had to be careful with poison oak.

On a couple of successive weekends, we spent one night in town in an old hotel, where we took baths and slept in beds. On one of those evenings, the older, heavy-set woman who ran the place took a couple of dollars out of the bosom of her work dress and forced the money on us boys. We tried to refuse it, as we were earning our own money and were proud of it, but she said, "Take it. It's my way of getting into heaven."

After about three weeks of camping, we moved into an old auto court in town near the Pajaro River, which separated Watsonville from Pajaro. Even in Watsonville, many signs were in Spanish, while in Pajaro, the town was like Little Mexico. The businesses were smaller, the colors and lettering were different, and almost all the signs were in Spanish. On payday, hundreds of braceros from the labor camps thronged the streets. I enjoyed reading the signs and practicing Spanish that way, and I was interested to see this other part of humanity.

When the blackberries, or olallieberries, as they were called by their proper term, needed a day or more to ripen, we picked raspberries with the same owner. This work was lighter and slower, as one had to squeeze the berries off the core and put them into one of a pair of cans hooked to one's waist. Raspberries paid less as well, and most of the time, only women and children did it.

At other times, we picked boysenberries or loganberries with other farmers for a day or two. We used wooden laths to push aside the boysenberry vines, as the thorns were large and sharp. The fruit had a stronger and more interesting taste than the blackberries did. The loganberries were milder fruit, being a cross between a blackberry and a raspberry, and they grew in very sandy soil. Picking them for a day was like being in a different locale.

My father was good at finding us work on a day that might have been a day off. We picked strawberries more than once, and we picked cucumbers for pickles and put them in burlap sacks. My father said the same thing each time. "It's better to work. When you get a day off, you spend a day's wages goin' to the zoo. Better to work. Even if you don't make much, you're not spendin' it."

My brothers and I shared this wisdom among ourselves with some irony. As well as I can remember, our family never went to a zoo when I was growing up.

———

The truck picked us up near the auto court early in the morning to pick green beans. We were the only *gabachos*, or white North Americans. All the rest were braceros. We sat on benches in the back of a canopied truck and later in a bus. One of the men poked an egg with a matchstick and sucked out the contents. Others rolled and smoked cigarettes. Many of them wore sandals and loose cotton clothes that looked like peasant garb from the textbooks. Some of them were very dark, and some of them spoke in rough accents that I assumed came from remote places. They asked us questions, which we answered in Spanish. "Are you boys brothers? How old are you? How many home runs does Willie Mays have?"

In the fields, it was all work. Sandy had told us stories about the workers throwing strawberries at each other when the boss was away and leaving red marks on one another's clothes, but strawberries had low-lying vines. Green beans grew on wires, higher than blackberries. Also, the bean growers' association had serious rules about not fooling around in the field, not fighting, and not taking green beans for personal consumption. The workers called back and forth and sang, but they worked hard.

Green beans paid two and a half cents a pound. We picked in wooden baskets, which in other places were called hampers. *Canastas.* When I filled my basket, I boosted it up to my shoulder and carried it out to the edge of the field, where an employee weighed it and punched a number on my ticket. I tried for 36 each time, but sometimes I had no more than 32, and sometimes I went down to 28. Some of the braceros heaped their baskets to 38 or 40. The ticket was a long piece of cardstock, yellow or green or beige according to the field, with vertical rows of numbers. We tried to average more than a dollar an hour, which meant a basket in less than an hour.

We brought our own lunches. The rest of the crew ate hot food that came out of large stainless steel pots that arrived by truck at noontime. The two-syllable call went out and was repeated through the field. "¡Lonche!" Footfalls thundered as the workers ran to the edge of the field.

The braceros were a happy bunch. They came to this country for a limited time on a work permit, made as much money as they could, and went home. Some of them seemed primitive in their appearance and mannerisms and rough accents, but they were all nice to us. "You boys are brothers? How old are you? How many home runs does Willie Mays have?"

———

We went to the show, as it was called. During berry season, the girl taking tickets took Sandy's hand and held it open.

"How did you get that?"

"Picking blackberries." He took his hand back.

"Oh."

When we lived in Half Moon Bay, Sandy knew a girl who

was Portuguese or Mexican or perhaps a mix, whose family picked peas. She had won the spelling bee that he and I participated in. She told us that picking peas defined a person. Some people did that kind of work, and some people did not.

We were now of the people who did that kind of work. It did not seem to make a difference when my brothers and I went to the park on a day off and played baseball with the kids from town. People who took our family's money for groceries, gasoline, and room rent did not treat us as a different class. Watsonville, like many, many towns, was full of workers at that time of year, and we were part of daily business. All the same, I imagine they perceived us as migrant workers.

I am sure they did on at least one occasion. My father read the want ads for a better place to stay, as the room in the auto court was small and two of us had to sleep in the back of the car. He found a basement apartment for rent. When we pulled up in the old Ford station wagon, a person inside the house pulled the "For Rent" sign from the window. In that moment, I felt more defined than in all the rest of the time we spent in Watsonville and the surrounding area.

———

Marilyn Monroe died in early August of 1962, on a weekend. Her death was big news. I did not know her as a movie star, as I had not seen any of her movies, and I did not know her as a sex symbol, as I did not read magazines that carried that kind of portrayal. To me, she was a pretty, blonde woman who died early, like my mother. She was thirty-six. My mother had been thirty-three.

Several years later, I would remark to a friend in college, as a way of saying that I did not have a cultural awareness of Marilyn Monroe, that she reminded me of my mother. He said, not in a prudish or lurid way, that no guy should say something like that. I think we were even in not knowing about some aspects of life.

We went back to the old farmhouse in Gridley in mid-August. The weeds had grown up all around the house and were dead and dry. The weather was hot. We had a month of summer vacation left, and my father had a prune-picking job lined up for us in the Colusa area. He was going to be the row boss, and the four of us boys were going to pick prunes.

My father had a new white straw hat, such as field foremen wore. My brothers and I had hats of the cheaper variety, made of flat, rough straw with an orange plastic band stitched around the edge of the brim. Such hats sold for thirty-nine cents in a supermarket. We kept them in a stack on the way to work and back.

We arrived at the prune orchard at dawn, having done our best to sleep as our father drove. We crawled out of the car in the cool air and put on our hats. Mosquitoes whined. The sweet aroma of fresh fruit was pleasant at this time of day. The prunes lay like a carpet, light blue with a tinge of purple. They had been shaken the afternoon or evening before. Ahead of us in the orchard, in the early morning air, the shaker rattled like a machine gun.

We unstacked our buckets and went to work, side by side like the hand of a clock, picking the ground clean all the way around underneath the tree. As we filled the buckets, one of us carried them, two at a time, to empty them into the bin. It was a plywood box, four feet square and two feet tall, that held about a thousand pounds of prunes. In the early part of the day, when the fruit was cool and firm and we were not worn out, we could fill a bin in an hour or a little more. In the latter part of the day, when the fruit was warm and soft and had more of a fetid smell, it seemed as if a bucket of prunes disappeared or even pressed the level lower. If the forklift driver moved a bin from one set of six trees to another, the impact settled the fruit two to three inches or more—work lost, energy and spirit cast away.

My father, who did not eat breakfast, had an egg sandwich at ten, which in the prune orchard was more like eight-thirty. We took a break together. The bread in the sandwiches was damp. Our hands were already encrusted with prune juice and dirt, and the smudge of mosquito repellent made its way into an occasional bite of food.

As the day wore on and the temperature increased, the work became more miserable. The mosquitoes never went away, even if they thinned in the afternoon. Fruit that had fallen a week earlier was soft as jelly and often moldy. One's fingers went through the skin into the warm pulp. There was no point in washing our hands. We had no water to spare, and our hands would be dirty again in no time. We rubbed our faces because of the heat, the sweat, the dust, or the mosqui- toes, and so we all four had dirty faces.

Our water jugs were now Clorox jugs. Gone were the glass wine jugs in burlap sacks. Every night we filled the plastic jugs with fresh water and put them in the freezer. In the orchard we kept them in the shade, but by afternoon the water was warm. We learned not to drink too much.

All day, every day, we crawled along the ground and picked it clean of fruit. Prunes that had been mashed by tractor wheels went into the bin, along with all the rest. Our picking buckets took on a crust of dirt and dried juice.

Sandy was our boss and to some extent our slave-driver. He kept a record at home of how much we picked each day and how many hours we worked. A typical day was ten hours and eight bins. At least once, we picked ten bins. A bin paid six dollars. Our goal was to average about $1.25 per hour each. Sandy kept his eye on his watch and on us even as he worked and picked the most. He hollered at us, swore at us, and when he thought it was necessary, he hit or kicked us.

It felt like slavery, and in later years I thought of it as being similar to slavery, but of course it was much less. It lasted only during the season, and we earned money. But to a boy, it was oppressive. The hot afternoons seemed endless, with the trees holding in the heat as the dirt floor of the orchard almost burned one's hands. Time slowed, and it seemed as if the end of the day would never come. An always-present aspect of that work, of that way of life, was that one had no choice but to do it.

The rest of the crew, with a couple of brief exceptions, consisted of Mexican families from Texas. The whole family spent the long day in the orchard, from the parents down to the small children. In the cool part of the day, little boys with no clothes on ran back and forth. They had not yet learned not to eat the fresh prunes, and going naked was an expedient. Mothers called. Babies and small children cried. People talked among themselves and called back and forth. The forklift roared, and the shaker rattled in the distance.

The women and girls covered up to keep out the sun. They wore straw hats with sloping brims, scarves, long-sleeve shirts and pants, and gloves. Some covered their faces, and when I would come near a girl or young woman, as I picked beneath my tree and she picked beneath hers, it seemed as if I saw only the eyes of a person who did not want to be seen. As I got to know them in later years in other crops and in labor camps, I learned that they did not want to be burned by the sun and thus be identified as a person who worked in the fields. There was no hiding in the fields, but even among people who knew one another, I had the sense that some of them did not want someone else seeing the real person at this work.

My brothers and I were exemplary workers. We worked all day without adult support and adult supervision. We were the first to arrive and the last to leave, staying, as my father would say, until the last dog was hung. As the row boss's sons, we had to behave. There was no question anyway. We were there to work. Sandy turned fifteen that season, I was thirteen, Bob was twelve, and David was not yet eleven.

At the end of the day, we stacked the four straw hats in the back of the station wagon. Depending on where the orchard was, which road we took to go home, and how late in the day it was, sometimes we stopped. One route took us through Princeton, where the ferry took us across the Sacramento River in the morning and in the evening. In that very small town on the river, a store sold ice cream. None of us wanted to go in, as we were grimy from work, but one of us had to. My father had told me more than once, "Never be ashamed to be seen in your work clothes," so I was armed with pride when it was my turn to go in and buy the four ice cream cones.

A girl about my age said, "Your face sure is dirty."

Too much came up at once. I said, with words I had learned from my father, "Is that any of your business?"

The proprietor turned to the girl and said, "I guess he told you."

Afterwards, I did not resent the girl. I was something unknown to her. She was young, and when she opened her mouth, words came out.

More than sixty years later, on a hot summer day, I drove south on the river road, Highway 45, from Hamilton City to Colusa, to visit my grandmother's grave. The Princeton ferry was long gone, as was the store. I thought it would have been interesting to talk to that person about how she saw life as a girl in a store in a tiny town on the river.

———————

One day when we finished an orchard before our usual quitting time, we drove over to Williams, ten miles from Colusa on the west side of the valley. The town was on 99W, which would become Interstate 5 a few years later. On that day, my father was looking at property. He found one place, a rundown house with a rundown shed smaller than a barn, with dry weeds grown up all around. My father, not always a master of slang and idiom, said, "What a shamshackle son of a bitch." On the way back to Gridley, he said it a few more times.

On a couple of other occasions, we looked at possible places. My father said he could build a house if he had to. He had done it before. In Orland, forty-two miles north on 99W, we found a more plausible piece of property.

————

The Gridley schools, like many schools in that era, postponed the opening of the school year in order to allow students to work another week in the harvest season. We were included in that benefit, even though we worked in another school district.

We earned more than a thousand dollars in the prune harvest. We averaged well over a dollar an hour each for the whole season, and we had no days off. We paid for all of our school clothes and had most of the money left over.

On the night before the first day of school, we took baths and put on the clothes we would wear the next day. The pleasure of the experience had a mixture of elements—the smell of new clothes, the sense of having bought those pristine garments with our own labor, and the prospect of leaving the prune orchard behind and going back to the encouraging atmosphere of school.

————

I began high school in Gridley with my friends from the year before. Some of them expressed surprise at seeing me. They said they thought we had moved. I did not remember giving that expectation, but a couple of my classmates had seen the packed station wagon. The new Spanish teacher had come from Orland, where we were planning to move, but I did not say anything about going there, as our father had taught us not to tell our business to other people.

I liked all of my classes, but the time came for a change. We moved to Orland on October 12, Columbus Day, when the fall rains had brought up new grass at the same time that they had brought down walnuts for us to pick up. We moved to a five-acre parcel with two small houses, an older house that might work as a rental, and a barn. The down payment came from my father's inheritance from Aunt Jenny. The rest of our money from picking prunes went into the general pool for moving expenses, living expenses, and a 1956 Buick station wagon that far excelled the old Ford. Having our own property was a new experience, and it might serve as a base for getting back into the cattle business. The auction yard was in the same place as it was when we lived in Orland the first time.

———

Sandy and I enrolled in Orland Joint Union High School, referred to as Orland High; Bob enrolled in C.K. Price Junior High, referred to as C.K.; and David enrolled in Fairview Elementary School, referred to as Fairview. Mill Street Elementary School, referred to as Mill Street, had the earliest or primary grades.

At the high school, the principal and vice-principal looked over our records. Gridley had a track system with both a university track and a college prep track, and Sandy and I were both in university. Orland had only a college prep track, and something prompted the two men in charge to put me in biology, a sophomore course that Sandy was taking, instead of freshman science. My other classes were normal, from algebra and English on down to typing and P.E.

A boy from the student council led us around on a tour. He wore a school sweater, dark blue and white, with the emblem of a Trojan warrior in a helmet. His name was Ken, and he was courteous with us.

Before long, I had an impression that Orland High School was more casual than the Gridley schools. The buildings were old, the light was dim in some places, and the maintenance in some classrooms was dingy. My English class was full of lads who did not pay attention and did not do their work. The teacher, an old man nearing retirement age who sat at his desk with his head resting in both hands, summoned the energy to give a lecture on the direct object. The history teacher was young and tried to compensate with a show of authority. He caught one dull boy cheating off the test of another boy, not much brighter, and he made a public example by evicting the offender from class. The student was back the next day, in a different seat.

My best class was biology, taught by Mr. Penner. It was a serious class, with clear lectures and explanations, sharp quizzes, and interesting laboratory exercises. Sandy was not in the same class as I was, but we had the same material, and we compared notes as we tried to earn the best scores in all of Mr. Penner's classes.

For newcomers, at least, Orland was not as friendly as Gridley. I was the youngest in my class and short for my age, still under five feet, and one student after another, boy and girl, laughed at me and pointed south, saying, "Mill Street is over that way." I responded as if I thought they were referring to a street and not a school.

One day during our first week there, Sandy and I were eating lunch together in the cafeteria. Across the table from us, a clean-cut fellow with the number of the junior year sewn on his school sweater sat across from us. He was polite and observed that we were new at the school. He finished his lunch and waited a couple of minutes for us. As we were about to leave, he asked if I would take his tray for him because he had injured his leg in football. I was familiar with the superiority of football players, and I was tired of people making fun of me. I thought he was trying to con me, so I said no. He asked Sandy if he would take his tray, and Sandy declined as well. As we rose from the table and took up our own trays, the fellow across from us reached down and picked up a pair of crutches from the floor. He straightened up, rose from the table, and carried his tray to the window. I felt guilty. I told Sandy, and he said that he thought the guy was trying to take us in, just as I did. To the student athlete's credit, he must have understood that we had some reason for reluctance, for he was never unfriendly to me after that. He was a leader in student government the next year as well as an accomplished athlete in three sports. He went on to become a distinguished professor of medicine. Orland had good leaders in the student body. I just didn't see them at first.

I attended Orland High for a little more than two weeks when an interruption appeared on my horizon. Since the middle of the year, my father had been corresponding with women from Mexico. He had found a classified ad for a listing service in a men's magazine, and through correspondence, he had received photos and letters. Through the summer, Sandy and I had read and translated letters that came in unfamiliar air mail envelopes with red and green stripes around the borders and exotic postage stamps. We wrote letters at our father's bidding. Now he had a short list of candidates, and, with money in the bank from his inheritance, he wanted to meet some of them in person.

As with the trip to Santa Barbara, we had discussions about who would go. We observed that I had more interest in Spanish and in speaking with Mexican people than Sandy did, and I think he did not want to be out of school for a month. Also, my father could leave him in charge of money, bills, groceries, and anything that came up with our new property. Grandpa and David were living in the smaller of the two newer houses, and the rest of us were living in the other, also a one-bedroom house but with more room for the four of us. The two houses were perpendicular to one another and close together, each facing the driveway as it came in along a small canal and turned at the barn.

I talked to each of my teachers to let them know of my planned absence and to ask about how I could keep up. My history teacher gave me a nod of assurance and told me to read and study a chapter per week. The algebra teacher gave me an estimate of what he might cover. The Spanish teacher, Miss Gurrola, was happy that I was going to have such a great opportunity. My other teachers told me I could catch up when I came back. No one seemed concerned about a long absence. My father was sure I would have to give a speech to the whole school when I returned, but I did not think my adventure was seen as that important.

Fog was hanging low throughout the Central Valley at the end of October, so my father took us on a route he knew from earlier times, when he would speed from eastern Oregon down through the deserts of Nevada. First, we climbed up out of the valley and arrived in Reno, where an arch over the street proclaimed it to be The Biggest Little City in the World. From there we turned south, toward Mexico.

SEVEN

The Buick station wagon cruised right along. We drove through towns whose names I would see later on maps and would hear in songs, such as Fallon and Tonopah. We drove through Las Vegas, which even in 1962 looked large and glittering to me. My father remarked that it had grown.

He exclaimed even more as we drove past Phoenix and Tucson and read the posted populations. We arrived in El Paso and crossed over into Ciudad Juárez at two in the afternoon on October 31, having left home two days earlier. We presented our birth certificates and proof of smallpox vaccination, and we were on our way to the city of Chihuahua in the state with the same name.

We stopped in a town that had a market out in the open. My father found a pair of pants he wanted to buy, so I had my first immersion experience in speaking Spanish with no help. I also had to convert pesos to dollars, which was not hard because our father had taught us to do math problems in our head all along.

We arrived in Chihuahua in the dark, and after securing a modest hotel room, we found our way to Avalos, a village that lay a few miles south of the city. We found the house and knocked on the door. We were met by a household of women who seemed to be in a strange state of mind. After holding the door ajar and determining who we were, they invited us in. We determined which one was Carmen, the young woman whose beautiful handwriting I had read and translated and whose long, dark hair and full features I had admired. We would not have recognized her, for she was pale and thin and distraught. She did not seem to be happy to see us, or happy about anything, and she let a couple of her sisters do the talking.

They showed us a newspaper and a separate photo of their late mother, who had been killed on the street in Chihuahua during the summer. I had read about it in one of Carmen's letters and had translated as best as I could, but I had not made complete sense of it. Even now, with the newspaper article and more than one person explaining, it was a strange story. Their mother, Eusebia, had gone into Chihuahua for shopping, and while she waited at a bus stop to go home, a group of auxiliary policemen, who may have been drinking, fell into a dispute and began shooting. A couple of the policemen and three or four bystanders died. As for the policemen themselves, I understood them to be something like private policemen or security guards, not part of the municipal police force.

The family was still in shock and consumed in grief. The mournful faces and sobbing voices were strange to me. Three months had passed, yet these people acted as if the event had happened the day before. Their sorrow was contagious. My father instructed me to tell them that it was hard for us to express, but we were very sorry. I said it as well as I could.

———

Back at our hotel room in the center of the city, my father smoked a cigarette and shook his head. "I don't know, Johnny.

I sure am disappointed. I wonder if we should give up on this one and look up the Apache."

Among the candidates, further down the list but also living in Chihuahua, was a stern, almost warlike-looking woman with straight hair and Native features. People did not smile much in photos in those times, and Mexico was more old-fashioned than the rural U.S. The photos my father had received, most of them taken in photo booths, were serious in expression, and this woman's was no exception. But she had a boy who was about five or six, and her handwriting was not very impressive.

————

We went back to Avalos the next day. We met the family members again and began to differentiate them by learning their names and their relative ages. There were ten children in the family together, "y ocho muertos" (eight dead). Six, all girls, were still living at home with the hard-working patriarch, Papa Alejo. Hortensia (Tencha) was twenty-eight, Andrea was twenty-three, Chuy was fifteen, Patricia was fourteen, and Chayo (Rosario) was twelve. Later I would learn that some of these ages were inexact, as teenage Mexican girls at the time often gave their age as the one that was coming up. Also, most of these sisters had the first name of María.

They said they were going to the cemetery the next day, and they invited us to go. We said we would.

————

November 2 was and still is a national holiday, El Día de Los Muertos, or the Day of the Dead. We found ourselves in a vast cemetery, not manicured with lawns and cypress trees but an orderly expanse of dirt and gravestones and crosses. Thousands of people had come. A sea of voices filled the air— people praying, people sobbing and crying and wailing, and people buying and selling tacos, tamales, fruit, candy, sugar cane, and water. People bought pails and cans of water to sprinkle on the dust. The Salas family gathered at the grave of their late mother, Eusebia. They prayed with the rosary, which was a new phenomenon for me, and they had an outpouring of grief. For a short while, I went with Papa Alejo and his son José Concepción, or Chon, to another part of the cemetery, where they sprinkled water and pulled a few weeds at what I understood to be the grave of Papa Alejo's first wife.

Carmen had a little boy, Jesús Manuel, age two. Andrea had two boys—Jorge, age two, and Javier, age four. They all lived in Papa Alejo's house, one of a tract of houses for workers at the local foundry. Chon worked there as well. He was about twenty-five or twenty-six. He had a pretty wife, Gloria, and a few little kids. The one whose name I remembered was Óscar. Gloria played basketball, and Chon played soccer. He and I became friends.

Papa Alejo took me in as a friend as well. He was a dark man, not very tall, who wore a flat-brimmed hat and working clothes. He had a horse named Reina (Queen) and a wagon with water barrels. He filled the barrels in Avalos, where the restrooms and water faucets were located in the center of every two blocks. He drove the wagon across the highway to Ranchería, where he sold the water. He invited me to go along, and I did. It all seemed normal, like stories from my childhood, with different details.

My father, meanwhile, had advanced in his courtship with Carmen, and he invited her to go with us to see more of the country. With me still acting as interpreter, we proposed the idea to Papa Alejo. He determined that a chaperone would be appropriate, so Andrea was to go with us.

Andrea, at twenty-three, was already well known in

Chihuahua as a singer with a mariachi group. She sang live on the radio as well as in nightclubs and at other venues such as the Palenque, where the rooster fights were held. My father and Papa Alejo went to see her in a program at the Hilton Hotel in Chihuahua. She was also voluptuous and turned men's heads wherever she went. I saw no irony in her being a chaperone, but I was only thirteen and was happy to have the pleasant company.

———

With my father and Carmen in the front seat and Andrea and me in the back seat, we put the Buick station wagon out on the open road. We drove south through Jiménez and Gómez Palacio and southeast to Saltillo, where I had a memorable serving of roasted goat. My father drove, and I practiced my conversation and vocabulary with the two young women. Andrea sang. My favorite song of hers was "Rebozo de Santa María."

As we traveled south at night, we saw what looked like fireworks far in the distance, to the southeast. The Cuban missile crisis had occurred in the last two weeks of October, and we were warned of the possible dangers of traveling in a country not far from Cuba, but the crisis passed. Upon seeing the lights, Carmen and Andrea made a humorous reference to Castro.

We drove on to San Luis Potosí and Querétaro, curving back toward Mexico City, and my father and I became sick with an intestinal disorder. A doctor came to our room, questioned us about what we had eaten, and pronounced that it was the cheese we had eaten at a truck stop restaurant. "Ah, sí. El queso," he said. Later, when I came to understand that the tepid coffee might have been made with tap water, I formed my own opinion.

At every place where we stayed, Andrea and I went in to ask about rooms. She talked, and I listened and learned. I paid, and we occupied our rooms—my father and Carmen in one room, Andrea and I in the other. In almost every place, we slept in the same bed—my innocent self, young for my age, and this distant, worldly woman in a beige nightgown. I would never have dared to touch her, but I marveled at the mystery.

Years later, when I played a record of Andrea's "Flor de Anis" for a girlfriend, she asked, "Who's that?" I told the story of who Andrea was and how we traveled together. I concluded by saying, "It's a woman I used to sleep with." But that was a joke for later in life.

———

We spent three days in Mexico City. My father paid a policeman twenty dollars to drive the car and show us the city. We came through it without a scrape, though at moments I had my doubts. The highlight for me was the Basílica de Guadalupe, the ancient cathedral in honor of la Virgen de Guadalupe, where penitents approached on their knees from a long distance away.

When we were in Mexico City, I saw a newspaper in Spanish with a photo of Richard Nixon and the news that he had lost the governor's race in California. I paused long enough to read the first part of the article and to learn that Nixon had announced that he was retiring from politics.

We spent a couple of days in Guadalajara, in a room above a bus station. I watched with great interest as buses came in from the country with goats tied on top, chickens and ducks in burlap bags, and people in provincial sombreros, sarapes, long dresses, and sandals.

On the street, vendors had rows of barbecued cow and goat heads. A man with a large knife chipped meat for tacos and called, "¡Pásale birria! ¡Pásale birria!" Years later, I would eat birria in the peach orchard with a family from Jalisco, and I would tell them how I had visited their state.

Traveling north through Aguascalientes, Durango, and Hidalgo del Parral, we returned to Chihuahua. Our tour had been about 2500 miles. We had seen a canyon full of Monarch butterflies, two naked boys bathing in a small waterfall in view of the highway, burros with large bundles of sticks for firewood, indigenous people carrying burdens, people plowing with oxen (one man very happy to have his picture taken with Andrea), many a horse and cart, and an array of people who made us feel welcome and were happy to speak Spanish with me.

During our next few days in Chihuahua, I became friends with Patricia. She was about my age. I went with her to buy corn and firewood, and I helped her start a fire in the back yard, where she boiled the corn. Early in the morning, I helped her carry pails of boiled corn to a mill, where it was ground into dough, or *masa*, and I helped her carry the pails home. I watched as she and her sisters made tortillas on a small press, cooked them on a griddle, and sold them to other people in the neighborhood.

Patricia and her older sister, Chuy (María Jesús), took me to meet a girl named Petra. I had green eyes, and so did Petra, in a world of people with brown eyes, so it was only fitting that we should meet. I saw her only once. I met the oldest brother and sister in the Salas family, Pedro and Ramona, who were married and had children. The only sibling I did not meet was Aurelio, between Andrea and Carmen in age, who lived in Tampico.

During this time in our visit, we visited the small museum maintained by Luz Corral, the widow of Pancho Villa. She was a courteous, hospitable lady. She showed us the general's saddles and guns and swords and uniforms as well as his automobile. She spoke English to my father and Spanish to me and my stepmother-to-be. She told us that the bullet-riddled car in which the general had been riding when he was assassinated in 1923 was a 1919 Dodge. My father, who was born in 1919, appreciated the detail. We took pictures with my father's

Polaroid, the kind that produced photos on the spot to be coated with a pungent liquid. In one picture, as I recall, Doña Luz had her arm around me, an old, well-mannered lady being nice to an American boy.

With Papa Alejo's permission, Carmen left with us for Ciudad Juárez, where she and my father planned to get married and arrange immigration papers. I said goodbye to all of my new and dear friends, and we left Chihuahua.

We stayed in a motel called Mi Ranchito, where the highway came in on the southern edge of Ciudad Juárez. From there we went to the downtown area, where my father began his inquiries. We met a lawyer. Having seen his sign, we went in and heard him deliver his name and title in a soft voice and lilting tone as he shook hands. *Edmundo Castillo Acuña, Licenciado y Abogado.* We met his associate, Ayub Ayub, a larger man in less formal attire who did the speaking in English. He had a harsh voice and a brusque way of speaking.

My father learned that he would need either divorce papers from his first wife or her death certificate as well as his own birth certificate. He had the latter. We would have to go to El Paso to send for my mother's death certificate. I was taking in the vocabulary. My father did not mention Donna or the marriage in Tijuana.

We were about three weeks into our trip when we arrived in Juárez. Now we were strung out from one day to the next with one complication after another. Carmen stayed at Mi Ranchito while my father and I crossed the border into El Paso every few days to check our mail at General Delivery. On one trip, we were crossing the street with pedestrians going both ways when a coarse-looking man hawked and spit a big gob of spittle right where I was about to place my foot.

In a letter from Sandy, I learned that he had been kicked off the bus for a week for getting even with a boy in my grade who was picking on Bob. It was a two-mile walk into town and back. Bob walked with him every day for the solidarity.

At the hotel, I spent some of my time reading and outlining chapters in my world history textbook and looking into my algebra book. I went on errands for groceries and cigarettes, and I took amusement in buying Tequila Sauza for my father. It was a clear substance in a bottle about the size of a fifth of whiskey or vodka, for the equivalent of eighty cents.

I also spent periods of time with boys my age from the neighborhood. We wandered the dirt lanes and chatted. They taught me a few words I would have learned somewhere else anyway. They asked me about Chubby Checker and the Twist. "Big Girls Don't Cry" by the Four Seasons was at the top of the charts, and I translated the title for them. I learned a little more vocabulary as they showed me how they made slingshots with the rubber of automobile inner tubes; I enjoyed the soft puffs as they shot small round stones into burning tires.

Downtown, I wandered the stores and marketplaces while my father and Carmen sat in the lawyer's office or went to government offices. President Kennedy was very popular, as was his wife, and I saw many portraits of him painted on black velvet backgrounds. Cowboy boots were popular, also, and in the morning when the shoppers were not yet about, a store-keeper hollered, "Cowboy boots! Cowboy boots! Nobody wanna buy cowboy boots?" On December 6, when I was out strolling, my father and Carmen found me. He was perturbed. They had looked all over for me, the opportunity was upon them, and they had gotten married without me. They showed me their rings, which they were now wearing.

In El Paso, I sent a telegram to Sandy giving him the news and asking him to send more money.

After a few more visits with Edmundo Castillo Acuña and Ayub Ayub and an interview in the American Embassy, my father saw that Carmen was going to have to go back to Avalos and wait while we returned to California.

We left El Paso on the morning of December 14, my fourteenth birthday. The weather was warm and sunny as we drove across the Southwest in the Buick, laden with blankets, sarapes, steer horns, wallets, coin purses, belts, and a couple of wooden chess sets. I had also bought pennants all along the way, my most memorable being from a wizened old woman who asked, in a shrill voice, *¿No quieres comprar una banderola de San Luis Potosí?*" I repeated that line, a line or two from "Rebozo de Santa María," the ingratiating self-introduction of *Edmundo Castillo Acuña, Licenciado y Abogado,* and other words and fragments that had struck my fancy. After I had taken a bath in the town of Aguascalientes, Andrea told me, smiling as always, that I could now say *"Me bañé en Aguascalientes,"* which had an alternate meaning of "I took a bath in hot water." I repeated that one, too.

We read off the names on the road signs as we passed—Las Cruces, Deming, Lordsburg. Out on the desert in Arizona, we stopped at a roadside café. On the front door, after we opened the screen door, was a sign I did not understand. It read, "No Colored Trade Solicited."

"Well, to hell with them," said my father.

Back in the car, I asked what the sign meant.

"It means they don't want to serve colored people."

"I thought that was against the law."

"It's supposed to be."

Towns in Arizona came and went—Tucson, Casa Grandes, Gila Bend. We stopped in Yuma after dark and went to the bus station, which in those days was a reasonable place to eat. A sailor in uniform went through the line up ahead. Not far behind him, a Black man in a jacket and slacks ordered. As he found a place to sit, I saw that the employees had served him his coffee in a paper cup, while they had served the white customers in crockery cups.

After our meal, we crossed into California and drove to El Centro, where we spent the night.

———

We had a long drive north the next day. By the time night fell, my father was working on a bottle. He said it would be a great joke if I went into the house and spoke nothing but Spanish, as if I had forgotten how to speak English. I said I didn't want to do anything that corny. Now he had something to harangue about. What was wrong with a little joke? I just didn't like to have any fun. And after all the Spanish I had learned. On and on.

In the end, I went into the house in the middle of the night, waking up Sandy and Bob where they slept in the front room, and I spoke a few words in Spanish.

Sandy said, "Where's Carmen?"

"She had to stay there, to finish getting her papers."

"After all that time and money."

My father came in behind me. "What do you think of all the Spanish your brother speaks? After you taught him."

Sandy said, "It's late."

"You need to see all the stuff we brought."

———

Back in school, I settled into my classes. I was weeks ahead in world history, weeks behind in algebra. Typing was almost hopeless, as I did not yet have good control of my fingers. I was a star in Spanish. Miss Gurrola, neat and trim in her jacket, blouse, skirt, dark glasses, and white cane, was delighted to have me back in class. She called me Juanito.

I did not have to give an oral report to anyone.

———

Sandy told me that while we were gone, he tried out for junior varsity basketball. He told me of all the exercises they had to go through on the gym floor, and afterwards, his name was not on the list. "I was cut."

Bob and David told me that Sandy had subjected them to discipline and bullying out in front of the barn. He had made them do strenuous calisthenics, and then he had slapped them and hit them.

I told Sandy about sharing a room with Andrea, and he was exasperated.

"And you didn't do anything?"

"No."

"You didn't even touch her?"

"No. Nothing."

"You fool. You stupid idiot. By God, I would have done something. I can't believe it."

"Well, I didn't."

———

My father took to developing a new line of thought that he had begun on the trip. When he had a few drinks in him, his voice relaxed.

"Sandy could marry Chuy. They're the same age. She's the darkest one, but she's pretty. And she's a *señorita* already."

"I don't want to marry some Mexican."

"We could invite her to come up and stay. Maybe she ends up with a big belly."

"I don't want to talk about it."

"And Johnny could marry Patricia. They're the same age, and she's got a lot of spirit."

I did not find the idea so disagreeable, but anything like that was a long ways off in time for me.

"Sandy with Chuy, Johnny with Patty, and Bobby with Chayo."

Sandy was steaming. "I don't want to talk about it. It all sounds stupid to me."

Up and down the aisles of the grocery store, as we picked out items on the list and no more, my father took a quart of buttermilk from the dairy case. When he made sure it was churned buttermilk and not cultured, he shook the waxed carton, pulled the circular tab that was stapled to the top, and drank from the carton. A white spot from the tab remained on his nose. I shrank in embarrassment. This was my father, who was self-conscious most of the time, keeping us from talking or pointing or moving away from the cart. This was my father, anti-social by nature, who squatted on a floor in another person's house rather than sit on the couch, who set his bottle in its brown sack on the floor in front of him and tipped his ash in the cuff of his pants.

I knew better than to complain or criticize. It was over in a few seconds, and no one would say anything at the cash register.

I spent long hours of Christmas vacation doing algebra problems I did not understand. In the eighth grade in Gridley and now in the ninth in Orland, we were being given a new math, in preliminary textbook editions with plain print and cardstock covers. Sandy was not familiar with the approach, and he couldn't help me. He was in geometry with Mrs. Walker, and he was doing fine.

Back in school with the new calendar year, I went into the typing room as soon as I arrived at school, and I practiced. My frustration was not improved when a student a year ahead of me leaned over me. We were painting rooms at home, and I had a white paint stain in my hair. This older student, Dennis, looked down at my head and said, "Who shit on you?" He continued to lean over me and taunt me about my typing. The typewriters were old Remington manuals that rang at the end of every line, and the keys bunched up on me. The teacher, Mr. Knotts, came along and said, "That's all right. Just keep practicing."

——————

I was moved into a different English class, where I met some of the more academic students in my grade. The teacher read us "The Gift of the Magi," which suggests to me that I was moved into that class before Christmas. As the days grew sunny and warm outside the classroom window, we read Hemingway's "Big Two-Hearted River," a story entitled "Leiningen Versus the Ants," excerpts from *The Odyssey*, an abridged version of *Great Expectations*, and *Julius Caesar*. I had memorized "If" by Rudyard Kipling in the eighth grade, and I had a good proficiency for reading out loud, so the teacher put me to recording "Gunga Din." Left to myself, I made a mess of the tape, and it came out of the machine in curls and knots. I felt embarrassed and clumsy, but I was not as ashamed as in my failure with the trumpet in Colusa.

——————

In late winter and early spring, Sandy practiced for the annual boxing show. He tried to convince me to sign up, but I was the smallest boy in school and didn't feel like being pummeled in front of a gym full of people. I sparred with him, though, as did Bob, and we all went to see the show. Sandy's match was the first of the night, and he fought to a draw with a boy from my grade. The featured matches of the night were in the heavier weight classes, where some of the boxers were much more developed in muscle tone and five o'clock shadow.

A year earlier, Benny "Kid" Paret had died after a fight with Emile Griffith. The event caused a great national dialogue about boxing, and it helped bring about the end of boxing in the high schools and in many colleges. The boxing show of 1963 was Orland's last.

———

Sandy and I were doing well in school. We had our textbooks wrapped in the heavy brown paper of grocery bags rather than in the laminated blue-and-white book covers with the Trojan warrior, but we were not the only ones. We both excelled in biology, and Sandy was one of the top students in geometry. We did not get into any trouble. However, Sandy fell into a disagreement with his mechanical drawing teacher. Sandy had received praise and encouragement from the revered art teacher, he was at the top of the class in geometry, and he was always meticulous in his charts and graphs, so I do not think he was doing poor work in mechanical drawing. But something was wrong, something like a personality conflict or an authority problem. Sandy told our father that the teacher was unfair with him and had given him a low score in a major assignment. He told me that if the teacher gave him a *D* or an *F* for the semester, he was going to hit him with a water balloon.

On the last day of school, when classes were out, I saw Sandy in the lower hallway of the main building. He had a water balloon in his hands and a comrade at his side. I asked him what he was going to do, and he said school was out, and he was going to hit the mechanical drawing teacher with the balloon.

Through the chaos and clamor of the last day of school, I caught the bus and went home. A little later, two juniors in a fixed-up Chevy dropped him off at the house. He said he had done what he intended, had taken off running, and had been offered a ride.

Later that day, the principal and vice-principal arrived at our house in an old Chevrolet owned by the school district. They were wearing white, short-sleeved shirts and neckties. My father was at home, so Bob and I made ourselves scarce. A few minutes later, the two school officials were in retreat as my father hollered abuse at them, including some unkind remarks about the mechanical drawing teacher, who had a Middle Eastern last name.

Six days later, a letter on high school stationery was addressed to my father from the principal. It began with, "You are aware of the problem presented when your son, Sandy," and went on to summarize the offense and to state the school's course of action. Because school had closed at the time of the incident, Sandy would be readmitted on probation, "Should you return to Orland next fall."

I do not remember our precise timeline. We might have already been in Watsonville, picking blackberries. Perhaps, as in Gridley, the people at school thought we had moved.

EIGHT

I n the latter part of the school year, after spending part of
the winter unemployed, my father had returned to work
in the Colusa area, doing carpentry work on a small labor
camp and then driving tractor. On more than one weekend, I
had taken my turn at going to Maxwell on the bus and
spending a weekend in a camp trailer next to a tractor shed
and an old overhead water tank that I think gave me a case of
hives. On one weekend, I was by myself. On another, I was
babysitting my new stepbrother, whom I called Chumel, a
shortened form of Jesús (Chuy) Manuel. Carmen had arrived
in April, and the little boy came a while later.

In June, with Sandy's encounter with authority in the
recent past, we were camped in the tan trailer at the edge of a
different berry patch from the year before. A couple of us slept
in the station wagon. Carmen kept house and took care of the
child, whom we now called Manny. Sandy and Bob picked
berries after the evening meal, while Carmen and I, with the
owner's permission, cooked and canned quarts of blackberry
jam.

As time went on, Carmen worked in the fields with us, and
we shared the housework. The berry grower was also experi-

menting with chives, so when the berry picking slowed down for a day or two, he put all of us to work at weeding chives. It was like picking strawberries, in that a person knelt in damp furrows all day long, but it was more detailed, as one had to use a paring knife to cut out the weeds and try to leave the thin, young chives intact.

We also picked strawberries and peas. On one job, where the rest of the crew and the row boss were Mexican, my brothers pushed me into the lead to do the talking when we changed rows. I had learned to use my hands when I spoke Spanish, so on one occasion, I made a sweeping gesture as I asked, "¿Empezamos aquí?" (Do we start here?) Sandy and Bob mimicked me, in voice and in gesture, for the rest of the day.

I said, "To hell with you. I don't care if you make fun of me for this. You made me do it to begin with."

Sandy said, "It's just because you're better at it, John."

I was learning that one, too. When it was convenient to him, I spoke Spanish better, I had a better memory, or I was better at this household task or that. I went shopping with our father and Carmen. We went through a great deal of sugar making jam, and when it was on sale, I stood by while my father asserted to the employee that there was no limit per customer.

We returned to the Sacramento Valley in time for peach season. We parked the camp trailer in the labor camp my father had worked on in the spring, a few miles north of Colusa on the river road. My father was going to be the row boss, and Sandy and I were going to pick on the crew. The foreman was a man named Al, whom we knew from before as arrogant and irritable. He gave my father the authority to fire people on the crew.

"If you don't like the way someone parts his hair, fire him," he said.

Most peach picking was piece work, paying sixteen cents

for a fifty-pound wooden lug box or $3.50 for a bin, and workers picked into a canvas bag slung over the shoulder. Al was doing things different. He had a crew of almost all men, with few women and no children. The workers were paid $1.50 per hour and used metal buckets. The buckets were new, with holes drilled in the bottom, a red number painted on the side, and a hook attached to the handle for hanging the bucket on the side of the ladder or on a branch. As the workers filled their buckets, they poured the beaches into bins, where employees sorted out any bad ones.

My father secured work for Sandy and me, though we were both under sixteen, the standard age for working above five feet on a ladder. I worked for a while with a man from India. He wore khakis and spoke in a soft, almost monotone voice. He taught me how to say, in Urdu, the equivalents of "Don't pick green peaches," "Don't pick little peaches," "Water," "Drink of water," and "Here, have a drink of water."

I also worked with a talkative man from one of the Southern states. He had a face like other men I had seen who sobered up for the work season. He made fun of men who held signs on road construction crews, and he told stories from his time in the Navy. In one, a man named Red had come sliding into the ballroom, breaking wind all the way, as was his talent, but rose with his dress whites stained brown. In another, one sailor had urinated between the legs of a sailor in front of him at a field latrine, and the sailor in front turned around and punched the other one smack in the forehead.

When people worked piecework, they were responsible for picking their own trees, and nobody was supposed to pick someone else's bottoms and steal the easy picking. Working by the hour, pickers did not have those boundaries. In one orchard, where the fruit was green and the crew moved fast in the first picking, my father put me to picking bottoms. The fruit is often greener on the bottom where it is in the shade and riper on top where it receives more sun, so I got ahead of the crew, trying to find ripe peaches.

Peach orchards were worse than prune orchards for heat, humidity, and mosquitoes because the trees took more water and had denser foliage. The day was oppressive, and I felt detached and isolated. Just once, I thought, just once I would break the rules of being a serious worker.

I picked a hard, green peach about the size of a baseball and hurled it at the trunk of the next tree in the row. I hit it dead center.

The foreman, Al, stepped out of the cover of Sudan grass and the foliage of a neighboring tree. He said something like, "Uh-huh."

I told him, in an apologetic tone, that it was the only peach I had thrown since I had been on the job, which was true, because a person just didn't throw peaches.

He told me to get back and work with the rest of the crew.

We worked on twelve-foot wooden ladders, which were heavy for me, and even more so when mud built up and clung to the steps. I did my work, though, sometimes struggling beneath the blazing sun, straining to keep the ladder from falling over as I moved it around the tree. I wore a wristwatch, which I looked at every few minutes, yet I could not remember what time it was. The day dragged. I asked myself, why do I work? Why do I keep picking? I answered, because I had to, because I could not fail in doing my part for the family, because I had to show that I could be a good worker. The main reason was that I had to. I had no choice.

———

Sandy had passed driver's education and had his learner's permit. My father was a good teacher, but Sandy had always had a temper and was becoming impetuous. He had taken to arguing with my father and criticizing him for having spent so much money on the trip to Mexico. Some of these arguments took place in front of Carmen, with whom I had more of a bond than he did, so I felt mortified.

One evening, the three of them went into town with Sandy driving for practice. On the way back, as Sandy told me, my father, having had a bit to drink, gave a command in the pidgin Spanish he had become accustomed to using. Sandy did not understand it or perhaps did not want to understand it, and from there the conflict grew.

They argued into the night. My father said Sandy was getting too big for his britches. Sandy said he was tired of being bossed around, working like a slave, and not having anything to show for it. We were always broke. We wouldn't be if my father hadn't spent so much money on the trip to Mexico.

I knew that some of his argument was valid, as we were behind on our payments and were likely to lose the place in Orland.

My father told him that if he didn't like it, he could go live somewhere else.

Sandy said he would. He would go stay with Suzi.

Suzi had stayed in touch. She was married again and had a little girl. She lived in Lancaster, where her husband was a roofer, and she had a standing invitation for any of us to go for a visit or to work.

Sandy left on the bus the next day.

My father was not subdued. That evening, with the help of liquid sustenance, he fashioned a phrase to repeat to us. "It'll just make it harder on the rest of you."

We went into prune season, working for the same company and living in the same labor camp. David came to join us to pick prunes, so our crew consisted of Carmen, Bob, David, and me, with Manuel toddling around. Our father was the row boss. I was the leader of our little group.

We were an unhappy bunch. The prunes did not fall as well as usual that year, so I had to spend a large portion of my time stripping the trees with a long pole. I also carried the full buckets to make the work lighter for Carmen and David. I had derived the idea that I had to prepare myself against the possibility of even hotter weather, so I wore a jacket zipped up through the hot part of the day. Perhaps, at a deeper level, I felt that I had to suffer. Bob and David made fun of me for the way I wore my hat, the way I tipped my head when I knocked prunes, the way I zipped up my jacket, the way I spoke Spanish, and anything else that occurred to them. I tried to make them work the way Sandy had done, but they were not afraid of me, and I was new to the role. Sandy's birthday came and went. We did not talk very much about him.

Life in the labor camp became tiresome. There was very little privacy, and some of the other residents were giving Carmen advice. She shouldn't let her husband discipline her son. She shouldn't have to cook and clean for all his boys. We did our share of the housework as always, but people talked as they saw fit.

I had developed sympathy for one family during peach season because the father contrived an excuse not to go to work, yet he sent his daughters out. They were about sixteen or seventeen, very attractive, and stricken with the shame of having to work in the fields, in a crew of almost all men, while their father loafed at home. He stated his case to me as he smoked a cigarette, wearing a clean shirt, with a dull glow on his face that I thought came from drinking in the daytime. The peaches gave him such a rash, he couldn't bear it. A person couldn't see it now because he wasn't in the field, but it was terrible.

In prune season, he was at the helm as his daughters, his wife, and the smaller children picked prunes. He stripped trees, carried buckets, and talked to others in the orchard. At one point, our white, five-gallon plastic water can disappeared from outside our trailer, right next to that part of the camp where that family lived, and it showed up under their tree. I could not believe how brazen it was, and the task fell to me to

get the water container back. I was still on speaking terms with
the daughters, so I told them the jug was ours. When it came
back, the cap was missing, and a rag was stuck in its place. In
addition, relations were now strained with these two girls who
had had my admiration and sympathy.

Prune season came to an end for us at last as we went back
to Orland for the beginning of the school year.

————

My course of study for the sophomore year, which had been
decided in the spring, included three junior classes—chemistry, Spanish III, and shorthand. I had skipped over Spanish II
because of my proficiency, and although Miss Gurrola was
gone, I was still recognized as a top student. My father had
urged me to take shorthand because it would be a valuable
business skill, like typing. My other classes were normal—
English, world geography, geometry, and P.E. I was glad to be
back in school, and I was ready for the challenge of new
subjects.

In geometry with Mrs. Walker, I began by sitting with a
basketball and football player with whom I had made fun of
algebra as a defense for not understanding it. My clowning
around in geometry did not last long. Stern, almost-militaristic
Mrs. Walker, whose pre-marriage name had been Kaiser, separated us and made me sit in the front row. It was one of the
best things that happened to me in a lifetime of good educational experiences. Mrs. Walker was nearing retirement age,
and she had taught many of our older brothers and sisters. She
knew her students and brought out the best in those who
wanted to learn. Her action also helped me remain serious in
my other classes.

In shorthand, I was in a class with older girls. Most of them
were juniors, but several were seniors. Among them were the
cheerleaders and song leaders, young women of poise and
beauty. Although they were distant from me in age, maturity,

appearance, and status, they made me feel welcome. We took dictation side by side. When my stenographer's notebook was full and I had to staple in some paper I picked up in another class, the girl next to me said, "Oh, that's a good way of doing it."

Shorthand was an enlightening subject for me. Through the exercises, I also learned how to write a business letter. Also, because of the formation of the symbols, it gave me another way of working with language.

———

Somewhere during this time, and I think it might have been before things were resolved with Sandy, an event occurred that David told me about later. Our father, who had always picked on David and struck fear into him, took David over by the barn and told him that he, David, was not his son. David, not yet twelve and somewhat frail and sheltered, was bewildered. My father, as was often the case, did not worry very much about how someone else took things.

———

Early in the school year, I was surprised one day to run into my brother Sandy. I was glad to see him, of course, and glad to see him in school, a natural place for him as well as for me. As it turned out, we were in the same chemistry class.

I asked him how he came to be back in school in Orland, and he said he was staying with a family that he and I knew. Two brothers close in age were in Sandy's grade, and the four of us had worked on biology together. One of the brothers had been with Sandy when he threw the water balloon at the teacher. Their family was irregular, also, with their mother in a second marriage with a couple of half-sisters. They lived in the country and raised their own calves and chickens, so they were like us in a way. The two brothers had a strange rivalry that almost ended in serious injury one time when Sandy and I visited, but the family was still together, and Sandy was staying with them.

When I went home that day, I told my father I had seen Sandy, and I told him where Sandy was staying.

My father, who was half-crocked and was changing the tire on the old Ford station wagon, which we still had, flew into a rage. Spit flew.

What the hell was going on? What the hell was he doing, staying with someone else? I was to go over there and tell him to come home, or our father would send the cops for him.

I stood dumb.

My father hit me with a hub cap and said for me to go get him.

I ran across country, from where I had been standing to the place where the other family lived. I ran through irrigated pastures. I climbed over teetering fences. My side ached as I ran along gravel roads. I arrived at the place where Sandy was staying, and I told him he had to come home.

He was only sixteen. He could see he had no choice. So he returned home.

He told me stories of roofing in the hot desert climate of Lancaster, at a time when roofers still drove every nail by hand. He told of acquiring a rash from handling bundles of redwood shakes.

I told him how we had made it through prune season.

I do not know how happy he was to be at home again, but as brothers, we were all glad to be together. I am sure my father was satisfied in having his number one son at home, and our family was at peace for a while.

The dread that had been creeping along stood up and became undeniable. The bank had foreclosed on our property in Orland, and we had to move. I had known for a few months in the middle part of the year that we were not making payments, but I could not understand how things had gotten to this point when we were all working. Prune season had not been as good for us as the year before, but we had all worked, all summer.

We moved into a rental house about two hundred yards away on the same side of Highway 99W, where the trucks roared by our bedroom window. It was part of a frontage property with our house on the south end, a little store in front of a two-unit cabin-court-style rental in the middle, and the owners' house on the north end. The owners had three children, including a boy in my grade and a boy in David's, and we had all waited for the bus together the year before. Grandpa and David moved into one of the two cabin units, and the rest of us moved into the house for forty a month.

My father rented an open trailer to move our belongings. On one short trip, he left us at the house on the highway while he and my grandfather went to Corning, eleven miles farther north, where the gasoline was cheaper and the station gave double trading stamps. It would have been a place to pick up a bottle as well.

We were standing in front of the house, a few yards from the highway, when the yellow-and-white Buick came into view. My father slowed down, honked, pointed with a cigarette in his left hand, and hollered for us to go to the other house. He was preparing to turn into the road by the canal.

As he was turning, a car that was trying to pass hit the rear driver's side of the station wagon, turned it, and sent it sliding and skidding backward, with the trailer jack-knifed, until both vehicles ended up in the dry concrete canal with the front end of the Buick sticking up and facing north.

I ran to the scene, fearing the worst as the dust cleared. I believe Bob was with me, calling out, as Sandy had stayed at the other house. My father and my grandfather were sitting in the front seat, looking astonished. They climbed out unhurt.

My father had me hide a wine bottle in the nearby orange orchard.

Cars and people gathered. A man with a twisted face and a shiny puffed cheek squatted at the edge of the highway, forearms on his knees as he smoked a cigarette. Our landlady, who had been standing in the little store, had heard my father honk and had seen him stick out his arm. The highway patrolman listened to everyone. A tow truck pulled the car and trailer out of the canal. No one was hurt, and no one was cited, but the best car we had had in many years now had a greenish crumpled dent in the rear panel.

For the next few weeks, as our father waited for us after school to go pick walnuts, we winced as we crossed the street to get into the dented car. Somewhere deep inside, I knew that life would change, but this was the way it was now. And I could always go back to school the next day.

———

Sunday, October 6, 1963, was a sunny day. We were able to go home early from picking walnuts so we could watch the fourth game of the World Series. Sandy had made a Dodger fan of me the year before, and we had suffered together when the Dodgers lost the pennant to the Giants at the end of the season. Now, Sandy Koufax was back with a good arm, and the Dodgers were on top. They beat the Yankees in four straight in the World Series. Koufax won two games against Whitey Ford and was voted the Series' MVP. After the game, my brother Sandy and I went outside and played catch.

———

As the days became shorter and the weather became gloomier, we learned that Orland High was going to have its first wrestling team. Sandy tried to convince me to go out, but I resisted. I had just reached five feet in height, and in spite of working in the fields, I did not have good muscle tone. So he went out for the team by himself, and he practiced with the boy who had been his opponent in the boxing show.

Sandy kept at me, and I felt guilty for not cooperating. One day I was loitering at lunchtime with a few other lads inside the back door of the gym, and the wrestling coach came by. He said no one could be in the gym at that time of day unless he was out for a sport. I said I wanted to go out for wrestling, so I was able to stay inside out of the rain. By the end of the day, I had a pair of baggy sweats to wear.

I was not a good wrestler at first. I did not have good strength in my arms, and I ran out of energy on short notice. In addition, I had to starve and run extra laps in order to qualify for the lowest weight class, so I was already tired when I weighed in.

When we went on the first trip to a meet in another town, I had not been on the team long enough to wrestle, but I was allowed to go along. Sandy and I had to get up early and walk into town, as our father was working elsewhere. We were told to dress well, so I put on a pair of greyish-white dress pants. As we were leaving the yard in the dark, I tripped, and I came up with a muddy spot on the knee of my pants. I was stuck with it for the day, as those were the only good pants I had.

On the return trip that evening, the bus stopped at a restaurant. The coach had told us our dinner would be a dollar each, so Sandy had the two dollars for us. At the end of the meal, word came down the table that we could have German chocolate pudding for dessert, for another twenty-five cents. Sandy looked at me, and we did without.

Sandy and I were sitting in chemistry class on November 22 when a message girl came from the main office. The teacher, who was a droll fellow who told teenage allegories about ionic bonding and who read us his original poetry from his Army days, turned very serious. He read to us that President Kennedy had been shot in Dallas, Texas.

The world hung in suspense. Later in the day, news came that the president had died. Everyone went home to follow the news on television. The assassination took place on Friday, and school was canceled for the beginning of the next week. After that came Thanksgiving, so we were out of school for the whole week. Oranges were coming into season, so I spent a great deal of the week slicing oranges and cooking them for marmalade to go along with the blackberry jam from the summer. As I worked, the television covered all the events of the procession. The words "rotunda" and "cortège" came into my vocabulary. I saw, as did the rest of the world, John-John's salute, the riderless horse with inverted stirrups, and the mourning family. With the rest of my family, I saw, on live coverage, the shooting of Lee Harvey Oswald by Jack Ruby. For the country, it was a large, unifying moment in history. For members of my generation, born after the attack on Pearl Harbor, it was the most important event in our growing up.

My father was working for a big company called Mills Orchards, off the highway near Hamilton City, between Orland and Chico. He drove tractor and did other work as needed, including in the prune packing plant where Carmen had a job sorting on the conveyor belt. Sandy and I went to work picking oranges on weekends and on Christmas vacation.

For orange picking, we were issued a picking bag and a pair of clippers. The bag was of canvas, with a padded strap that went around the neck and one shoulder. The mouth of the bag, at elbow level, was firm with a heavy piece of rope hemmed around the top of the canvas. The bottom folded up and attached to the body with a trigger snap on each side. The clippers, for cutting the stems flush, had a small leather strap that went over the middle finger. When a picker had his bag full, he hurried to the bin trailer, stepped up onto the running board, swung the bag, undid the two snaps, and let the oranges flow into the bin. As he did so, he called out his number. The checker, holding a pen in his gloved hand, made the tally on a clipboard. Sandy and I picked on the same number. We earned sixteen cents a bag, and there were not many shortcuts.

We had to use sixteen-foot wooden ladders, but the ladders did not have a third leg, so they were not as heavy as they might have been. Orange picking took place in the cold, damp time of the year, so we slipped in the mud as we balanced the tall, upright ladders in order to move around the tree. It was good exercise for the stomach muscles. We had to be careful climbing the ladders. Mud built up on the steps worse than in the peach orchard, and we had to knock it off. We also had to be careful when we stepped up onto the running board of the trailer, as we often had mud on our shoes. The tractors that pulled the trailers through the orchard were diesel tracklayers. The engines ran all day, and diesel smoke drifted among the trees.

More than once, we picked oranges all day on a Saturday and wrestled that night.

———

For the last meet of the season, I not only had to starve, but I had to sit in the whirlpool to try to get down to ninety-eight pounds. I still had a soft, juvenile body.

The coach asked me what we ate. I gave him a guarded summary and asked what kind of food we should eat in order to keep our weight down.

He looked at the scale and at his clipboard, shrugged, and said, "Steak."

———

I looked on the bulletin board where Mrs. Hart, the English teacher, posted the best writing assignments. I had made it twice before—once for an essay about the yo-yo craze of 1962, which I had lived through in Gridley, and once for an essay about Christmas. Now my fictional story appeared. It was called "To Find a Killer," a title I had borrowed from a murder mystery I had read in an empty upstairs bedroom in the big house in Gridley. In my version, I had to track down the killer of Charlie Brown, and my trail led me to my brother as the perpetrator. In the final sentence, I disclosed that I had to exact revenge for the death of my guinea pig.

My story was based on fact. After the mice in Gridley, I had guinea pigs. To save on money, I fed them kitchen scraps and feed I salvaged from the fields, such as milo, or sorghum. When my father brought home green pears from the orchard, I fed some of those to my pets, and they died. My story, as I recall it, was a clever exercise in not disclosing that the murder victim was a guinea pig until the final words. I did not have a grudge against any of my brothers; I may have been working out my own guilt for letting my animals die. At any rate, the story was fanciful, and I was happy to see it posted. Recognition on Mrs. Hart's bulletin board was a memorable step after having my juvenile poems included in the collection in Mrs. McNolty's class two years earlier.

My father and Carmen, with Manuel, moved into the company housing at Mills Orchards. My grandfather and David moved into the rental house with Sandy, Bob, and me. My grandfather had had a low blood sugar episode, called "insulin shock" at the time, and David had been so nervous and uncertain that he had delayed in coming to our house for help. Grandpa was out of the hospital, with funny stories about the old people, but it was just as well that he should be with us older boys.

Carmen went to the hospital in Willows, and our sister

Carmen was born on March 5, 1964. To help with the baby and the housework, Bob went to stay at Mills Orchards and to spend part of his eighth-grade year in Hamilton City. Sandy and I did not want to interrupt our classes and activities in Orland.

Bob and I traded places during spring vacation, and I spaded up a garden plot in back of the company house. The house itself had metal sides, no insulation, and plastic windows, so the inside fogged up with condensation. The shared bathrooms were outside. All of that was tolerable to us, and I took an interest in the garden as I dug it up and planted it.

———

After wrestling and spring break, I went out for track. Having run laps on so many afternoons for wrestling, I thought I might be a distance runner. The longest race for sophomores was the 1320, or three-quarter mile. I could run it, but I was still small, and I discovered that I ran out of energy if I pushed myself too much.

In my first race, which was held in Orland, I ran out of breath and energy as I tried to keep up with the other runners, and I had to drop out behind the bleachers with a boy who was quite a bit bigger than I was. He was flabby, and his face was flushed. I don't imagine I looked much better.

After that, I finished every race, even though I came in way behind. People applauded. At one meet, in Chico, I was almost in tears because a bigger crowd saw how much I lagged. But I finished. As I walked away, a man came up to me, put his arm across my shoulders, and said, "That was good." I looked up and saw Mr. Knotts, my typing teacher from the year before, who had moved to Chico.

———

One of the neighbor kids who played football with us was a fast runner, so I told him he should go out for track. When he did, the coach took my sweats and gave them to him. I was no longer on the traveling team.

My friend came back from the last meet of the year. He told me that on the bus, they had voted for awards, and I had been chosen for the sportsmanship award. However, the coach gave it to a senior who had done well in the shot put and had been a good football player under the same coach. The rationale was that as a senior, the other student was having his last chance for an award.

The coach was also my world geography teacher as well as the head football coach. For him, football was more important than anything else at school. In order to support the new wrestling team, he pressured football players into going out for wrestling. He wanted my swift-running friend to go out for football. Now he was giving a track award to one of his football players. I had nothing against the senior. He was a quiet sort who kept to himself and competed in his event off in a corner of the track meet. He did not exude sportsmanship, but he was not a bully or a braggart, and he was a far better athlete than I was, so I found it in me to be pleased for him that he received the award.

———

By participating in sports and earning letters, Sandy and I became members of Block "O," the athletic club. We went on the spring picnic with a busload of other boys. The event was a wienie roast with willow sticks, on the gravel shoals of Stony Creek, with no hidden costs.

On the way back, I fell into a conversation with a boy from my class, a well-to-do, above-average student. The subject of going to college came up. I asked him if he planned to go, and he said, oh, yes. He asked me what I planned. I thought, if this fellow can make it through college, I sure can. So I said, yes, I thought I would go to college, too.

———

Under Sandy's influence, I read biographies and autobiographies of famous baseball players, and so I became conversant in the careers of John McGraw, Christy Mathewson, Walter Perry Johnson, Ty Cobb, Bob Feller, Roy Campanella, and others.

I also read Jesse Stuart's *The Thread That Runs So True*, an autobiographical account of the author's working in a small country school in Kentucky. I read this book on the recommendation of the librarian, as I had expressed an interest in becoming a teacher.

In the spring, we had Career Day. I went to the session for teachers, and I saw Sandy there. The speaker, from Chico State College, gave a good presentation that included some of his experiences. On the way out, I told Sandy I wanted to be a teacher.

———

The student who impressed me the most that year was the valedictorian. She was among the cheerleaders and song leaders, less flamboyant but very steady and modest. From a distance, I admired her as a great inspiration for students to achieve their best.

Ten years later during my graduate work at UC Davis, when I went jogging at a certain time of day, I passed her a few times going the opposite direction as she walked along the edge of campus. I did not think she recognized me as the little kid who took shorthand and graded papers for the Spanish teacher, but I nodded to her, and she nodded back. She had the demeanor of someone in a subsequent phase in life, married, perhaps with children and a career. I did not know her last name or what she did, but I was sure she was still inspiring those around her.

———

For most of my life up until then, I had received all *A*'s except for a *B* in science and health and a *C* in handwriting. In the sixth or seventh grade, I practiced my handwriting for one semester and brought my grade up to a *B*. Handwriting was no longer on the report card in high school, and I set myself the goal of earning all *A*'s.

For the first time in my life, I sat down and did all of my homework when I came home from school. My brothers and the neighbor kids organized games of football and baseball, but I did not go out and play until I had my schoolwork done. I had heard of other students following this kind of discipline, but no one had ever imposed it upon me until I did it myself.

———

By the end of the year, my father had pulled up stakes at Mills Orchards, leaving the garden plot behind, and had gone to work again in Colusa. He and Carmen and the two young ones stayed in the trailer at the same labor camp, and Bob finished the eighth grade at C.K. Price.

On the last day of school, I bumped into Bob on the high school campus. I asked him what he was doing there.

He was brimming with energy. He had graduated earlier in the day, and he and a few others had come over to step on the grounds of their new school.

I thought it was a little presumptuous of him, as he wouldn't be in high school for real until the fall, but I could see he was happy.

So was I. I had all *A*'s on my report card.

NINE

andy and I had already been to the labor camp on a couple of weekends, so I was familiar with the work I was going to be doing. Some varieties of peach trees needed support for the branches as the fruit became heavier. One method of support was prop boards, for trees that had low-spreading branches. Another method was tying, for trees that had branches growing upward. That was the method we were going to employ, here in the same orchards we had picked the summer before.

With a ball of heavy jute twine and a pole with a hook on the end, the worker placed the twine about nine or ten feet up, all the way around the tree. After cutting the twine and mounting a ladder, the worker put the free end through a loop on the other end, pulled, and tightened and tied it like a girth. Some individual branches had to be tied with a separate strand, but for the most part, the single twine held the tree together, and the branches on one side helped support those on the other side by counterbalancing the weight.

My father, Carmen, and Sandy were doing the work to begin with, and I was going to be added onto the crew before long. My father had fashioned the hooks and poles, and he supervised the work as well as tying trees on his own row.

A friend of Sandy's came to stay with us. He was one of the two brothers in the family that Sandy stayed with when he came back from working with Suzi's husband, and he was the one who had been with Sandy on the day of the water balloon incident. The family had moved to the Burney-Fall River area northeast of Redding on the route to Oregon, and Sandy had stayed in touch with his friend Avery. Now Sandy had persuaded our father to let Avery live and work with us. It was an irregular arrangement, as our family was insular. We stuck together and kept to ourselves.

Avery was outgoing and talkative, self-assured and some-times sarcastic. When Sandy and I had visited at their place, Avery goaded his brother Webb into a rare show of temper when we were all in the barn. Webb picked up a wooden pallet and was about to bring it down on his brother when Avery fended it off with a pitchfork. I thought something terrible was going to happen, but the flare-up passed over.

At the labor camp, I was left to hang out with Avery for a day or two as my father waited for Al, the surly foreman, to approve adding to the crew. Avery wanted to know what was in the old barn on the west side of the camp, so I went with him to poke around where the picking ladders, knocking poles, scrap lumber, and old grease barrels gathered dust. While we were in there, Avery noticed an owl perched on a cross-member up on an end wall. With some stealth, he set up two ladders. He found a scrap of canvas about five feet square, and he induced me to help him trap the owl. I did not know what he had in mind, and I had not yet developed my own ideas about leaving wild animals alone, so I assisted him. We captured the owl with the canvas. Seeing how sharp its claws and beak were, Avery had me find a pair of side-cutters in my father's tools. With my assistance, he cut off the tips of the owl's claws and beak. He tied a rope around the owl's leg and set the bird on a tree branch near the camp trailer.

When I came back to look at the owl a while later, it was hanging upside down. I had the feeling that the bird had lost its will, and I felt guilty for my part in disabling it. We set it on the branch again, but before long, it was hanging as before. When my father came home from work, he told us to let the bird loose, so we took it out in the orchard and released it. I did not think it would fend for itself very well.

I do not recall Avery expressing any conscience about what we did to the owl. At the beginning, I thought he had a plan for making the bird into a pet or something like that, but after a short while, it seemed to me that for him, it was just something to do. For the rest of my life, I have remembered the owl and have regretted what we did. In my perusal of bird books, I believe I have seen him in representations of the barn owl.

———

We all went to work, and when the first payday came around, Sandy lobbied with my father to be allowed to take the car on a date. He and Avery had arranged with a girl in Orland to set up a double date. We still had the Ford station wagon, so my father let them take the Buick. Sandy had not yet gotten his driver's license, although he had turned sixteen in August of the year before, so Avery drove. They went on their night out and came back.

A few days later, I awoke to find my father in a great state of agitation. Sandy and Avery had left in the night, taking the Buick. Sandy had left a note saying that he was leaving home for good and that he was sorry.

My father had to take off work to deal with the problem. He filed a complaint for a stolen car so that he could locate the Buick and get it back. He went to Orland and had some kind of a confrontation with Sandy.

Meanwhile, I was sent out to work in the orchard by myself. I was threading the twine along the upper branches of a peach tree when Al, the foreman, found me.

He said he understood we had a problem in the family.

I said, yes, Sandy had taken off, and my father had gone to take care of things.

He said that in situations like that, when family members fought with one another, brought in the cops, and missed work, he fired the whole bunch of them.

I gave a minimal answer as I processed what he said.

He went on to say that that meant me, too, working out here alone with no supervision.

Now I worried. I did not want to see this edict as a reason to quit early and then give my father a reason to chew me out. I asked Al if I should go ahead and finish out the day.

He said, no, we were all fired as of now.

I asked if he wanted me to finish the tree I was working on.

He said, no, he wanted me to leave right now.

I left my ladder where it was, with the thread started in the branches and the brown ball of twine sitting on the ground, and I walked a long way through the orchard to the camp.

I spent the afternoon alone. I had a feeling of great emptiness. A huge loss had come to our family, and I had a hard time trying to make sense of it. My father and Sandy had not had a big argument this time. Sandy had chosen to do what he did, and he was gone from us. He wanted to be on his own, away from arguing with our father and not having his own money, so he left. I doubt that he was aware of the magnitude of his action. He had broken up our family unity. I would come to feel later that he had turned his back on his family, even though he did not forget about his brothers. At the moment, I just felt that something big had happened that could not be fixed.

My father came home with his news of confronting Sandy and getting the car back. He said the Buick wasn't running right, that there seemed to be something wrong with the transmission. I recalled Sandy saying something about Avery making a bad shift on the transmission when they took the car on the river road for the date in Orland. I told my father. He showed me the problem. The car's speedometer consisted of a horizontal orange line that grew to the right as the speed increased. My father put the car in gear, stepped on the accelerator, and the bar went past twenty with the car not moving.

My father said that Sandy was adamant about wanting to leave home, and he told him not to come back. He had said something of that nature the year before, but it seemed more definite now. He had also gotten it out of Sandy that he and Avery had plotted some of this action during the school year. My father had nothing good to say about Avery, but he did not blame it all on him.

The next day, I went with my father to the Department of Motor Vehicles in Colusa, where he canceled Sandy's driver's permit and any future driver's license while Sandy was a minor. I sensed that it was a combination of my father protecting himself from liability and exacting a bit of punishment. He parked the crippled Buick, and we used the old Ford station wagon to move the camp trailer back to Orland.

In the interval, Sandy and Avery had stayed with Grandpa and David for a few days as they picked apricots. Grandpa said that Sandy's friend had been smart-mouthed and had told Grandpa, after one meal, "By God, that was pretty damn good." Now they were gone, perhaps to Watsonville.

The man for whom they had been picking apricots came to the house when his fruit was ripe again and he needed pickers. We went out to work for him for a couple of days.

We were out of work and without a plan. The Buick was gone. I had acquired my learner's permit as soon as I could, right after school let out, more as a matter of wanting to get a perfect score on the test than of wanting to drive. (I missed one question.) We had a 1952 Cadillac for a short time, the first car registered in my name, but it did not last long, so it went to the junkyard.

Bob and David and I worked for a few days at cutting apricots while our father and Carmen planned our next activity. Cutting apricots was easy, low-paying work. Almost all the workers were women and children. They worked in a shaded area, open on the sides with a corrugated metal roof. We needed a group of four, so a girl we knew went with us. Her name was Tommie.

The work consisted of cutting open an apricot, pushing out the pit with one's thumb, and laying the two halves face-up on a lightweight wooden tray about three feet wide and six feet long. The work table consisted of a tray set up on lug boxes, and one tray would go on top of another. The workers had a break when they filled six trays and called "Trays away." The full trays would go into a sulfur chamber and then out into the drying yard, where the fruit would dry in the sun.

A worker sat on an upended lug box, or field crate, and took apricots out of a horizontal lug box that sat on two other upended boxes. The work was monotonous, and in spite of the shade, the atmosphere was warm and soporific, with occasional whiffs of sulfur. A radio played Beatles songs interspersed with other hits of that summer, the most memorable being "We'll Sing in the Sunshine," and chatter went on at all the work stations. Near ours, a faucet ran a slow stream of water all day for people to wash their hands and knives. When one of us would finish a box of fruit, he or she called out, "Fruit!" and set the box aside with the pits rattling in it. One of the yard boys would bring a full box and punch the worker's ticket, which was pinned to the person's shirt or blouse. At "Fruit" or "Trays Away," a person washed up.

We were paid fifty cents a box and made about six dollars a day each for a few days, until our next move. At that time, field work in our area began with the apricots in the latter part of May in Winters, about ninety miles south of us. It moved to the Orland area in mid-June, and when it finished, there was not much work for people like us until peach season, which began in the middle of July. It went up to and overlapped with prune season, which lasted until the third week of September or a little later.

We returned to the plan of going to the Watsonville and

Gilroy area for part of the summer, with the exception that Carmen wanted to leave Manuel and Carmen with her family in Mexico so she could work in the fields with us. I did not like the idea, but I was not used to the custom of the family raising the children together with a combination of parent figures. With time, I came to understand this extended family system, which, among other things, provided a contingency plan for children whose mother died early. For the present, I translated, even though my father and Carmen had their basic communication worked out, and I went along with the plan.

Bob traveled to Mexico with Carmen and the two young ones, David stayed with Grandpa as usual, and I went to the Santa Clara Valley with my father to find work.

We landed in the Morgan Hill-Gilroy-Hollister area, where there was work in a variety of crops. One might have expected to go to Watsonville, but the easy work of picking berries did not pay as well as the work I was now big enough to do, and I think my father preferred not to cross paths with Sandy or to talk to the berry and chive grower from the year before and tell him that our family had broken up.

For the first week or so, we lived in the car. We were flat broke. We slept behind service stations and ate canned goods. Each morning, my father parked out of sight and sent me into a café to ask for a thermos of hot water so we could make instant coffee. I was used to having to go into a business since the days in Grimes, when we owed money at the little grocery store and hoped that the owner did not have the heart to turn away a child. Now I was fifteen, and instead of asking for groceries on credit, I was begging hot water. M father let me choose the place so that I did not have to face the same waitress each day. They all seemed to understand, however, as I am sure I was easy to read, and they all treated me with kindness. They rinsed the thermos and filled it, then assured me there was no cost. I saw some of them more than once. From a long distance, I thank them all once again.

———

Among the day-labor jobs we found, one was in the garlic fields. Gilroy has since proclaimed itself to be the garlic capital of the world, just as Castroville, south of Watsonville on the way to Monterey, in those days called itself the artichoke capital. I had heard of topping garlic, and now I took part in it, using a large pair of springy metal shears to cut the stalks and roots off the garlic heads. In the course of a day, I found it strange to be out in the middle of a vast field of garlic, trimming heads into a hamper, breathing the fumes of Gilroy's potent product. We were staying in a cabin court by then, and when we went home at the end of the day, I fell into a deep slumber.

My father told me a story about a man in Lompoc who raised garlic on a couple of lots in town during the war, when some products were scarce and when he could not do anything else with the property because of the shortage of building materials. The man made a good sum of money. I was impressed by this story as an example of how a person could raise a crop on a small scale in an unexpected place. Many years later, when I raised my own garlic (and called my few rows "little Gilroy"), I saw that even one city lot would entail a great deal of work and would produce a large amount of garlic.

———

We also picked peas. The year before, we had picked peas as a family, in an orderly operation. A field boss traveled across the rows, lifting the vines with a stick to see if we missed any peas. He spoke to us in Spanish and humored our dog, a half-

Chihuahua, half-fox terrier named Cocoa. She growled at his stick, and he called her *perra brava* (fierce dog).

Now, we worked in a chaotic setting. The labor contractor brought down busloads of people from as far away as Oakland, some two hours or more away. Most of them were Black and were dressed in clothes and shoes more fit for the city streets than for fields and furrows. They boarded the bus in the early hours of the morning and arrived at sunrise, when the Mexicans were burning hampers for a cheery blaze to start the day. Some of the city people did not last long. By the middle of the morning, some of them would be sitting in the shade of the portable outhouses, passed out with an empty bottle between their sprawled legs. Most of them worked, even if they were not in their element.

This work paid two cents a pound, a little less than green beans, and less weight fit in a basket. When a picker brought a basketful to the sorting station, he or she dumped the contents at one end of a slanted, slatted table. Pods that were too thin fell through to the ground. A Mexican woman or girl on each side, dressed in full covering and with rubber gloves, pushed the peas along, pulling out more thin pods and spoiled ones. Meanwhile, the picker moved to the lower end with the basket and shook it as the pea pods fell in.

A foreman walked back and forth, calling out in a cheerful voice, *"Sacudan las canastas, parnitas,"* then in English, "Shake your hampers, partners." I learned soon enough that *parnitas* was an invented word, but the phenomenon was not new to me. Words morphed in this world. I had heard a water jug called a *yoga* in Spanish, and in English I would hear a set of trees called a "clam."

Sacudan las canastas, parnitas. The sorting girls were impassive, crunching the pods to be thrown aside. The tide of humanity flowed around. When the last peas fell into the hamper, the picker moved it to the scale, where he saw it weighed and was paid for it on the spot. By the end of the day, I had a sock full of coins in my pocket. Others did, too, but a worker could quit at any time with no ceremony. Some did. They sat in the shade of the bus that would take them back to the city.

———

When we went out on a new job, my father sent me to talk to the foreman or owner. I learned to present myself, to be assertive and businesslike.

During this time, I became my father's surrogate oldest son ("elder" and "eldest" would be terms for a later, educated era) and confidant. He told me many of the stories of his life. Some of them I had heard before, in greater or lesser detail, and several I would hear again. I had read a number of biographies, and I had begun to read obituaries, aware of the saying that reading obituaries was a sign of middle age, so without conscious effort, I put together something like a history of my father, along with several stories about people from my mother's side of the family.

He told me that his mother had had another baby a few years before him and that the child had not survived. His father had told him about it much later in life. He had grown up as an only child, and he had understood that his mother's nervous and reclusive nature was caused by her having given birth to him at the age of forty-five (in reality, she was forty-six). She also blamed her nervous condition on his chasing the chickens around the yard one day, waving a large feather. She refused to have her picture taken, with the inferred reason that she was much older than her husband, and she did not answer the door very often.

When he was growing up, he was often on his own. He had his own horse and rifle and set of traps, and he made his own money by trapping and selling pelts. He bought his own clothes, including a leather jacket. This narrative, or set of stories, was a model for us in the early years, as we had the aspiration of having a horse and gun and learning the self-sufficiency that those things brought. When we had our newspaper routes, one idea we had was to buy leather jackets, but when the time came, we had only enough money for cloth jackets. The rest had gone for living expenses in the meanwhile.

He told me of having scarlet fever and missing part of the eighth grade. The one teacher who did not pass him on was the English teacher. In his first year of high school, he had to go to the junior high every day to make up English, which included public speaking. Having grown up as an only child in the country with an eccentric mother and a not-very-communicative father, he was not outgoing, and he struggled with speaking in front of a group. He opened his mouth, and no words came out. The speeches mounted up, but in the end, he completed them all and passed.

Like me, he was young for his grade. When he was a senior, he had a girlfriend who was a sophomore. They went steady until he graduated. At that time, girls or young women could marry without parental consent at eighteen, while young men had to wait until they were twenty-one. My father had an uneasy relationship with his father, as they did not have confidential conversations. (He said he learned his personal male hygiene from his Aunt Jenny, who was a nurse of some kind, and he learned about sex by going to a whorehouse.) Furthermore, my father's girlfriend was Catholic, which my grandfather did not approve of. So, rather than ask his father to sign for him, my father decided to wait until he turned twenty-one. By then, father and son were partners in farming and in buying and selling cattle, but they did not have this basic compatibility.

When he was a few months short of turning twenty-one, members of the girlfriend's family came to the ranch one day where my father and grandfather were working together on a windmill or water tank. The visitors conveyed the news that the girl had died after her operation for appendicitis.

My father's world fell apart. He said he never drank before

that. He looked old for his age, and he bought liquor for his friends, but he did not drink. Now he did. On many occasions, he bought a fifth of whiskey and sat on her grave at night to drink it. Her open casket would appear in his headlights as he drove his cattle truck on lone stretches of highway in the middle of the night.

Interspersed with my father's narrations were stories about his own father not coming home until late at night after drinking and rolling dice and winning handfuls of cigars. By my father's account, his father was too drunk to attend his high school graduation, so he gave his two tickets to his girl-friend's parents.

I met the girl's parents one strange night in 1969 when my father had me drive him and my grandfather into their yard, unexpected. The parents observed the ravaged man, now fifty, and me, reserving my comments. They showed us a picture of the girl. In 1992, my sister Suzi sent me a copy of the 1936 Lompoc yearbook, *La Purísima* (named for the nearby mission), which she had bought at the historical society's flea market. My father's signature appears on his senior picture, and on the page for the sophomore class, the students all together and not listed, I recognized the girl who died, as she was always called in his stories.

My father threw himself into the cattle business. He drove his cattle truck, single-decker in those days, up and down the state of California and on into L.A., as I had heard many times. At any local sale, he ran the figures in his head, so he knew how much he had to pay when he went to the window. He paid with a three-day draft, which meant he had three days to haul the cattle to Los Angeles, sell them, and put the money in the bank. There was a thrill to it, a mystique, that being sharp and taking risks and working long hours was going to make him successful and looked up to. And it did.

He made time each year to ride in the Fourth of July parade in his home town. He had horses, and he knew how to rope, although he did not compete. I knew he could rope, because he roped Sandy and me as we ran up and down the driveway when I was about four, much to my mother's chagrin.

When he was loading cattle and had his clothes smeared with manure, he bought new garments. "That's how I kept myself in clothes." He wore black shirts and Frisco jeans to go along with his black Stetson. "They called me Blackie in the stockyards." I do not know how many times he bought new clothes that way, but it became a generality, like the oft-repeated statement that "If someone asked me for a dime, I gave him ten dollars."

He told me of raising crops, fresh market tomatoes foremost among them and most relevant to our working in the fields. And he told me how he met my mother.

At the end of World War II, he hired a man named Chuck Schneider. Chuck had been in the Air Corps, which was part of the Army at the time and would become the Air Force. Chuck finished his military service at Camp Cooke, which would become Vandenberg Air Force Base and bring economic growth to Lompoc and Santa Maria in the late 1950s and early 1960s. During the war, it was a regular military base. Elizabeth Short, the "Black Dahlia," had worked there in 1943.

When Chuck was discharged, he was married with two daughters. He had done farm work growing up, so he fit in with my father's needs, to keep up the farming while my father was on the road. Chuck and his family moved into a house on the ranch.

Chuck had a sister named Elizabeth, or Elsie, who also had the nickname of Dutch. Pictures show her with a bandanna or head scarf around her blond hair, in the style of war-era women, and although the family was Hungarian, Dutch was an easy stereotype, and one can see how the nickname stuck.

Elsie came to stay with Chuck, and she met Dunville, as my father was called. She was four years younger, born in 1923, and she had a little girl, Suzi, born in 1942. She had been married to a man named Foster, a horseman and cowboy, but he drank too much, and the marriage had not lasted long.

Elsie and Dunville took an interest in one another. When she stayed over with him one night, Chuck became furious. My father felt that both of them were compromised, and he thought he should offer to marry her.

I said, "Didn't you think you were...making a mistake?"

"Well, yes. But I was twenty-seven, which was kind of old not to be married yet, and I didn't think I would ever find anyone perfect again after the girl who died, and your mother had this little girl that needed to be taken care of, so it seemed like the thing we ought to do."

They were married in 1946. Sandy was born a little over a year later, and I was born fifteen months after that, all in Lompoc.

I asked my father if my mother had always been a drinker.

"Sometimes she cooked and kept the house in order and kept you kids clean, but sometimes I would come home from a trip, and she would by layin' around drunk. The house was a mess, dirty dishes piled up, and you kids runnin' around dirty."

He also told me more favorable stories about my mother—how she liked to dress in a white blouse and blue jeans and enjoyed the ranch life, and how she told him stories about her family, which he now retold to me. Many of her family members, including her parents, her sister, her brothers, and a couple of cousins, had skeletons in the closet—affairs, disastrous relationships, infidelities—as they put up a proper front and altered facts such as marriage dates and parentage. I came to appreciate my mother as a person who didn't mind telling the truth and laughing at pretense. When I came to meet some of these people later in life, I might have enjoyed my knowledge a little too much; when I came to my own difficulties even later, even though I did not lie about them or try to gloss them over, I saw that there was not much room to feel superior.

Life on the ranch in Lompoc had a possible undercurrent. Chuck and his family had moved to San Diego County not long after my parents married, at the time when my grandparents were building the motel. My father and grandfather had had several hired hands, sometimes a crew for bean or mustard harvest. When my father was on the road at about the time I was born and later, they had a man who was hired on steady and lived at the ranch. He was middle-aged or older, but he seemed to get along well with my mother.

My father said that another hired hand gave him a discreet tip. "I could tell you something, Dunville, but I won't."

My father told me he had a pretty good idea of what was going on. When he and my grandfather decided to make the big move to Oregon, my mother stayed behind for a while. She suggested that they take the hired man to work on the ranch in Oregon, and the man was willing to go. But my father "put the kibosh" on that idea, and the man dropped out of the family operation. One picture of him remains in David's collection. I do not know who took it, but it survived among a mass of photographs of cows, bulls, horses, trailers, trucks, cars, dogs, babies, and other family members.

My father told me a fuller version than I had heard before of how he went broke. We were living on the ranch in Oregon, with Grandpa and Grandma in town. Bob and David were born in 1950 and 1951 in Lakeview. My father was driven to rise to the top of the cattle business, to do more than just have a ranch and support a wife and kids. He did not want to be one of those men he talked about who "made a shit pot full of money and then laid down and died." He wanted to make a million dollars, a grand ambition in those days, and see us all live a good life.

The government was going to set the price on cattle. My father's bookkeeper, a man named Stanley, proposed to my father that they collaborate on a plan. My father would go out and buy all the cattle he could. Stanley had a place to put them. When the price came back up, they would sell all the cattle and split the profits.

My father went out and bought the cattle. He had them

waiting in pens at various auction yards, and he needed money to pay for them. He called up Stanley and asked him where to take the cattle. He had been given to understand that Stanley had secured a big acreage of good pasture that other cattlemen hadn't been able to get hold of.

According to my father, Stanley said, "What cattle? What are you talking about?"

The ruin was swift. My father had to sell all the cattle where they were, at a loss of several cents per pound for every animal. He lost everything in a very short while—not overnight, but in a couple of weeks.

He told me that he sat in a chair with his deer rifle, put cartridges in it, and thought about going to kill Stanley. "But one thing kept me from doing it. I thought of you four little boys and what would happen to you, how you would be brought up, and I couldn't do it."

This part of the story did not have any mention of my mother and Suzi, I would realize. It was the four boys that mattered.

The dénouement was a now-familiar series of events, how they lost the place in Oregon, ended up in the Sacramento Valley, tried to get back on their feet buying and selling cattle on a smaller scale, and couldn't make it. In the telling this time, he gave more emphasis to my mother and my grandfather drinking. Here he was, running all over the valley and trying to hold things together, and there they were, sitting around and drinking what little they all had left.

He told me about one Christmas during this time. He said he had a little bit of money from something he salvaged and sold, and Christmas was coming up. He said to hell with it, at least we'll have a good Christmas, so he bought presents for all of us. That may have been when Mama burned her finger on the Christmas tree, and it may have been where the toy fire engine came from.

One narration was new to me. He told me about a winter when they were broke. In the supermarket, my mother would put packaged steaks under her armpits beneath her coat, and she would do the same with a carton of cigarettes. He said it scared the hell out of him. He also said that was where I inherited the tendency to shoplift. My mother was a kleptomaniac. I did not know how much he was taking the opportunity to blame her, as he would do years later, when he said that my getting drunk came from my mother and her side of the family.

My father told me again how he and my mother separated and then divorced and how he ended up with the four of us.

Some of these stories he told me when we were living in the station wagon. Others he told me when we were staying in an auto court, driving back and forth from work, or sitting in the car after a day of work, he with a half-pint of Ten High and I with a can of Seven-Up. He told some of the vignettes in the next place we stayed.

―――

We found work with San Martin Vineyards, a large company that had orchards as well as vineyards. We went to work picking apricots and stayed in a labor camp. We had one half of a Quonset hut, the likes of which showed up in many places after their use in World War II. Our half was a good-sized dwelling for two people, and the boss might not have let us have it if my father had not told him that we were expecting two more workers to join us when they came back from Mexico.

Now we did not have to pay rent or drive distances, although the driving itself was not altogether bad. It put a buffer between getting up in the dark and going to work at sunrise, and it allowed a boy to hear songs on the radio like "The Cowboy in the Continental Suit" and "The Yellow Bandana." The latter song was stirring because it featured a pretty Mexican girl who died.

In the apricots, we worked on ladders and were paid by the

bucket. We took the fruit to a checking area where we poured the apricots from a picking bucket into stacked lug boxes, or field crates. A girl sorted, and a checker punched our tickets. A foreman's younger brother was our field boss, and he offered me work for a while as a sorter. There I got to know the checker, a man in early middle age named Cristo Salinas, who sang in a more subdued style than Andrea and was pretty good. He told us to watch out for him because he was going to be famous. I did not ever hear him on the radio, but in later years I saw 45's on YouTube by a person with his name and in the bolero style of that time and earlier.

I went back to picking with my father. We had become acquainted with another white family who had boys the ages of me and my younger brothers, plus a little girl or two and a large woman who might have been in a higher weight class than June's. The boy who was Bob's age looked a great deal like Bob, which was remarkable in itself, and his name was John. The boy my age was named Jim. The woman and the younger children stayed in their house in the camp, one of several old houses in a row, near the Quonsets, while the father and the two older boys picked apricots. They were from Texas, where the father said the boys earned all ones and two in school. My father took out my folded report card with all A's, which he carried in his wallet, and he handed it to the man.

"See what Johnny did?"

The man looked at the unfolded paper as if it was counterfeit or did not have any bearing on the current conversation. It was not the only time my father showed off my achievement that summer, and it was not the only time the other person regarded it with little interest.

———

On my own in the orchard, I sang a song I had learned a few years earlier in school.

When I was a lad I served a term
As office boy to an attorney's firm.
I cleaned the windows and I swept the floor,
And I polished up the handle on the big front door.

He polished up the handle on the big front door.

I polished up the handle so carefullee
That now I am the Ruler of the Queen's Navee!

As office boy I made such a mark
That they gave me the post of a junior clerk.
I served the writs with a smile so bland,
And I copied all the letters in a big round hand.

He copied all the letters in a big round hand.

I had to skip a few verses I did not remember, and I resumed.

Now landsmen all, whoever you may be,
If you want to rise to the top of the tree,
If your soul isn't fettered to an office stool,
Be careful to be guided by this golden rule.

Stick close to your desks and never go to sea,
And you all may be rulers of the Queen's Navee!

I sang this song in a low voice as I stood near the top of my ladder, picking apricots with both hands. From time to time, I heard the Texan boy named Jim singing a single line from a song of his own:

High in the treetops, where the chickens wouldn't
pick.

———

Bob and Carmen returned from Mexico, and the four of us worked in the apricots until the end of the season. We arranged to pick pears for the same company and stay where we were. The pear orchards were in Gilroy, and our camp was east of the highway near Morgan Hill, so we would have to drive each day.

In between crops, we went up to Orland and brought David back so that he could contribute to the family's earnings. David was only twelve, and he was smaller for his age than the rest of us had been. He was also afraid of my father, who harped on him and intimidated him even when Grandpa was present.

Grandpa would bite his pipe and say, "Ach, leave the kid alone!"

Now Grandpa was far away.

In the pears, we picked into canvas bags similar to those we used in the oranges. David picked bottoms, and the rest of us worked on ladders. The pears had to be picked green, and they were hard and heavy. David lagged.

Our father took it upon himself one evening in the Quonset to give David a long, overbearing complaint, including a threat to send him back on the bus. In his style, he said it all more than once.

The next day, David worked in a frenzy. He picked fast and ran to empty his bag into the bin. I was afraid for him. I did not think he could keep up the pace, and although the weather was not as hot as in the peach and prune orchards, I was afraid he would do harm to himself. After that day, he worked at a more reasonable pace.

My father expressed his satisfaction that his "little pep talk" had gotten good results. I was afraid David's production would sag and we would have another blowup.

———

Time came around for me to practice driving. The old Ford station wagon was nothing fast and nothing precious, so I was allowed to drive it from the highway into the labor camp, which was about a mile with one right turn.

My father, Carmen, and I went into Morgan Hill for groceries and a bottle, and I took the wheel when we pulled off the highway. My father sat on the passenger side, with Carmen in the middle. He began to rag on me about something I don't remember now, but it was not my driving. It was something else, and he went through it over and over. I got fed up and said something like, "Oh, shut up," and he began hitting me. His hitting any of us was nothing new, but Carmen, in the middle, received some of the impact of his arm. I was not only fed up but wound up over events of a couple of months, so I grabbed his hand when it hit my mouth, and I bit into his finger.

Now he hit me with more earnest and cursed me for being the little son of a bitch and animal that I was. I turned into the labor camp and parked the car. My nose was bleeding. We unloaded the groceries and went inside, and my father continued to rage.

The police arrived and came inside. They wanted to know what happened. My father said I had gotten into a fit and had bit him on the finger. I said I was just defending myself the best way I could while I was driving.

One of the officers asked where the drops of blood on the floor came from.

I thought that if I told the police the true story, they would take my father to jail for hitting me and drawing blood. Like many people I have heard of since then, who were afraid of what would happen, I kept quiet.

My father said, "It came from me. He bit my finger."

The cops took me outside and said they knew it was hard sometimes, living in a situation where people got mad. But in the future, when I felt things getting to me, I should try going outside and throwing rocks.

The argument continued after they left, and my father said that if I couldn't get along and behave myself, I could leave.

I said I would. I said I would get on the bus the next day and go back to Orland.

I did not sleep well. I spent half the night thinking about what kind of turn things had come to, how I had taken a step that was going to make things worse than they were. I had already told myself that none of this was going to last forever, that I would be able to run my own life some day, and that I just had to wait. Now we were at a breaking point, and I did not know what would come of it.

In the morning, my father asked me if I was going to be decent and go to work with the rest of them so we could make a living.

I said I would. I didn't want to fight, and I didn't want to leave my two brothers behind. As for being decent, I was used to my father using that term for making peace and not fighting anymore, regardless of where the argument had come from.

TEN

The pear season ended, and we were at that point in the summer when we would have gone north for the prune harvest. However, I had heard some of the girls in the camp talk about picking grapes, and it did not sound as bad as picking prunes. I told my father about the prospect, and he thought it might not be a bad idea.

Bob and David were mad at me because it would take us farther from home. They thought I was persuading my father because I wanted to see more of the girls, but there was no provision for me to see them in the Fresno area. They were going with their group, and they would be swallowed up in a vast area of vineyards and labor camps. We would have to find a place on our own once we got there.

We had just bought a 1953 Cadillac and had left the Ford at the car lot to be dealt with later. The Cadillac was a good car, in much better condition than the '52 we had had for a short while. We packed up the few things we had and drove a hundred and fifty miles to the grape country.

We found work, with a camp to stay in, near the town of Sanger. This was new country and new work for us. I had heard of picking grapes in the Stockton and Lodi area, where workers picked wine grapes and poured them into large vehicles called gondolas. The work at hand in the Fresno area was different. These grapes went for raisins.

I have read that no work is unskilled, and I suppose it is true. Some fruit picking has tricks and time-saving methods, but the harvest tasks in most crops can be learned in a short while. With raisin grapes, the picker had a knife and a pan. The knife had a curved blade, similar to that on a linoleum knife, and it hung from one's wrist by a thong when the person was not cutting stems. The pan was a dull metal basin like a dishpan. A person cut bunches of yellow-green seedless grapes and put them in the pan. When the pan was full, the picker tipped it upside down on a tray and spread out the grapes to be dried right there in the sun.

The tray was no more than a sheet of heavy brown paper, about two feet wide and three feet long. The picker laid the trays side by side on a slanted bed of ground between the rows. Later, when the grapes had dried into raisins, crews would come and roll up the trays to be collected. We were in the picking phase and only heard of the rolling that would take place in the future.

The trick was to cut the bunches fast, spread out a sheet or tray, put a couple of bunches on the lower end, maybe a couple on the sides, and spread out the grapes so that they covered the tray and were not piled.

It was not hard work, but the weather was hot, and not much breeze stirred between the rows of vines. On several evenings, Bob and I went back out after dinner to pick for another hour or so. I felt like quite a wage-earner, not having to do any house or kitchen work.

The housing itself was demeaning. We did not know what it was like until we had already accepted the situation. The camp consisted of a large, old, single-story farmhouse that was shared by a few parties—three families and a man and his son.

The man had a job in a shop or business in Fresno, but he had picked grapes earlier in life, and now he and his son came to make some additional money during his vacation time. They were Hispanic, as were the other two migrant families.

All parties were supposed to share the kitchen, but one family that had been there in past years dominated it, taking it over at a very early hour and barging in when they felt like it.

The bathrooms consisted of portable field toilets, which we called outhouses and are now called porta-pots. I could not be in there for very long without one of the other teenage boys asking what was taking me so long and what was I doing.

The showers consisted of sun-warmed metal tanks of water raised above enclosed stalls with the sky above.

Our father and Carmen had one small bedroom. Bob, David, and I slept in a lean-to, on top of upside-down field boxes. The boxes were wide and shallow and would be used for the rolled-up bundles of raisins later on. Through the wall, we heard the dominant family's radio when it blasted in the morning.

I believe that this camp, with its abject lack of privacy, was the most dehumanizing place we stayed in during our migrations. Four years later, when I was a student at UCLA, I stopped at a table where activists were protesting the living conditions for workers in the grape harvests. The famous Delano grape strike had taken place in the meanwhile. The students at the table had pictures of housing such as I had seen in person in many places, such as rundown wood houses, screened dwellings, canvas cabins, and the like. I wondered if the activists had done such work or were taking up the cause of those who did. I asked some questions of a young Hispanic woman, and I may have seemed impertinent, with my proprietary sense of the experience, and she said, "I've picked more grapes than you have." I said, "I doubt that you have," even though I had worked in that crop for only one season. Afterwards, I wished I had treated her with more courtesy, but that was the way of having worked in the fields. One had a bitterness and a stubborn sense that someone in a comfortable environment could not know what it was like. We might have thought that of each other.

———

Our family stuck out the season and went back to Orland in the 1953 Cadillac. On the way home, the main highway took us through downtown Sacramento and skid row, where, as in years past, I saw drunks lying on the sidewalks and in doorways. On 99W, on our side of the valley, we drove through Dunnigan, where the old neon sign in front of Bill and Kathy's had a woman flipping a pancake into the air and a man raising his rifle to shoot it.

I do not recall anyone being happy, although, even in the most miserable places there was often something that offered amusement.

The pea fields with the busloads of people from the city had a stream of incongruous scenes and sounds.

In the apricots, my father and I heard an inscrutable statement when the man from Texas said that he kept the Mexicans from stealing their picking buckets overnight by putting a cigarette paper in the bottom of each one.

In the grape-picking camp, the intrusive nature of the other residents had some inadvertent humor. Among the migrant people, the young folk had a general awareness that at sixteen, they could drop out of school and work without being worried about truant officers in the field. Young people knew one another's age and what their respective privileges were. One day, a couple of the lads who called out to me when I was in the outhouse were engaged in a conversation with David and me. They asked me how old I was and what grade I was in. When I told them I was fifteen and a half and was going to be a junior, one of them said, "You be crazy to quit now." David and I found it memorable, as if it was assumed that, because I was in a migrant camp, I would consider dropping out of school and needed encouragement not to.

By this point in our lives, my brothers and I had a bit of cynicism and something like a shared fatalism. In the early days, as in Grimes when we raised animals and sold them, we had the illusion that the money would come back when times were better, and we would be able to fulfill some of our wishes. With the newspaper routes, we thought that a little later on, we would be able to use more of the money for ourselves, but we never progressed. Now with working the fields for three seasons as well as on afternoons and weekends during the school year, things weren't getting any better. The one short flourish of prosperity was gone, and with it went a place we had for once called our own. Now we were living in a rental house where the owners would not fix the roof or the toilet or the septic tank.

Working for the communal good had a positive aspect, as it taught us not to be selfish. We shared everything. We divided food or dessert or treats four ways—or now three. But when all the money went into the pot, most of it disappeared. My father didn't drink it up. A half-pint of Ten High or a fifth of Gallo Port did not cost much—each of them in the neighborhood of a dollar. Cigarettes cost twenty-five cents a pack. The money went down holes, like moving to the next crop, paying rent for an additional place to stay, or meeting basic expenses in between jobs.

We knew that that was the way life was. We had to work. We dreaded getting up early in the morning and going to another long day in the fields. We hoped for delays or cancellations. In the field, we didn't do anything we didn't have to. In piece work, there was a saying that if a person wasn't doing something wrong, wasn't cutting a corner, or wasn't being chewed out, he was doing too good a job and wasn't making enough money. In hourly work, we never wanted to start a few minutes early, work a few minutes late, or do anything for free. And in the end, we worked for free anyway, or close to it. In a broad way, we learned the value of work because we had to work in order to eat and have a place to live, but in another, almost perverse way, we did not learn the value of work because we did not see the reward.

We received our necessities, including new clothes at the beginning of the school year and at Christmas, but we did not see a reward beyond that—no leather jacket, no horse, no rifle. And the illusion of going into the cattle business had died like an animal that wandered off by itself.

————

One thing that Bob and I did salvage out of the summer of 1964 was a car. I was approaching sixteen, and we were going to need one to drive back and forth from work or to take Grandpa to the store when our father and Carmen went somewhere else. We went with our father to a car lot in Willows and settled on a 1959 Vauxhall. We had never known of one before. It resembled an English Ford in size, and in body style it resembled a 1955 or 1956 Chevrolet. We came to understand that it was the English equivalent of a Pontiac. It had four cylinders and a three-speed manual transmission, and it cost us a hundred and fifty dollars. I was not old enough to drive it by myself yet, but we were prepared.

————

As the school year got under way, I had a normal schedule of classes. One afternoon, I was called to the principal's office.

This was not the same principal who had written my father the letter about Sandy's behavior. He was not any more personable to me, but he told me that the manager of Sprouse-Reitz, a variety store that many people called the dime store, had come to him to ask for a recommendation for a student who knew Spanish and could communicate with Spanish-speaking customers. My name came up. I could go see the manager after school. His name was Mr. Hodge.

My first reaction was something like my reaction to a good score on a test or assignment—this was something I deserved. After all, I was the best Spanish student in school. With time, however, I had a fuller realization. This was the first time I had been offered a job on the basis of my education or my academic ability. It was the first job to lift me from field work and dependence on the weather.

———

The manager of the Sprouse-Reitz store, Mr. Hodge, was new to Orland. He was in his mid-twenties, clean-shaven with a flat-top haircut. He wore a short-sleeve white shirt, a narrow tie, loose slacks, and common black dress shoes, like any other small-town merchant. He was cheerful to the point of being jaunty at times, but business was business. He was Mr. Hodge, and the store name was Sprouse-Reitz, with a long *i*, not a short *i* or a long *e*, as some people pronounced it.

Before long, I learned that he had a wife, a small daughter, and another baby on the way. They had a late-model Plymouth, bronze with a black top, one car between them, as was the case in many families.

I was the stock boy, which meant that I worked in the back room, unpacking merchandise, putting prices on items, doing small assembly tasks, and sometimes cutting a window shade. I also worked on the floor, and I spoke Spanish with customers. Sometimes I walked home, and sometimes Mr. Hodge gave me a ride.

———

On days that I did not work at the store, I rode home on the school bus with Bob and David. When the bus pulled off the highway, David's flock of chickens came out to meet him.

Grandpa, who was a pragmatic old butcher, had let him breed up a flock of twenty or more, but it was understood that some day, some of them would meet the fate of the washtub and hot water.

———

One day at school, I was surprised to meet up with Sandy. He had enrolled in classes. I asked him what he had been doing, and he told me that he and his pal Avery had gone to Watsonville and had worked the summer for the berry and chive grower. They had bought a car, a 1955 Ford convertible, which Avery still had. They had gone back to Fall River Mills and had worked in a potato shed after school and on weekends. Now Sandy was working for Mrs. Harris, a large, ungainly woman who had a dairy of eighteen or twenty cows out on the highway north of where we lived. I had heard of other young people working there. Mrs. Harris preferred that they stay with her so that she could depend upon their getting up at five in the morning.

I told him how we had spent the rest of the summer, and I told him, with some pride, of my new job.

"John the Mexican," he said.

In spite of that small note and his air of independence, I was glad to see him and to know that he was staying in school.

———

My father and I were going home from town after dark. My father was driving. Less than a mile out of town, a hitchhiker appeared on the side of the road. As we passed, I saw that it was my brother Sandy.

I do not think my father saw him. I do not think Sandy recognized the 1953 Cadillac or could see into it to recognize us. It was a strange moment, full of dread and uncertainty for me, holding my tongue as my brother glanced at one more car that passed him by.

———

A couple of days later, my father told me he had driven past Sandy in the daylight. My father was worked up.

"What do you think it made me feel like? To drive past my son and not be able to stop."

I could not know what it felt like. I could not know what mixture of emotions—anger, guilt, fear, stubbornness—worked in both of them.

At school, Sandy told me of the same incident. He began by asking if the old man was driving an old Cadillac now.

I said yes without making any remarks about the Buick.

"I thought that was him. He drove right past me, wouldn't give me a ride. What a prick."

I thought it was unrealistic of Sandy to think that our father could have stopped, in a matter-of-fact way, and given him a ride to somewhere else. It seemed to me that it was Sandy's way of keeping up a front, as if to say that nothing all that serious had happened in June.

———

Olive season came, and we found a new crop to pick. It was slow work, pulling olives off the branches and always having to separate them from the leaves. Many people had small orchards of a few acres, and Blevins, the man we worked for, had a couple of orchards separated from one another. He was about my father's age and was of that generation of people who came out during the Depression and did the work we were doing now. My father, having grown many crops, often took interest in the grower's point of view, so we had an agreeable time working in the quiet countryside, in the autumn when the weather was neither hot nor cold.

———

We came home from school one day to find out that our grandfather and our father had a big blowup. Our father was passed out, so we heard our grandfather's version of the incident.

My father had gotten drunk earlier in the day, or perhaps had stayed drunk from the day before, and was sitting on the floor with his legs out, moving them as if he might get up and go somewhere but couldn't. My grandfather rebuked him for being worthless and a disgrace, and my father came back with some of his own unkind comments.

Later in the evening, my father woke up, and the argument began anew. My father brought out some of his old recriminations, such as my grandfather selling his pinto horses and sleeping with my mother. This last part was more than my grandfather would tolerate, as he now had Carmen for an audience as well as us boys, who were old enough to understand such things.

The outcome was that my father and my grandfather were not going to live under the same roof anymore. My father and Carmen would go somewhere else to work.

Then came the crux. My father wanted Bob and me to go with them.

Bob and I conferred, and we gave him our answer. We were tired of moving around and did not want to continue doing it during the school year. We were both in high school and wanted to stay in one place.

My father said that if we all worked together, we could make it all right, but if he had to work somewhere else and send money back, it would be difficult if not impossible.

We said we would support ourselves, pay our own expenses.

Our father accepted the offer, and he and Carmen left to find work elsewhere. Bob and I made an agreement with our grandfather that we would pay him for our share of the living expenses. Grandpa received $135 a month for his Old Age Survivors pension.

Bob was fourteen, and I was still a couple of months short of sixteen. We were now partners in paying our own way.

After my father and Carmen left, my grandfather told us the story of how they went broke. My father must have brought up enough from the past that my grandfather felt compelled to give his version. His Irish *r* came out in his pronunciation of the president's name.

"Truman set the price on cattle, and your fahther had a deal to go out and buy all the cattle he could. But the fella he had the deal with was a crooked son of a bitch, and your father and I got stuck with hundreds of head of cattle. We had to sell 'em at a loss of ten cents a pound, more than a third of what we paid for 'em. We lost everything. And then we came down here, and your mahther and your fahther took to drinkin' and drinkin' [more of the Irish *r*], and they drank up all that was left."

Bob and I compared notes and came to no definite conclusions, but we thought our grandfather's version might be closer to the center.

He also told us that he had gone broke once before when he was in the meat business. His partner ran off with all the money. "I made two fortunes, and I lost them both." When his second loss came, he took his retirement pension and said to hell with it.

He was not one to rue the past or long for it. More than once, he held up his hands to observe all of his fingers intact. "Never lost a bit off of any of 'em. There's a lot of butchers can't say that."

One Friday evening, Mr. Hodge gave me a ride home after work. I believe he was concerned for me, as he asked a few questions about how I was getting along. I was defensive in my answers. We had learned not to let in much of the outside world, and I did not care to talk to an outsider about my family circumstances.

The next day, he asked me if I was all right.

I said, "Yes, why?"

He said, "Last night you seemed like a young man with a lot of problems."

I did not think I had all that many, compared to what I had seen. "I'm all right," I said.

———

Between the property we had once owned and the frontage property where we now rented, an older couple lived on a strip of land that reached from the canal on the south to the county road on the north. The field consisted of two to three acres, undeveloped. The couple allowed the young people in the neighborhood and from across the highway to play baseball and football in their field.

My friend who took my place on the track team was the older couple's grandson. He came to stay with his grandparents during our freshman year. He said he had a brother a little older and a sister a little younger. I asked about the sister. He said she was "an ignorant savage." In our sophomore year, their mother moved from somewhere else to a house in town, along with the other two kids and a truck driver husband who was not around much. So our friend Walt was living in town with them. He was almost a year older than I was. His brother, Robert, was a year and a half older than he was, but they were both in the same grade as I was. Their sister, Sue, was in David's grade but was a little older, and she happened to be the girl who set up the double date for Sandy and his pal before everything broke apart.

Walt and Robert had acquired a 1951 Chevrolet with a "slip-and-slide Powerglide" transmission. Robert allowed me to drive it around in his grandparents' field, to add to the little practice I had had during the summer. Next, he coached me on the use of the clutch in the Vauxhall, which was rough going at first but improved.

His grandfather gave me permission to practice with the Vauxhall on my own, off the public road, so I did. My brother Bob went along with me. After driving around the field several times, I took the car out on the county road, came back, turned into the field between a pair of eucalyptus trees, and went out onto the road again.

Bob became impatient and insisted on driving the car. I told him he was too young and didn't have a permit, but he kept insisting. He said the car was his as much as it was mine, and he deserved a chance to learn to drive it. I relented.

We went down the county road, with Bob driving. He turned around and came back, driving faster than I would have. When he turned off the road toward the field, I saw the eucalyptus tree on the right coming straight at me. The car slammed into it.

I had an immediate sense of disaster. We had no insurance, we were not even of legal age to drive the car, and we had already wrecked it.

We got out and looked at the damage, and it was very demoralizing. Now we had to tell our grandfather and find a way to get the car fixed. We found a shop that would replace the hood and fender and headlight door, as it was called, and paint the replacement parts. We were in debt, but we had no option.

———

Walt and Robert were mobile in their old Chevy, and Sandy was now hanging around with them. The other boys smoked cigarettes. The first time I saw Sandy smoking a cigarette with them, my heart sank. We had all pledged to avoid the vices of our father and Donna and some of the deadbeats we had known, and here was Sandy, acting like a tough guy.

Robert had dropped out of school. He had been held back once or twice in his earlier years, and he did not do well in our sophomore year. I saw him as something like the frog in the story puzzle that is hopping toward a wall and hops half of the remaining distance each time.

Before long, Sandy and Walt had dropped out as well. Sandy had quit milking cows for Mrs. Harris, which was not surprising, as everyone I knew of had lasted a short while. Sandy rented an apartment above the Orlando, a bar that sat on the corner of the main intersection downtown. He was trying to make enough to pay his own rent and other expenses.

He worked for a while at a supermarket, but the owner said she was missing money in the neighborhood of a hundred dollars. She implied that she thought Sandy might have taken it, so he quit. I do not think he took any money, because I could see how his money came and went. There was an older fellow who worked there, twenty-five or so, who seemed like probable suspect to Sandy and me. If he was the culprit, he was good at it. If he was, he wasn't the only one. A year later, two boys from my grade were discovered for stealing a thousand dollars, an enormous amount, from the same store.

———

I was called to the office at school, and Sandy was there to meet me. I asked him what was up.

"Uncle Chuck and Aunt Anne are here to see you."

I had an idea of who they were. My father had mentioned them in his story from years earlier. Sandy had met them the year before when he was staying with Suzi, so he spoke of them with familiarity.

He led me to the parking lot, where I met a middle-aged,

middle-class-looking couple in a bronze-colored Rambler Ambassador. Sandy introduced us. My uncle told me they had come to take us boys to live with them. He said he had been out to the house to talk to Grandpa.

His wife, who sat in the car with the door open, showed me a picture of one of their daughters. They were all the same to me. I knew there was one about my age, and I had had to kiss her one night when I was about four. I swallowed a moth in the night and threw up on my Lone Ranger sweatshirt, and I associated it all together, as if the first event caused the second. The person in the picture was a different cousin.

"She sends her love," said my aunt.

I thought that was nice, but she didn't even know me. I didn't know what to say, so I nodded.

My uncle clarified that they were going to take Bob and me.

I told him that Bob and I had already decided where we wanted to live. This was our home, and this was where we wanted to go to school.

We talked a little more, enough for them to understand that we were not going with them. Aunt Anne closed her door, Uncle Chuck got in behind the wheel, and they went back to their house, about seven hundred miles away.

Sandy made a comment to the effect that I wasn't very polite with them, and he implied that Bob and I could have taken them up on their offer. I said I didn't know them.

My grandfather told us that evening that Chuck had visited. They were still on good terms from the old days. He said Chuck had some idea of taking us with him.

I said that I told them that Bob and I were staying here.

Grandpa nodded, and we had our evening meal as usual.

———

Sandy found an employment opportunity with the San Francisco *Chronicle*, a big newspaper, much thicker than the San Mateo *Times* or the Sacramento *Bee*, the main newspaper we had known through our growing up in the valley. A man working for the *Chronicle* had come to town and had increased the subscriptions in town from a handful to over two hundred. Sandy was in charge of delivery.

At first, he collaborated with Walt and Robert, but they didn't like to get up that early in the morning, and the old Chevy was too expensive to maintain with gasoline and repairs, although they both claimed to be adept at working on the car. Sandy asked me if I would like to work with him, using the economical Vauxhall. I conferred with Bob and said I would.

Not many mornings passed until I was stopped by the police, who saw me as a young boy in an unfamiliar car. I still did not have my license, so we had to make a new adjustment. I could not drive back and forth, so I moved into Sandy's apartment. I had to have someone at least eighteen ride along with me, so Robert joined us. Sometimes he drove, and sometimes I did. I picked up his habits of peeling out, hanging sharp turns, and rolling through stop signs. But we delivered the papers.

Sandy had little social gatherings at night in the apartment. Walt and Robert's sister, Sue, came, as did a friend of hers named Tommie, whom I knew. I was obliged to play spin the bottle and to kiss Sue, who drooled with beer and cigarette breath. I was glad when I turned sixteen and was able to drive back and forth again.

I had to take my driver's test three times, thanks to the habits I had picked up from my mentor, plus having to learn parallel parking for the first time, but I received my license. I knew the man who operated the DMV (Department of Motor Vehicles) because he went for coffee with Mr. Hodge and his wife worked with us at Sprouse-Reitz. He also knew my father and Carmen, and being Hispanic, he spoke Spanish with her. He was a patient and brave man, sitting through hundreds of driving tests with young people like myself.

The subscription boom did not last. People were willing to take the *Chronicle* for an introductory free month, but when they had to pay the high subscription rate, they began to drop. Before long, Sandy was not making enough from his share.

He turned over the newspaper delivery to me, gave up his apartment, and went to work at Mills Orchards. There he picked oranges, stayed in the bunkhouse, and bought his cigarettes and work clothes on credit in the company store. He came to Orland by thumb, wearing a nice, thick flannel shirt and a new Levi jacket.

Wrestling season had begun. I was delivering newspapers, working at Sprouse-Reitz, and going to wrestling practice. I was falling asleep at school. Algebra II was harder than geometry. Physiology was not as interesting as biology had been, two years earlier with the same teacher.

In a conversation with another fellow at school, it came out that he drank beer. I asked him what he got out of it.

He said it made him feel good and it helped him forget about his problems.

I wondered what problems he had. He came from a secure family life. I admitted to myself that I had a few problems, but at least life was sane. I wasn't arguing in the middle of the night or listening to other people flinging insults.

Mr. Hodge and I were reviewing a list of figures. He knew I liked to run sums in my mind, so he was calling out the numbers as he tapped them into the adding machine. In conversation, he touched upon my family situation again, and he came around to a question.

"What's your father going to leave you, then? His picking buckets?"

"I don't know," I said. I didn't want to talk about it. For one thing, I didn't think my father or anyone should have to leave me anything. I expected to make my own way. But I also knew I would be arguing against a set of societal assumptions, and I did not feel prepared for that kind of argument.

Bob and I had our fingernails trimmed and ready for our wrestling match. For most of my life, I had not known finger-nail clippers. My father trimmed his nails with a knife and made jokes about his toenails to anyone who needed a knife to cut up a peach or pear or melon. I had not become adept at trimming my fingernails that way. In the earlier years, I bit or chewed them off or tore them when they broke. Now I felt quite civilized, prepared to curl my hands and present my nails to the referee, as we did.

Sandy said he did well at picking oranges, but I knew that with the weather, one did not work every day, because oranges discolored if they went to the packing sheds with water on them. Also, he spent some of his money ahead of time by charging items at the store and selling them to his bunkhouse acquaintances for a little less, sort of like paying interest in reverse.

In the latter part of the winter, Sandy and Walt announced their intention to go into the Navy. They were both seventeen and would go in on the buddy plan, which meant that they would stay together. Each of them would get out the day before his twenty-first birthday.

Two weeks after they went in, Walt became ill and went to

Sick Bay. They did not see each other again until they were both out of the service.

My grandfather signed for Sandy and became his beneficiary. A little over a week after Sandy went in, I received a package with a note from him saying I could have all the contents. The package contained a comb, an empty wallet, a pair of shoes, a pair of worn socks, unlaundered underwear, pants, a flannel shirt, and a Levi jacket.

ELEVEN

After my good showing at the end of my sophomore year, my grades took a drop in the first quarter of my junior year. I had joined CSF, the California Scholarship Federation, the previous year. It was what some people call an honor society, but I did not know that term. I knew CSF offered the kind of recognition I hoped for. A member had to maintain academic courses and had to keep up his or her grades in order to qualify for life membership or Sealbearer status. To be a Sealbearer was a serious goal of mine, so I had to bear down and improve my grades. I was taking German and Spanish, which were not hard classes for me, but Algebra II was difficult. I had dropped Physiology when it came time to prick our fingers for a blood test, but inside, I knew it was one rigorous class too many for me at that time.

I did my homework, but not in as disciplined a fashion as the year before. Like other students, I did homework for one class when we had work time in another class. I dashed it off at lunchtime.

At home, I spent long, sometimes sleepy hours reading *Uncle Tom's Cabin* and *Moby-Dick*, both of them high-point earners for U.S. history. In English, I was in with a group of lesser achievers, and we read only what was in the textbook. We read Jack London's "To Build a Fire" and a short story entitled "Footfalls" by Wilbur Daniel Steele, which Sandy had told me about when he read them the year before. These stories are on a level of "The Most Dangerous Game," which I think I read at about this time as well. On a little higher level, we read a short story by William Faulkner entitled "Two Soldiers," a short story by Ray Bradbury entitled "The Pedestrian" about the mindlessness of watching television, and a short story by Ernest Hemingway entitled "The Old Man at the Bridge." English class also had us read selections that I did not enjoy, such as poems by Vachel Lindsay and *In the Zone* by Eugene O'Neill. The class did have a good segment on rhetorical fallacies, however, and we had the opportunity to learn how to be skeptical of political and commercial messages. Some of this material served me well in subsequent parts of my education.

The English teacher used the restroom across the hall from his classroom. It was the first time I saw a teacher in the same restroom with students. I derived the idea that teachers were ordinary human beings.

With Sandy and Walt in the Navy, Bob and I formed a social group with Walt's brother Robert and their sister's friend Tommie. Robert and Bob both had a crush on Tommie, who was Bob's age but was in David's grade. All of us came from broken families, so it was natural that we formed our little group. It did not complement my academic aspirations, though. The most intellectual thing we did was go out to the old truck stop south of town, Greenwood Switch, and drink coffee as we listened to "Chapel of Love," "Mountain of Love," "Leader of the Pack," "Last Kiss," and "Pearly Shells."

Robert did not have a job. He was tall and slender, blond and pale, with low energy and a mumbly voice. He did small jobs for his mother and talked about getting a good job in construction, which he pronounced without the *t*'s. The old Chevy he had with his brother went the way of all old clunkers, so he did not have much mobility on his own. But he was eighteen and had lived in a more populated area like Hayward, and he presented himself as being experienced and resourceful.

We learned from him how to siphon gasoline. One morning after delivering newspapers, he and Bob and I conspired to steal some motor oil from the island of the service station when we checked the air in the tires. The attendant reported us, but when the police stopped us, we had already put the oil in the engine, so all the police found in the trunk was a red can and a green siphon hose. They were not illegal, just revealing.

————

At the end of the wrestling season, one member of our team, the heavyweight, qualified to go to the state tournament by taking second place in the section meet. The wrestling coach was happy, but the head coach, or athletic director, did not allow the wrestler to go. He gave the reason that the wrestler did not try hard enough. Those of us who were devoted to the team were dismayed, and I took up the cause by writing a letter to the Orland newspaper.

It caused a bit of a stir. I lived out of town and did not know many people, so my sense of who read it came from team members and other students. A friend of mine, who was destined to be our class valedictorian, lived in town and had parents who knew everybody. He said many people read the letter, and many of them thought it was written by an adult. I also understood that the athletic director, who was the football coach and had manipulated the sportsmanship award in track the year before, was displeased.

The wrestling coach stopped me in the hallway. He confirmed that I had caused some concern in the athletic department. I said I thought I had a right to express my opinion, and he agreed. He went on to suggest that I print a retraction.

I said, "You mean, take it back?"

This was not the coach who recommended that I eat steak. The first coach was a football and baseball coach who was filling in for our first wrestling team. This coach cared more about wrestling and seemed to be sympathetic to my case, but it was his first year at Orland. He nodded and said, "Yes."

I was only sixteen, but I knew that people didn't take back what they wrote with conviction. They didn't yield to pressure from people higher up who were exposed or criticized. I had learned about examples from history. People wrote for what they thought was right, for a sense of justice. To give in would be to do the opposite. I was a bit chagrined that someone would ask me to, but I told him I didn't think I would.

———

Our father was living in Porterville, down in the San Joaquin Valley east of the main route between Fresno and Bakersfield. Bob and I had gone there for a few days during Thanksgiving break and had picked oranges on eighteen-foot ladders. When wrestling season was past, in early April or so, my father asked for Bob to go down and help him. He still had custody of us, so it was hard to refuse, even though it was outside our agreement.

Bob came back in less than a month. He had a flood of stories as soon as I picked him up at the bus station. He had enrolled in school, but our father kept him out to pick olives more than half the time. Our father and Carmen had split up, so Bob spent much of his evening time as a go-between, relaying pleas and demands and refusals. He had to cook and do all the housework in the cabin court, and when he served dinner, our father told him to flush it down the toilet. Bob declined until our father shouted at him a few times. When he did flush the food down, our father berated him for doing it.

Bob repeated all of our father's vocabulary, which I could hear very well. It was worse than crazy, and Bob was glad to get out. I was glad to see him back, unhurt.

———

With the encouragement of Mrs. Walker, I competed in the county math contest. One of her seniors took first place, and I had the honor of taking second place. Mrs. Walker mentioned my achievement to the Algebra II class, and it made me feel worthy at a time when not everything else was going well.

———

Mr. Hodge gave me the unexpected news that he was leaving. He was going to drive a bread truck for two hundred dollars a week instead of manage the variety store for a hundred and twenty-five. He wagged his eyebrows and said, "Not hard to figure out which is the better deal."

I felt a disappointment that was not just for me. Mr. Hodge had seemed to have company loyalty. He spoke of Sprouse-Reitz with respect, and although he might have had a trace of irony when he mentioned Mr. Sprouse himself, he showed appreciation for the box of pears that the owner sent for Christmas to every manager in the chain. Mr. Hodge said he expected them to be ripe on Christmas Day, as they had been in the past. I thought managing a store had more status than driving a bread truck, but I understood the practical aspect.

The other employees were sad to see Mr. Hodge leave as well. And no one seemed impressed by his replacement, Mr. Slattery. He had the air and the accent of someone who came from somewhere else. My guess was Oklahoma or Texas.

One of my first tasks with him was to do an inventory of the merchandise at the beginning of his term. I had done inventory with Mr. Hodge at around New Year when he closed the store for a couple of long days, so I knew my part. I read off the quantities, and Mr. Slattery wrote them down. I did not give the name of the item, just the price and how many there were—three at twenty-nine, four at ninety-five, and so forth. As I stood on a short ladder reading some of the items on a higher shelf, I was able to see Mr. Slattery's clipboard and notations. It appeared to me that he was writing down a lower number of some of the items that were worth a dollar and more. My suspicion rose as I stole a few more glances. I was pretty sure he was short-changing Mr. Hodge.

When my next payday came around, I saw that my check was for less than I expected. I asked, and Mr. Slattery told me that I was employed at a dollar an hour, as per company standards. It was less than minimum wage, but some companies were able to get away with paying less to entry-level or training-level employees.

I told him that Mr. Hodge had paid me a dollar and a quarter and had made up the difference on his own—not out of his own pocket, I don't think, but out of another account.

Mr. Slattery said that he didn't have anything to do with that, and he wasn't going to pay me any more. If I didn't like it, I could leave. It was apparent to me that he did not care for employees who spoke well of Mr. Hodge, and I did not care for him, so I said I would go. I had some wages coming since the pay period ended, so I asked when I could pick up my check. He said to come back in a week.

I told him that under California law, the employer had to pay the same day for someone who was being fired, and the employer had to pay within three days if the employee quit. In all of my visits to employment offices, I had picked up some of the brochures and had read about employee rights.

Mr. Slattery said, "Come back in three days, then. I don't need someone workin' for me to tell me wot's wot."

I said, "I'm not telling you wot's wot. I'm just telling you what the law is." I knew I was being cheeky with him, and I didn't blame him for wanting to be rid of me. I thought he had a hunch that I had seen him fudging on the inventory.

After I received my final pay, I filed a claim with the state labor department for the amount I felt I was being shorted.

The days were getting longer, and the weather was warming up. The newspaper circulation was down to so few subscriptions that I made the deliveries myself on a bicycle.

On a sunny afternoon, I received a letter that had "Tulare County Jail" stamped in the return address area and on the first page of the letter. The handwriting was my father's. He wrote a short account of his ordering a hamburger at a drive-in and falling asleep. The police arrested him for being drunk in public, and they impounded his car. He needed help.

I sent him some money. Earlier in the school year, I had sold the camp trailer to some people who dropped in off the highway. A chunk of the money went toward a penalty for not keeping the registration current, but I made the sale and sent the proceeds to my father. My grandfather complained and pointed out that Bob and I owed him money. He was right. A little later, feeling the pinch and being pushed by my grandfather, I sold a roomful of my father's tools and belongings, including the deer head and the mounted antlers from Oregon. My father was furious when he found out, but it was done. Now, I had to send money that Bob and I had earned and needed.

Toward the end of the school year, I went down to Porterville on a weekend. My father was a wreck with his wife having left him. Part of the problem was that Andrea had come to Porterville and had been giving her sister support, telling her she didn't have to take all the verbal abuse and turmoil. So Carmen held out. My father blamed it all on Andrea.

I had a strained re-acquaintance with Andrea, and I did not succeed in persuading Carmen to return to my father.

He told me of his stay in jail, which included meeting

Tommie's older brother Jack. It was quite a coincidence, so far away. My father told me that some of the inmates, including Jack, mashed some aspirin pills, ignited them, and inhaled the smoke.

In what was for me an objective comment, I said I thought it would be interesting to be in jail for a short period to observe things.

With Carmen still holding out, I helped my father get his things together, and we drove the Cadillac back to Orland.

———

There followed a short, strange period in which our father stayed in the bedroom that Bob and I had. The room had a door to the outside, but my grandfather had nailed it shut when Bob and I were making free use of it. My father went in and out the window, just as Bob and I did on some evenings when we went to the truck stop to listen to the jukebox. During the day when we were in school, he hung out in our room.

My grandfather spoke to me. "I know your fahther's been staying in your room. I don't know why he can't be a man and show himself. But he's not fooling anyone."

The situation did not last long. My father, Bob, and I rented a house in the country south of town. The rent was ninety dollars a month, but school was out, and Bob and I had work, though low-paying, with a farmer who lived west of Mrs. Harris's dairy. (Minimum wage did not apply to farm work.) I was sixteen, so at least one of us had a chance at better wages.

———

My father found work at the Dodge agency, detailing cars. He was trying to hang on, not drinking. He had a haunted, detached air about him, and his skin was pale. Later in life, I would know what it was like to be sick with worry about a woman, and I would remember his way. At the time, it was life as I saw it from the outside. I stopped to visit him at work. I was impressed by his neat work with the dashboard and all the instruments and knobs. The window glass was immaculate. He was kneeling by the opened driver's door and was cleaning the edge that closed against the doorpost.

"This is real nice," I said.

He broke down. His lower lip trembled, and he sobbed. He said, "I wish Mama was here. It's just no good without her."

He had me call in sick for him. He was not drinking. He just did not have the fortitude to hold himself together for a day's work.

I found work for Robert and me, picking apricots where Bob, David, Tommie, and I had cut apricots by the running water faucet a year earlier. Bob continued to work for the farmer, but he was only fifteen and could not drive, so my father drove him to work every morning. As he did, he went past the Dodge agency on his way through town.

He had me talk to his boss to arrange for a little more time off, and the boss said, "I think he's been going to work somewhere else." I said, no, he was just taking my brother to work, and the boss said, that was all right, he didn't need my father anymore.

———

One day when we were out of money, I received a check in the mail. It was from Sprouse-Reitz, making up the difference in my pay, and it included a short notation from Mr. Slattery, indicating that the check was for wages promised by Mr. Hodge, as if Mr. Hodge had not kept his promise.

I was glad to get the money. It came at a time when we needed it.

My father said, "Always darkest before dawn."

———

The man who owned the house we rented was in late middle age, close to retirement age. He and his wife lived on the next property, north of us. He came over to visit and to tell a couple of off-color jokes. He had a smooth voice and seemed to consider himself a humorist. He offered Bob and me the job of stripping the old wood shingles from his barn roof. We put on leather gloves and ran our hands between the roof slats, pulling the shingles upward. The work took us a couple of days.

A year later, we read in the paper that he was arrested for child molesting. I was not shocked. There had been something beneath the surface.

My father, Bob, and I went to work thinning beets, south of Orland and Willows where the open field crops stretched for miles under a blazing sun. Thinning beets paid by the acre. Depending on the length of the field, a row equaled a portion of an acre. Some fields were so long that a row equaled an acre.

We worked with a short-handled hoe, always stooping, moving from left to right, swinging the hoe with short strokes, leaving the seedling plants spaced the width of a hoe head, and picking out the doubles with our left hand.

It was the hardest work I ever did in the fields. The rows seemed never to end. The hot sun was relentless, pitiless. My father's urine turned the color of coffee. Bob did not take the heat well when there was no variety of movement and no breeze. We worked for a few days, finished our block of rows, and drew our pay.

A year or so later, a woman who had thinned beets told us that one way to lessen the strain on the back was to keep one's legs crossed in stepping sideways. I felt that I should do the work again and try that method.

I found out some years later that the short-handled hoe had

been outlawed. I was glad for the people who continued to do that work.

About thirty years after our experience, I was at a Wyoming Council for the Humanities conference for writers. I was talking to a writer from Worland, Wyoming, which was in a sugar-beet-growing area, as was Torrington, Wyoming, where I lived. The subject of thinning beets came up, and a woman from the Humanities Council asked how the work was done. The other writer and I, as if by compulsion, both bent over and gave a demonstration, hoeing with one hand and pulling doubles with the other.

———

On one day in mid-summer, we had to drive quite a ways to pick plums. My father, Bob, and I worked all day and did what we thought was a good job, but the plums had been pretty ripe, and a great many of them fell as we set our ladders and picked. At the end of the day, the owner paid us and sent us on our way.

———

The farm labor office gave us a referral to pick peaches. My father and I went to Nord, across the river past Hamilton City and north into an interior country of row crops, walnut orchards, prune orchards, and peach orchards. The foreman, who drove an open Jeep between the rows, was a man named Monte. He was a Texan about my father's age, with cutaway shirt sleeves and a crumpled straw hat. All hats in orchard work were knocked off and run over at some point. His lower eyelids were puffy, and his pale-blue eyes peered through slits as he waved at the peaches on the tree and nodded to us. Sixteen cents a box.

I invited our friend Robert to work with us. A person could work alone picking by the box. The three of us worked together picking a set of trees, so he moved through the orchard with us.

Every morning, I had to go into Robert's house in the dark and wake him up. Every morning, my father would bark, "Leave the son of a bitch here. You drive him back and forth, and he can't even get up in the morning. Lazy son of a bitch."

———

In another orchard, where the peaches were durable and went to the cannery, we picked by the bin. It was harder for a person working by himself, but it was still much better than picking prunes, as the bin filled faster.

At the end of an orchard or at the end of the job, it was common to have to wait around at the edge of the orchard or at the office for the checks to be made out. On one such day, my father and Robert and I were waiting in the car when a commotion arose in the car next to us.

It was a common scene—a Mexican family in a station wagon, the parents with the reserved air of people who did not speak English, and a young man about my age who drove the car and managed the business aspect. With his status, he was something of a tyrant. The ticket for one bin was missing, and he was shouting at the others in the car. *¡Falta uno! ¡Falta uno!* One is missing. He went to the office window, came back, and shouted a few more times.

I reinforced the grammatical construction for myself. Inverted subject-verb order. The verb form agrees with the subject to follow. If there had been two tickets missing, it would have been *Faltan dos*.

A couple of years later, I saw the same young man in the parking lot of a store in Chico. I recognized his fierce features and his prominent teeth, and I remembered the way he had thrown his authority around with his family. *Falta uno*, I said to myself, out loud.

My brothers and I had sworn never to eat store-bought blackberry jam—or worse, strawberry jam—when we saw what kinds of moldy and rotten fruit went into the cannery crates. After we saw the mashed and mushy prunes that went into the bin, and heard of the rats that chewed the prunes at the dehydrators and packing plants, we made a more solemn vow never to eat that product.

Peaches were different. I knew that some of them went for jam and baby food, but we didn't put the junk in the boxes to begin with. The fruit would spoil too soon. None of the peaches stayed in the field overnight. They had to go straight to the cannery.

Maybe I was growing into more of an awareness of my place in the world. Maybe I was on top of my job enough that I did not have to hate it and its product. Maybe my father's sense of the food producer's perspective was rubbing off. I began to feel a bit of pride in doing my part to help bring food to the world. Later in life, I would read about the difference between gainful employment and useful employment. I would wonder if I had a Calvinist streak in me. For as much as the heat, the humidity, the mosquitoes, and the itch of the peach fuzz made life uncomfortable, I did not feel the futility I once did.

———

Life was calm for a while at the house we rented in the country. I had an old junior-high-school literature textbook, and I enjoyed reading poems such as Alfred Noyes's "The Highwayman." I had read it in the seventh grade or so, and I had read "The Cremation of Sam McGee" perhaps a year earlier. I had an enduring interest in writing poetry, thanks to Mrs. McNolty in Gridley, and I aspired to write something grander than I had in the past.

In another small episode from the golden past, my father told me how he and a friend invited two young women to go horseback riding for a day's excursion on the ranch. My grandfather went along to grill steaks on open coals. My father told the story as if it was an activity that happened more than once.

In another story, he told me how he and his friends used to rent the Santa Rita schoolhouse, a rural school that was no longer in use. He would bring a battery and set up lights, and they would put on a dance. Nobody drank inside. They left their liquor in the cars and went out to drink. Everything was clean and orderly.

I heard the first story more than once, and I heard the second story several times. In the second story, the theme was more explicit. "You young people don't know how to have fun anymore." These stories had more application now that I was of dating age.

We caught up on living expenses well enough to buy a yellow-and-white 1959 Nash Metropolitan, a tiny car with room enough in the back seat for a lunch pail. But it got much better mileage than the Cadillac. Bob and I had heard the terms "hoopy" and "whippy" applied to our Vauxhall, and of the two, "whippy" sounded more diminutive, so we used it to refer to the little Metro.

My father's spirits improved for a short while when Carmen came back to live with us. Andrea, who may have come to the U.S. to have her baby, had done so and had gone back to Mexico. Carmen had discontinued whatever social life she had in Porterville, so we were all under one roof again.

It did not take long for the old patterns to return. My father and Carmen argued day and night. He drank. She was erratic and unreasonable—not that he was rational in his harangues.

The argument reached a pitch one hot afternoon when Carmen said she was going to leave.

My father said, "If you leave, I'll burn everything you've got."

She began walking down the county road, where the heat rose from the asphalt, and the countryside all around baked in the August sun.

My father said, "Johnny, go get her."

I started up the Cadillac and went down the road after her. I pulled alongside, let down the power window, and told her to get in.

She kept on walking.

I puttered along, trying to persuade her to get into the car. I told her she couldn't walk all the way to town in such heat.

She and I had always gotten along well and had reasonable communication, but her mind was different at this time. She had even promoted some of the argument with my father, which was not characteristic of her. I was exasperated. I told her to get into the car and not be a fool. But the word I used in Spanish (it begins with a *p*) was stronger than I realized, and she took offense. She looked away and would not speak to me as she kept walking.

At last I gave up and went home. My father was still on the rampage.

"I told her I'd burn everything she had if she left. By God, I will. Help me take her stuff out of the house."

Bob and I were fed up with all of the recent fighting, the nonsense and conflict in Porterville, the argument between our father and our grandfather, the rupture with Sandy before that, and all the little flare-ups in between. So we helped carry things out of the house. My father lit the fire, and it burned past dark.

He was not done. He was drunk, but he was not down and out. He got in behind the wheel of the Cadillac and said, "I've got a telephone pole picked out between here and Artois, and I'm gonna run into it at a hunnerd miles an hour."

As he peeled out of the driveway, I let go of the window ledge and ran alongside with Bob next to me, both of us saying, perhaps without full feeling, "No, please, Dad, don't!"

He gave the car full acceleration, but it had not reached a high speed when he plowed it into a brick column on the right side of the driveway entrance, continued across the county road, and plunged into the ditch on the other side.

He climbed out of the car, his left hand on his ribs. "Son of a bitch. Didn't even hurt me."

Bricks and rubble lay where he had hit the column. The right front quarter of the once-sturdy Cadillac was crumpled.

A police car came, then a tow truck to pull the car out of the ditch. The Cadillac was registered in my name, out of a long-standing practice of my father not having things in his name that could be repossessed or seized. I received a citation for improper parking, and my father was cited for failure to drive on the right side of the roadway.

We did not know where Carmen went.

Later, I discovered the extent of the damage in the fire. All of the photographs from our trip to Mexico, including those of me with Pancho Villa's widow, were gone.

———

We had to find another place to live, so we rented a house on the highway, north of Grandpa and David's house, north of Mrs. Harris's dairy, and on the east side of the road. Our rent was seventy-five a month.

My father and I found work across the river again, this time in the prunes. We drove back and forth in the little Metro. Much of the prune harvest was now being done with shakers and canvas catch-frames, but quite a bit of fruit was left behind. Workers were needed to pick behind the machine, as the saying went. We picked up prunes around the trunk and on the strip of ground where the two frames did not come together well enough. We also picked up scattered windfalls and used a pole to knock or strip the prunes that did not come down with the shaker.

We picked into lug boxes and wrote our number with chalk on the end of each box, as we did in other crops. I was in charge of knocking. The pole was long and heavy, and my neck became tired from tipping my head back. Hornets that had their nests disturbed sought retribution, following the pole to the source.

On one occasion, when I was holding the pole above my head and had finished stripping prunes up high, I relaxed my grasp to let the pole come down between my hands. As it did, the tip hit a branch and threw off the direction or angle of the pole so that the blunt lower end came down and hit my big toe. I was wearing tennis shoes, which offered no protection. The pain was terrible, as the pole hit me at the base of the toenail.

Over the next week or ten days, my toe swelled up and turned as dark as any plum. I had to cut the top out of my shoe in order to be able to work. The toenail at last lifted up at the lower end and came off, and I had a very tender toe to look after as the new nail grew in.

———

My father wanted to go to Marysville, so I drove the Nash Metro. We arrived in the evening in a part of town where people stood on the sidewalk in front of bars. Most of the people were Black. I got out with my father and loitered on the sidewalk. A well-figured Black woman about thirty walked past, turned around, came back, and lingered.

"I thought I was looking for someone," she said.

My father said, "Are you looking for me?"

She glanced over him and said, "Maybe."

I waited on the sidewalk in front of our car, beneath the street light. I was wearing an inexpensive admiral's or yachtsman's cap, white with little yellow anchors on a blue background.

A Black man who was loitering nearby spoke in a slow voice. "Hey, young blood."

I nodded.

He said, "Hey, young blood. You out to have a good time tonight?"

"Reasonably good," I said.

My father came out of the building he had gone into. In the car, he told me that was the nice thing about colored girls, you could get them to go down in price. Next time, I could go along if I wanted.

Not at all, I said. I didn't tell him much about my girlfriend, but she came from a family with two parents, and she was the type who kept her elbows and knees together. I couldn't think of doing something so impure with someone else.

My sister Suzi came to visit with her husband and their two small children. They had moved to the Sacramento area and lived in North Highlands, where Ken did roofing work and car repair. They arrived at Grandpa and David's house, so Bob and I went to see them.

Our father showed up a little while later. For some reason, he took it ill that Bob and I went to see Suzi. Perhaps he nursed a grudge from Sandy having stayed with her a couple of years earlier, or he may have been drawing from his grudge against my mother's family in general. I had told him about Uncle Chuck's attempt to take Bob and me to live with them, and he may have had that in his craw as well. Whatever the case, his state of mind had not been good for months, and on this day, he had been drinking. He pulled off the highway coming from the direction of the house we rented a ways north, and he honked the horn.

Bob and I went out to see what he wanted. He launched into a tirade of what the hell we were doing here and why we weren't at home where we should be. Suzi and Ken came outside. Grandpa and David lingered at the door.

The complaint continued. My father told us to get our asses home. Of Ken, he said, "I don't even know this son of a bitch," and he issued the obscene two-word insult to Suzi. Bob and I told Ken, who was in his mid-twenties and was making motions as if he was going to step forward, not to get mixed up in it. We told our father we weren't going to go home if all we were going to do was fight and argue.

He said, "To hell with you, then. If you don't come home now, don't come home at all. Just stay away. Don't come back."

After Suzi and Ken left, Bob and I went to visit our friend Robert. He was staying in a detached room in back of his mother's house, so we spend the night there.

The next evening, we headed for Chico, where there was a teenage nightclub that had loud music and pinball machines. Sometimes the bouncer stood on the sidewalk and sang with the music coming through the speaker.

> Come on in.
> Papa's gonna teach you how to
> Do the Swim.

Robert was driving, Bob was on the passenger's side, and I was stretched out on the short back seat of the Vauxhall. I smelled something burning, and I saw that the upholstery was glowing. We stopped, pulled the seat out, and snuffed the fire. As we were concluding that the fire was caused from Robert's cigarette, which he had been holding up by the open window, a sheriff's car pulled in behind us and put on the red lights.

The deputies said they had a warrant for Bob and me for running away from home.

We explained that we were told not to go home.

The deputies said they had to take us in. We gave Robert

permission to take the car, and we got into the back seat of the police car.

Bob and I had the opportunity to state our case with the probation office the next day, after spending the night in a cell. (We found out that juvenile hall was not a hall or a wing but just another cell in the county jail.) The probation officer, a prim lady who must have had cold water in her veins, listened to our story.

In court, we heard the favorable recommendation that we be placed in the custody of our grandfather and become dependents of the court. Our grandfather would receive fifty dollars a month for each of us—including David—and my father would be expected to pay what he could to the court. He was present, but he was not very disputatious.

Bob and I went back to live with Grandpa and David. We kept the Vauxhall and the damaged Cadillac, and our father kept the Nash Metro.

With a little bit of summer vacation left, Bob and I did what we knew how to do. We found a job picking prunes in Vina, off the main track near Corning, the next town north on Highway 99W. We invited Robert and Tommie to go with us, as they needed money.

Bob had taken Auto Shop I in his first year of high school, and he had done several repairs on the Vauxhall. Robert and his brother, Walt, had professed to be shade-tree mechanics in their own right, and they had done some work on their old Chevy before it came to an end. With me in attendance, and with the help of a person who had an arc welder, Bob and Robert put a grey front fender on the light-metallic-blue Cadillac. We had to leave off the front bumper, but we had it operable. The frame must have been sprung, however, for a highway patrolman stopped me and told me my car looked like a dog going down the highway.

We were driving down the main street in Corning with Robert at the wheel, Tommie in the middle, Bob on the passenger side, and me in the back seat with my girlfriend, a friend of Tommie's. A thump and a crunch sounded in the right rear, and the car began spinning. When it came to a stop and we all climbed out unhurt, we saw that the right rear wheel had broken off and the hub had served as a pivot point. Gasoline was leaking where a fuel line had been broken.

The police came. A fire truck came to wash away the gasoline. A tow truck came. And that was the end of the 1953 Cadillac, which had been a good car.

———

The labor office sent us about forty miles south, near Williams, in Colusa County, where there was an acute need for people to pick cannery tomatoes. Harvesting machines were replacing manual labor, but the machines broke down with frequency, and the growers needed a great number of workers for a short while. Bob and Robert and I drove down there for a couple of days and picked ripe, thick-skinned tomatoes into five-gallon plastic buckets. I had known five-gallon buckets all my life, but these were the first plastic ones.

When we finished the field, we had to wait around for our checks. A couple of older, bullying guys made fun of my admiral's cap, so I sassed them back.

On the way home, Robert said, "Johnny, you shouldn't have talked to those guys that way. They were hooligans. They could have kicked your ass."

"Aw, to hell with them," I said. "They're just tomato pickers like we are." To myself, I thought, maybe they could have. They were mean-looking like some of the people I remembered from Half Moon Bay.

We found work closer to home, picking up windfall almonds ahead of the knocking crew. Tommie worked with us again. We did a good job for those people, who had a girl who was a good student in my grade. We picked into buckets and emptied them into burlap bags, and when we were done, we helped the owners haul the bags to their barn.

Summer vacation was coming to an end. Bob and Robert each still had a crush on Tommie and were getting nowhere. My girlfriend and I broke up after an uneventful romance, and I spent a short while being morose. One night I decided to stay home while Bob and Robert went out to drive around. I went to bed early, but feeling restless, I climbed out the window, walked into town, continued to the edge of town where she lived, went past her house, turned, and walked the three miles home. It was nothing to tell anyone about, just a small way of putting something to rest.

As always, I was glad to go back to school.

TWELVE

On the first day of civics class, the teacher stopped at my desk and spoke in a low, ultra-sincere tone. He said, "Last year, I had your brother in class. He had a great deal of ability, but he didn't apply himself. I've heard that you have a great deal of ability, also. I hope you apply yourself."

I felt as if a sticky cloud hung over me. I had a sense of something that I would articulate for myself many years later in my own work: evaluate the work, not the student.

At the same time, I wanted to do well.

———

Driving old cars was a concomitant part of our way of life, and there were levels of old cars. The Vauxhall and the 1953 Cadillac had cost $150 each, while the 1952 Cadillac had cost about $50 or $60. Many of the common cars such as Chevrolet, Ford, Dodge, Plymouth, Oldsmobile, and the like were in that range. At about the time we went back to school, we saw a 1951 Plymouth station wagon, pale green, sitting by the edge of the highway with a "For Sale" sign. Robert did not have a car, and with Bob and me in school again, he needed one to drive back and forth to the work he was going to find. On an informal partnership, we bought the station wagon for $60.

We had been fond of the song "Eve of Destruction" and had sung it in memory of the Cadillac. A surfer song was playing when the Plymouth lost power and slowed to a stop.

Bob and Robert went to the parts house and came back with the triumphant announcement that they were going to overhaul the engine.

By the time they had it put together again, school was well under way. I was taking Auto Shop I so I would know something about engines, although I knew I did not have much aptitude. The Plymouth was still not running well, so Bob and I, with Robert as kind of a guest, took the car into the evening auto shop, which was an open time when various students came in to work on their cars or to watch and help others.

Bob and Robert finished their new repairs on the engine, and it was knocking worse than before. Robert came to me and said, "Johnny, follow me in the Vauxhall. I'm gonna take this thing out on the highway and drive it till it blows up."

The car was registered in his name. I could see that we had thrown good money after bad, but not a huge amount each time, so I agreed. I waited as he backed the car out of the shop, and when he did, it gave its last fatal bang.

Robert had a short temper at times. He got out and kicked the car and began hitting it with a wrench. Within a few minutes, others joined in. They hit the car with hammers, lug wrenches, iron bars, and anything else at hand. They climbed onto the hood and beat the roof. I watched them, silhouetted by the light inside the shop. A fellow from my grade was wearing what we called a hillbilly hat, with a round crown and a pulled-down brim. He made a grotesque figure as he jumped up and down with his back arched and brought an iron bar down on the roof of the car. Perhaps a dozen fellows joined in, venting themselves on someone else's hulk of a vehicle.

In the end, the windows were all broken, and the car's

whole exterior was rippled with the blows. Someone had a car big enough to tow it, so we took it out and left it at the junkyard on the highway, halfway to our house. It was an interesting sight on the way to school the next morning, and in the light of day, I recalled the legion of auto-shop enthusiasts who expended their energy and perhaps frustrations on someone else's car.

———

I received a message from the main office at school that our father wanted Bob and me to go see him. The message included the name and address of a hotel in Chico.

We found the hotel that evening. It was an old, dismal place that had been plain and inexpensive in its best days. We visited with our father in a dim room with drab-colored walls.

He was clean-shaven and sober, and he had the melancholy air about him that he had had when he was detailing cars several months earlier. He said the engine of the Nash Metro had blown up on him, and he wanted Bob to rebuild the engine. He would need help buying the parts as well.

Bob and I told him we couldn't do it. We said we had already split our assets with him; we had already made our deal and settled things. We had to manage our own expenses.

His mouth trembled, and he said, "You don't care about me. Do you want me to dry up and blow away like a weed?"

It was a sad plea, and he looked as if he was drying up already. But we had to resist. We said we were sorry. We had to look out for ourselves.

In the course of conversation, I told him we did not appreciate his having had us thrown in jail when he had told us not to come home.

He replied that I had said I would like to know what it was like to be in jail. He thought he had helped me find out.

I stated the obvious, that I hadn't meant that I wanted to find out in that way.

Bob and I drove back to Orland in the night. I felt sorry and guilty at not knowing what would become of our father, but it seemed as if we would be going backwards into more of the same conflict and disorder if we had to continue looking after him. A few years later, he would say to David that the trouble with Johnny was that he didn't care about anyone but Johnny. On that evening in the dingy hotel room, I had not heard of empathy. I did not know the word. I was not incapable of feeling, but I had learned, along with my brothers, that we needed to survive and to look out for our own needs. We did not dream for a fairy godmother or mother of any sort, and we did not dream of a fortune being dropped in our lap. We did not want to be adopted or patronized. But we had to take care of ourselves. In retrospect, it seems as if building a shell was something we had been learning to do all along.

———

Partway into the first semester of my senior year, I realized that I needed another academic class if I was going to qualify for CSF Life Membership. I had learned how an internal combustion worked, so I dropped auto shop and enrolled in public speaking. The teacher was young and lively, and she had taken over the German class, so now I had her for two subjects. I also had English, trigonometry, civics, physics, and P.E. I felt that I was on track.

———

Bob and I worked in the afternoons and on weekends. Sometimes Robert worked with us. People who had just a few trees, or a poor crop, or a scattering of nuts that fell late could not afford to pay to have their almonds or walnuts picked by the sack, so they had people like us pick on the shares. The pickers kept half or more of what they picked. We had done it before, so we knew where to sell a few sacks to processing plants.

The walnuts needed to be dried more, so Bob and I nailed a board along the edge of the roof of the house and laid out all the walnuts to dry in the autumn sun. It would have been a common sight to anyone who lived in the area.

I am sorry to say that we might have sold a few bags that we did not pick. I do not want to blame Robert, but Bob and I did not pull stuff like that when we lived with our father. When we ran around with Robert, we did. We began with gasoline and motor oil, what I might call perceived needs, and moved on to produce left on the doorstep of a store in the early morning. The winter before, we took a bag of onions and contributed them at home as part of our living expenses. We took a box of green bananas and ate them over a period of time in Robert's little room.

Now we were stealing for money. It was on a small scale, not close to home, and it seemed to be out of need. But it went beyond a flimsy boundary I had once accepted in shoplifting, which was that it was not taking something from an individual. Taking from a big company was not personal, and the loss was absorbed, as if it did not cost the company anything. I believe I lost sight of these distinctions, however contrived they might have been.

Although the court was paying our board and room, Bob and I needed money for ourselves—for our clothes, for our car, and for what little social life we had. We worked, but with next to no guidance, we strayed.

———

Bob and I came home from working one day, and David told us a man called Uncle Jimmy had dropped in for a visit. He had chatted with Grandpa and had put down a cup of Grandpa's caustic coffee without blinking.

I recalled who Uncle Jimmy was. We had called him Uncle

Butch when we were very small. He was our mother's younger brother. My father had told me that Jimmy was a smart-aleck who had come to the ranch not long after my parents were married. My father put him to work hoeing beans, and Jimmy whined. He wanted to drive tractor. He went back home, and as the story went, my mother did not disagree with my father.

My grandfather said that Jim Schneider had come to visit, to see how we were doing and to see if Bob and I needed a better place to stay. Uncle Jimmy was living in Sacramento now, and Suzi had told him where we lived. He told my grandfather a jolly story about Chuck working as superintendent on a big lodge and resort job in Lake Tahoe, where Chuck had cut off the ends of several expensive laminated beams and had been fired. I did not know either Chuck or Jimmy very well, and I did not know much about construction, let alone big commercial jobs, but I found it interesting.

———

Wrestling season began, and this year, David was on the team with Bob and me. David was very small, but he was learning. I had experience and was an average wrestler, but I was in the same weight class as the best wrestler on our team. The coach asked me to wrestle up two weight classes, from 127 to 138, for a three-way meet, and I saw what a great difference two weight classes made. I decided I would rather be second string in my own class. Bob was good. He and the fellow in my weight class won the trophies.

As a senior, I received a varsity letter. As a sophomore, Bob received his second varsity Block "O." From our shared means, Bob and I had found the money for a school sweater for me the year before. Now we bought him one, also.

———

Bob and I skipped school one day to pick oranges. In the early afternoon, we took a break and sat down with a couple of dropouts we knew who were not making a fortune at this work. A Mexican fellow came through with a ladder horizontal on his shoulder and his picking bag hanging at his side. He wore drab work clothes and had his cap turned backward. He stopped and smiled at the two dropouts and asked them if they were ready for their peanut-butter-and-jelly sandwiches. They replied with good humor, and he went on his way.

I asked our pals who he was. They said he was the trusty in jail who brought meals. Then I remembered him from the night that Bob and I had spent in the can.

Our friends went on to say that he was the one who had been driving when a short-time student at our high school had died in a car wreck when he was hitchhiking. I remembered the incident. The student had come from Hamilton City and had shown very good academic ability, but he was hitchhiking to Chico one night and was killed in a crash on the bridge. The driver was found guilty of drunk driving and manslaughter, and he had spent a year in jail. We had seen him there and again now, a polite fellow going about his work with a bit of humor. He had walked on into the trees ahead, and I did not see him again.

———

I received very good scores on the ACT, the SAT, and the National Merit exams, among the highest in my class. I also took the Air Force exams and received the highest scores possible in all four categories.

In English, we read *Hamlet* and *Macbeth*, which appealed to me in my intellectual aspirations. On a more casual level, I enjoyed copying lines such as "I prithee, take thy fingers from my throat." We read poetry including *The Rime of the Ancient Mariner*, and we had poetry memorization. After the first assignment in *The Return of the Native* by Thomas Hardy, I did not have my reading done. Students were passing around a copy of Cliff's Notes, and I had an early and useful lesson in not using those materials in lieu of doing the reading. As a class, we read *Lord of the Flies*, and I read Golding's *Pincher Martin* as well. For individual projects, I read *David Copperfield* by Charles Dickens and a volume of Boswell's journal, the latter recommended by my friend the valedictorian.

—————

In public speaking, or speech, one of the students was a girl in her junior year. She had three sisters, and they were all tall and womanly. They rode the bus with us in earlier days, and two or three of them had worked for Mrs. Harris. Her family had a small dairy as well, but as in generations past, family members of a small operation often "worked out" with other farmers. In one speech, the student talked about milking cows. She said that in this world, some people milked cows, and some didn't. People who milked cows were known as such. I understood. I had heard something similar about picking peas. With cows, one had no choice. They had to be milked twice every day.

—————

As it turned out, I worked for Mrs. Harris for a couple of weeks after wrestling season. Bob put in a stint as well. She gave her workers plenty to eat and a clean room, but the work was unending, up at five every morning and on the job again as soon as school let out. The weekends were the same. What little entertainment I had came in the form of Mrs. Harris's Southern voice, as when she would say, "John, that cow's milked out," or when she would go to the back door of the barn and call her cows by name, with stretches of "Sup, sup, sup, sup."

—————

My friend who had not been allowed to go to the state wrestling tournament worked for a family that had an orange tree nursery and a turkey farm. He asked me if I was interested in work, and I said I was. After a day of helping to plant the pink-coated orange seeds in warmed planter beds, I went to work in the less tranquil world of turkeys.

One of my tasks was to gather eggs out on the open ground, a small hillside that was bare except for a layer of turkey manure. Some of the hens would leave eggs out there.

After I brought in my gathering, I sat in a room with the owner and one or two other workers, cleaning the eggs to be sold for their use in bakeries. We cleaned the eggs with a brush and a light piece of emery cloth. The radio played songs by Lorne Green, of *Bonanza* fame. I enjoyed the song about the old tin cup and the battered coffeepot, and I tolerated the song about Ringo the gunfighter, although it became tiresome. I did not have much patience for "The Men in My Little Girl's Life," which was sung by someone else, but it was the boss's favorite. Each time it came on, he would sigh and say what a touching song it was.

Another task I had was gathering eggs from the nests, which were contained in wooden bunks on each side of a long, low barn. I went down the center aisle and took eggs from each side. After a while, I saw that the turkeys became territorial and aggressive. A large flock of them, a mixture of toms and hens, blocked the lane, clucking and gobbling. One tom, who appeared to be the leader, raised his head and let out a sharp gobbling cry. The rest of the group raised their heads and echoed in chorus. The exchange went on a few times, and a creepy feeling went through me each time. I had read, in one of my father's magazines, a story about a turkey farmer in Wisconsin or Minnesota who tipped over his tractor and feed trailer on a slick hillside and was pinned in the wreck with grain covering him. The birds came in great numbers to peck the feed, and he lay trapped, "waiting for one of those bastards to pick my eyes out."

The turkeys that faced me were hostile. They approached me and crowded me. I was wearing clumsy rubber boots, and I had to kick several toms in the chest about three times each, to keep them from mobbing me. Even that did not push them back. The leader kept at me until I hit him in the head with the flat of my fist. He went down and bounced back up, then turned and walked away. My anxiety settled down.

The best part came on a weekend in early spring when the bleak weather was improving. The owner hired a couple of more boys, including my brother Bob, to help load the turkeys. They were going to the processing plant, which was a very satisfactory thing for me to know. We herded hundreds of turkeys, most of them a dirty white, into a large pen that reduced to a "V" and sent them into an alley and a chute. The owner's son had a vaccinating gun and gave each turkey a shot. A few turkeys died during the herding, and I was told that it was a common occurrence. A heart attack. One of the regular workers hung them, feet upward, on a fence, for the upper-level employees to clean and take home. All the others went into the truck, headed for a destiny that I though they all deserved.

———

Another friend from the wrestling team came to stay with us for a couple of days. He had some kind of quarrel with his parents, and he did not quite ask to stay with us. He just hung around and ended up staying over.

While he was sitting on the couch, he asked my brother David to draw his picture. David was well known in his own class for being a good artist, and he had drawn some very entertaining sketches and cartoons of wrestlers on our team, wrestlers from other schools, and incidents during the tournaments, including one primitive-looking member on our team who sweated profuse amounts and starved to get down to weight, ate a huge amount before the match, and vomited a great volume into a towel at the edge of the mat. David could draw perfect pictures of his chickens, his friends, and our family members, but he had also been drawing grotesque cartoons since the fourth or fifth grade. Now he was a freshman, and our visitor, in a patronizing way, wanted his portrait done.

David drew what I thought was a nice, serious portrait of this fellow in his Ivy-league haircut and mohair sweater. The fellow took the paper in his hand, looked askance at it, and threw it into the wood-burning stove.

I was appalled. David did not say much. He and our visitor agreed that he would draw another one. Bob and I left him to his work as his subject held his pose for almost an hour. At last David showed his product.

A hag of a woman, with open eyes and reaching arms, had her mouth open, showing jagged, gapped teeth as she shouted his name and leaned forward to embrace our cringing friend. Bob and I laughed and laughed. The cartoon went into the flames as well. I think our friend understood the lesson.

Many times throughout the years, someone from Orland has told me of a picture that David drew during those years and that the person kept as a dear keepsake. It is too bad that the two he drew that evening were tossed into the fire.

——————

The Vauxhall was wearing out, and Bob and I found a Plymouth Valiant on a car lot in Chico that looked within our means. It cost five hundred dollars, and we were allowed a small trade-in for the Vauxhall. The salesman/owner offered us a payment plan, and we went to ask our grandfather to sign.

He rode to Chico with us. The owner's son had been in Bob's weight class, and Bob had beaten him in a tournament, so we were all good sports. The owner, noting my grandfather's accent, asked him where he was from.

My grandfather said, "Ireland."

The salesman said, "Oh, that's nice. A lot of good priests have come from Ireland."

My grandfather responded with a scorching commentary on priests and their sexual transgressions, with knocking up nuns and knocking the unwanted babies in the head.

Bob and I held our seats. The car lot proprietor sat it out and finished the paperwork. My grandfather signed, and we went home in the 1960 Valiant with a new paint job from a used car lot.

I drove Grandpa to school with us. He had an early appointment with the principal and vice-principal to talk about Bob skipping class. Bob and his friends went to the bowling alley to drink Coca-Cola and smoke cigarettes rather than eat a decent lunch. They sneaked off at other times, going across the street to smoke in the park.

I waited in the car until Grandpa came out, a large man in an old hat and button-up sweater, smoking a cigar and standing on the sidewalk as the students stepped down from the bus.

When the bus pulled away, I turned the car around and picked him up at the curb. He continued to smoke his cigar in the car as I drove him home.

In the company of Robert, Bob and I graduated into shoplifting. For me it was a return after four years. I do not think I would have done it by myself, and I do not think that Bob would have, either, although he had his own casual friends who might have done such things, and he indulged in other delinquency with them.

We went into a store but not together. Robert, tall and

sullen, went by himself. Bob and I, shorter and identifiable as a pair, went down a different side of the store. If a floorwalker followed us, Robert had an opportunity, and vice-versa. I discovered that there was a thrill that went along with what seemed to begin as a necessity. When I was younger, it was fear. Now it was a kind of surge.

We did not shoplift much or often—food, small items of clothing, maybe a car accessory. Cigarettes for them. Then we took a thing or two at night—parked down the street, where one of us would cover the dome light as the other two slunk out and heisted a tire or a gas can.

When Robert was drafted into the Army, we could have quit our unwise behavior. But I do not think it occurred to us. We invited one of our wrestling pals to join us. Now we were the bad influence, although I did not think of it in those terms. I think I was subject to a combination of lack of awareness, lack of guidance, lack of consideration for others, and lack of a moral sense. I did not smoke, and I did not drink, so I had some principles. I was blind to others. I was seventeen years old, at an age when others knew better, and I was stepping into disgrace.

I had a couple of opportunities to take warning.

Bob and I had gone out the window many times at night. As a practice, we waited until our grandfather went to bed. We climbed out the window, pushed the car back from the house, and hit the starter when a big truck went by.

We became impatient one night and sneaked out before our grandfather went to bed. As David narrated it to us, our grandfather went outside to see the stars, as he sometimes did before turning in. He saw that the car was gone. He asked David if he knew any reason for the car to be missing, and David said no. They went to our bedroom and turned on the light. As David told it, the curtains moved with the breeze through the open window, as in a movie.

The next morning, my grandfather said, "John, I don't want you to lie to me. I know you and Bob went out the window last night, and I don't think it was the first time. I don't want you to do it again."

Our second warning was less private. Wrestling season was well over. With our friend from the wrestling team, we formed the idea that we would take the chrome rims from the car of a fellow he knew who dated the sister of another friend and team member. The two friends conveyed the impression that the fellow with the fancy car thought too much of himself and could use a lesson.

I drove the car. Bob and our friend jacked up the back end of the fancy car and took off the rear wheels. At that point, the boyfriend came out, saw the work in progress, and ran back inside. That part was cinematic in itself.

The next day, I was called into the police station for questioning, as my car had been seen in the neighborhood. I characterized the action as something like a prank, and the police let me go. Nothing had been stolen.

———

I was rehearsing for the senior play when one of the girls asked me if I had a new little sister. She said she had seen in the newspaper that my parents had had a baby. It was the first I knew about a baby or that my father and Carmen were living together and in the area.

———

Because I was with the senior play, I did not go out on some forays. Bob came back with the news that he and our friend had taken a set of wheels in Willows, the next main town to the south and the county seat. They sold the wheels to a fellow in Orland.

The next evening, I went to the bowling alley after play rehearsal. Bob was to pick me up. As I waited inside by the pinball machines, a policeman came in and asked me to go outside. Bob was standing outside of one patrol car, our friend was in the back seat, and the second patrol car was waiting for me. I stopped to exchange a couple of words with Bob. I said it looked like we were caught. He said, "Tell 'em everything."

Now we were in jail for real. We were kept up late for questioning, under lights, and we were put into separate cells. We were arrested on our mother's birthday and would go to court on Bob's. We would spend all of our spring and Easter break behind bars.

———

After our initial interrogations, we were taken up front for questioning for other offenses we did not commit. In one, someone had stolen tires and left the car up on blocks. I told the policeman we did not do that one, as we did not use blocks. In another, someone stole some large spools of electrical wire, to sell it for the copper. That kind of theft was new to me, and I said so. In what I thought was an unfair accusation, I had to answer to Mrs. Harris's suspicion that I had stolen her camera when I worked for her. An investigator came from Chico and plied me with questions of a psychological nature. He said he was used to dealing with delinquents who took drugs. He said, "I can tell you're not on goofballs, though. If you were on goofballs, you'd be comin' across the table and tryin' to get me." With another investigator, I quoted *Macbeth* on vaulting ambition.

———

Bob and our friend and I were put into the same cell. Tommie came by in the daytime, outside in the sunny spring weather. She smiled and waved and said she had brought cigarettes for Bob. He had been tearing up old butts and rolling cigarettes with the leftover tobacco, like a real jailbird.

———

Carmen came by on another sunny day. She had a baby in her arms. It was my sister, whom I would come to know as Irene, born on March 17, 1966. She was about three weeks old. Carmen said that she and our father were living in that same town, Willows, where the hospital, the jail, and the courthouse were located.

———

I heard my brother call my name. His voice came from the dark outside, below the grated window.

"John. This is Sandy. I heard you and Bob got in trouble."

He had come all the way from San Diego. I gave him a brief account. I didn't have to tell him much if he had already heard it.

He said he would be there for our court appearance.

———

For more than a week, we heard The Mamas and the Papas singing "Monday, Monday" several times a day. On Monday, April 11, we were taken to the courthouse. We waited outside the courtroom, not speaking. Sandy, my father, and my grand-father sat apart from one another. I noticed that the soles on all their shoes were worn down the same, like mine.

We were given a year of supervised probation, with our juvenile records to be sealed if we kept out of trouble. We had to write a report every month and were to show up for any meetings we were called to. With that, we went home with our grandfather.

———

We returned to school the next day. I expected ostracism and hoped for acceptance. The reception was somewhere in between, and it did not happen all at once. Some of my friends treated me with sympathy. People our age got into trouble for one thing and another, but theft was not as venial as fighting or possession of alcohol. Two girls whom I called my social workers, who came from secure home lives and were cheerleaders as well as good students, undertook to understand me. They asked me questions and encouraged me to do my best. The valedictorian told me I could still be a good student. I told him I felt guilty for corrupting our classmate on the wrestling team, and he said that the other boy, who had also been a football player and was part of the in-crowd, had chosen on his own to do something daring. Another friend, who was more cynical but also among the high-achieving students, told me that some of the fellows who scoffed at me or criticized me were, in essence, hypocrites, as they wished in secret that they could do the same thing but they didn't have the nerve. I thought that was an interesting insight, but I wondered how true it was.

Some teachers welcomed me back into class in a matter-of-fact or non-committal way, and I did not mind it. No teachers made unkind comments, which I appreciated, as I had feared that some might.

The young speech and German teacher, who had come from an upper-middle-class family in Chicago, had attended Northwestern University, and had married a sailor stationed at Great Lakes, had taken an interest in my case earlier. In the first semester, she made a comment in class one day, in response to a smart comment of mine, that I must be one of those kids whose parents sent them to summer camp every year. The rest of the class laughed so much that she endeavored to know better. Now she wrote me a letter saying that my family background and the depravity of my father (a word I added to my vocabulary) had helped bring me to this point but I could overcome those disadvantages and try to fulfill my potential. She was very earnest and an amateur psychologist (she told me that a friend of mine was a latent homosexual). She was also the director of the school play, and in my absence, she had yielded to pressure and had put another student—a junior from the speech class—in my role. She put me back into the play, and although mine was not a large role, I avoided one more small humiliation.

My English teacher from the year before stopped me in the hallway and offered his positive comments. He said he understood that young people got into trouble, and he encouraged me to try my best to get over it and continue to pursue my goals.

The wrestling coach, who a year earlier had suggested I write a retraction, also paused in the hallway to offer a few words. He knew the three of us and my brother David as well. He had taken me aside during the season to tell me that Bob reeked of cigarette smoke and I should do something about it. This time, he showed what I thought was more understanding. Like the English teacher, he encouraged me to move ahead.

Mrs. Walker invited me into the separate office she had as a counselor. The old battle-axe and disciplinarian, who had sent Tommie home one day for not wearing a slip, was also a career counselor. She had reviewed my ACT and SAT results with me, and she had helped me with my admissions and financial aid applications. Now she informed me that my California State Scholarship, which would have paid my tuition and fees at Berkeley, had been taken away. Someone from town had notified the board. My other scholarship chances had become dim. It looked as if I was going to have to change my plans and go to Chico State College. But that wasn't all bad, she explained. I could work my way out of this. I just had to put my mind to it and do my best work.

———

A month later, on the Chico State campus with Pioneer Week music and festivities outside the open window, I competed again in the annual math contest sponsored by McClatchy Newspapers, publishers of the Sacramento *Bee* and others.

This time, I took first place. I received a pin like the one I received the year before, smaller than my little fingernail, round, with the letter *pi* on it. I put them on my school sweater, to be joined by my CSF Sealbearer lamp and a small, elegant pin from the Mathematical Association of America.

Mrs. Walker retired with the graduation of our class. Some students remembered her as an old harpy, but for me, she would always be a great educator. She motivated me to do my best from my sophomore year onward, she helped me become the top math student that year, and she helped me restore faith in myself. Many times, in later years, when Sandy and I were faced with a math or geometry problem, he would say, "How would Mrs. Walker have us do it?" or "What would Mrs. Walker say?"

———

The people for whom we had picked up windfall almonds at the end of the previous summer remembered me as a good worker. The girl from the family, a classmate of mine, conveyed the message that her brother Pat had work for me, lining bales. She explained that it was part of hay hauling.

I had hauled hay the year before when Bob and I worked for the cheapskate farmer. We stacked bales on the flatbed trailer, on a haystack, and in the barn. The farmer sent me in his place to do some work for a neighbor with whom he traded labor. The farmer's daughter drove the pickup, the farmer boosted the bales, and I stacked them. I ran out of energy, but it came back. In the barn, I carried bales on top of the stack, up near the roof, where the stifling hot air rose and stayed. The exertion almost finished me off, and I was soaked in sweat when I climbed down in my chaps with my hay hooks in hand.

I was a couple of inches taller and fifteen pounds heavier now, so I was ready to try again.

In lining bales, a person combined three rows at a time, moving the bales on either side into the center row. Thus the hauler did not have to make as many trips up and down the field, and the bales came off the elevator with greater frequency. The hauler made money by the ton, not by the hour. I was paid two cents a bale, I believe, and I was paid for every bale in the field, not just for those I moved. I was able to go out and line a field after school.

When I drove the truck, Pat stacked the bales. He was about twenty-eight, tall and well-built, with his sleeves cut away like most hay haulers. He had been in the Army, and in addition to working for his family, he was making money on his own. The whole family was efficient, and he was a dynamic worker. "Faster!" he shouted to me. "Faster!" He was good-humored as well. There was a little joke to making money, because he put it into his race car.

———

Before my incident with the law, I had developed a crush on another girl in my class, whose father also raised almonds. She was in the senior play, and she had a crush on one of the football players who played the roles of soldiers. (The play was *The Mouse That Roared*.) Undaunted, I wrote her poems.

When the time came for the senior ball, I understood that the football player had asked someone else. The girl I adored was available, and no one wanted to be left out, so she accepted my invitation, with the permission of her parents.

The ball was held at a place called The Blue Gum, a high-class restaurant for that area that sat amidst a grove of euca-lyptus trees on the highway between Orland and Willows, near Artois. We were to have dinner and then dance.

I did not know how to do either. For support, I had the valedictorian and his guest, something of a Platonic pair, to ride along in my car. I was not saved, however. I did not know one salad dressing from another, one steak from another, or one doneness from another. My father had his meat well done, as in the days before refrigeration, so that was what I requested.

When it came time to dance, I confessed that this was my first time. Dancing apart had become popular since the Twist, the Swim, the Mashed Potato, and others, so my companion did not suffer much. For most of the time we were on the dance floor, she was gazing at the one she wished she was with. But she was pleasant to me, even when I pushed the door open with my foot on the way out. "That was classy," she said.

I wrote her a poem in appreciation, a poem enslaved by end-rhyme.

———

With graduation not far away, I was keeping things in order. I had had my senior picture taken, and I had sent a copy to Suzi. Not having a suit or jacket, I had worn a dark wool shirt, and it looked all right. I did not think of a graduation suit, but someone else did.

Tommie's second-oldest brother, who had been in my grade, had dropped out of school, joined the Army, and gone to Southeast Asia. He sent home a couple of suits, one of which must have been too small for him, for his mother had me try it on and then gave it to me. It was of a shiny grey tone, and I thought I would wear it if I had to.

At about the same time, the principal sent me to a shop in

town where I was fitted with a more conservative-looking suit of charcoal grey. He said the Rotary Club was paying for it. A few days later, one of the members took me in his grey Oldsmobile Toronado to the Rotary Club luncheon, where I was introduced as one of the current graduates. Left unspoken, hanging in the air, was the knowledge that I was the recipient of their generosity. Some of the members looked me over in my suit, and one or two spoke to me in a perfunctory way. I had seen movies in which a felon received a new suit on his way out of prison, and I felt somewhere between him and the boy who had been the beneficiary of new shoes with Mr. Burchfield.

The weather being warm, we went to Stony Creek to frolic in the water. In the trunk of the car, I found the copy of *David Copperfield* that I had checked out of the town library. It was swollen and ruined from having gotten wet. I thought I had asked Bob to turn it in for me, but it had ended up in the trunk, and it was my responsibility. Now I had one more thing to feel guilty about.

At the awards ceremony, I was recognized for my math achievements, for CSF Sealbearer, and for foreign languages. The latter award came from Bank of America in the form of a framed certificate "for Distinguished Achievement and Promise of Future Success and Service to Society." The inscription seemed like words on a page to me, vague words that people delivered to embellish the moment. I also received a scholarship for $500 from the Luso-American Education Foundation.

Fifteen years later, I would learn that "Luso" meant relating to Portugal or the Portuguese language. Years after that, I would look at the Bank of America award and appreciate the sincerity of urging young citizens to be of service to society.

––––––

The weather was already hot at mid-morning as our class sat in chairs at the edge of the football field as part of our graduation practice. The principal and the head coach, both in short-sleeved white shirts and neckties, called for me to come forward.

In front of my classmates, but not quite audible to them, the principal said that the coach had some questions to ask me. This was the same coach who had intervened with the track award and who had kept our teammate from going to the state wrestling meet. He had also been my world geography teacher in my sophomore year and was my brother Bob's geography teacher at present.

The coach began his interrogation, which became an accusation. My brother was supposed to have written a term paper on Spain, but he handed in a paper on Denmark. I had done my paper on Denmark two years earlier, during my stellar semester, and now I was accused of conspiring with my brother. I explained that I had let him see my paper so he could see how to do his, but I also stated that I had not encouraged or allowed him to hand in my work. I had been appalled to find out that he handed in the very same report (the coach had not marked on it the first time through), but I did not mention that part during the confrontation.

I had pestered Bob for months to do his work, and now I was being taken to task. I think that, on the brink of graduation, I may have been sassy with the coach. I told him I had always done my own work and had a good academic record. I didn't have to answer to him.

The hot sun beat down on us. I squinted and sweated.

The coach was not much taller than I was. He had a dark, flat-top haircut and black-rimmed glasses, and he seemed constrained by his button-down collar and narrow necktie. He glared. Spit whistled out between his crooked teeth as he shook with anger and said, "I'd like to knock your teeth down your throat."

I was angry, but I had also been threatened and bullied. I went back to my seat and gave a brief explanation to my friends.

Later, I found the principal and told him that I couldn't beat the coach, but if the coach touched me, I would find someone who could. The principal looked at me and did not answer.

Bob received an *F*, but no one called him on the carpet. I thought it was unjust that I had to answer for his conduct, but it was not the first time.

Came graduation. After the ceremony on the football field, I went to the gym to hand in my cap, gown, and cords. The girl who had gone to the senior ball with me had succeeded in being invited to go to the graduation party with the young man she was stuck on. I had invited another girl, a junior girl with blond hair and impressive endowments, who had fallen from grace in another way and was trying to restore her dignity. With her at my side, I headed toward the parking lot.

My father appeared. He had attended the graduation, and now he congratulated me. With a look at my companion, he asked me if I needed him to buy me something to drink. I thanked him and told him I still didn't use any of that stuff.

We went to the dance and played miniature golf and stayed up all night doing nothing. The radio played the Four Seasons singing "Don't You Worry 'Bout Me" a dozen times. Daylight made my eyes heavy as I drove my companion home, past a field where I had lined bales. I drove back to town with a vague, drowsy sense that a door had closed between me and Orland Joint Union High School.

THIRTEEN

My father was driving tractor for a big farming operation out of Willows, and he told us there was an opportunity for Bob to drive tractor cultivating row crops. I did not like the idea very well, as Bob was only sixteen, and a person was supposed to be eighteen to drive machinery. Willows was sixteen miles away, so Bob would have to drive that far each day, plus the distance to whatever field he was working in. The hours were long, also. But Bob always wanted to do what the older guys were doing—or, to put it in terms I used at the time, he wanted to grow up too soon. So he went to work at a grown-up job.

Because we would be working in different places, we needed two cars. We bought a 1952 Packard, pale green, with a sun visor and a straight-eight engine. It was a good car and could run up to a hundred in no time, but the rear end went out, and we couldn't find a replacement, so the Packard went to the junkyard.

We bought a 1954 Oldsmobile, dark green, for about the same price—both of them in the sixty-dollar range. Bob drove the Oldsmobile for a while until one morning, when he was sleepy, he ran it into a telephone pole. He was not injured, but the car was ruined.

We found him a 1960 Ford Falcon, red and white, for five hundred dollars. Now he and I each had a car of about the same age and value.

————

I drove Grandpa to the barbershop in town on a hot summer day. I sat and listened as he told the barber how they used to skin sheep in the old country.

When we left the barbershop, my grandfather gave me twenty-five cents and told me to buy myself a soda pop while he had a beer. He walked across the street to the Orlando, which sat on the corner. I waited in the soda fountain until I saw him come out and stand in the shade of the overhang. I finished my soft drink and went out to the car to drive it around and take him home.

We went through this routine more than once. He told the barber more than once how they used to skin sheep. It was a comfortable routine, like eight or nine years earlier, when I went with him from Grimes to Yuba City to sell our animals at the auction. We ate beef stew in the auction yard café, and he bought me a soda pop afterwards.

————

Grandpa had cataract surgery in both eyes in the course of the summer, which required several trips to Chico for the surgery, for changing the bandages, and for checkups. I had to take time out of the work day, in the afternoon, when lunch and the heat would make me drowsy.

When I drifted off the shoulder and came awake, Grandpa would make a mild comment like, "Need to stay awake, there," or "Keep it on the road."

———

I was working at various farm tasks such as hauling hay, irrigating, building fence, driving tractor, and hoeing weeds. One of my pals, who was a bit of a hoodlum but was willing to work, went with me on a couple of jobs. In the middle of the summer, we found ourselves picking pears at Mills Orchards.

At this job, we worked on a crew, picking by the bag and emptying the hard, green pears into the bins on the trailer, or wagon. The crew took four rows through the orchard, two on each side of the drive. In other systems, when people picked by the box or the bin, they might each have a row or a set of four to six trees. With the crew system, as a general rule, people picked four rows across, and each picker or pair of pickers was expected to take the next tree in line. However, some pickers skipped trees that had poorer picking or jumped ahead to trees that looked better. A crew often had a row boss to make sure everything went well, and sometimes the row boss went from one crew to another.

As with many methods of harvest, moving through an orchard, whether it was by the tree, by the row, or by the set, worked well as long as no one took advantage or got out of order or cheated in some way. Working in the fields had its own law of the jungle if people were allowed to get away with things; and in places where there was an all-Mexican crew, or an almost-all-Mexican crew with two *gabachos* joining, and a Mexican row boss, it was just human nature for people to do devious things. Depending on the crop and the system, pickers sometimes left their buckets with their ladders in the orchard overnight. In the morning, a worker might find his bucket replaced with a damaged one, or his ladder exchanged for a broken or wobbly one. More than once, I scratched my initials in the side rail of a ladder.

During the day, pickers might try moves other than skipping trees. They might offer to help someone catch up, and they would pick the bottom or the better parts of the tree and leave the original worker stuck with all the cleanup. Some pickers would pick the best parts of their own trees and move on, as to the next orchard, and the row boss would assign someone else to clean up. All of these moves were facilitated by a foreman who sympathized with the opportunists. With a bit of distance, it is all rather amusing, but at the time, it was infuriating. When a person had to stay behind to clean up trees, he had to carry his fruit farther to the wagon. When he had to pick poor trees or half-picked trees, he made less money. When he knew that others were laughing at him, he resented it. The closed-in heat and humidity of the orchard, plus the always-running tractor engine, raised the aggravation a little higher.

When we reached the end of the orchard, my pal and I let the crew turn around and head the other way. We stood for a long moment with our ladders straight up, and we let them fall. We walked out to the car and drove back to headquarters.

We checked in our picking bags at the Dutch door where in orange season we would check out or check in our picking bags and clippers and where other workers would check out pruning shears or other tools. The woman who worked there knew us. Her son was the wrestler who didn't get to go to the state tournament. Her husband was the supervisor in the prune shed where my father had worked and where Carmen had sorted on the conveyor belt. We all knew each other, and there was nothing outrageous in our complaint that we were fed up with our treatment. There would be other times and other crops.

This was a liberating moment, far different from those endless earlier days when one had no choice. On my own, at seventeen, I might still dread some of the heat and drudgery of the day ahead, but the work and the wages were my opportunity. Leaving the field at the end of each day, going back to my own car, gave a small sense of freedom. Being able to say, I've had enough, I don't have to take this shit, gave a larger sense.

This same pal and I were referred to a small-scale job of knocking almonds for an old man about eighty years old who said he had run the bakery in town for many years. He had a small orchard and put us to work spreading canvas and knocking the almonds with rubber mallets and the usual long poles. After knocking a tree, we gathered the almonds by tipping the sheets and dragging them to bunch up the nuts into a shed drawn by an old grey Ford tractor. From there we shoveled the almonds into burlap bags.

My good-humored pal sang, "Bringing in the sheets," to the tune of the well-known church hymn.

We broke the handle on one of the mallets, so the old man lent us his car to go to the hardware store to buy another mallet. The car was a 1953 Plymouth with a maroon body and a grey top. (As with all cars, the registration was in clear view.) The car was in very good condition, as the old man kept it in a garage and did not drive it much. The radio had good reception and sound, also.

I found it gratifying to be trusted by the old man and to be trustworthy in return. About a year and a half earlier, this same pal and I had stood by and watched as a runaway kid of about fifteen broke the glass on the front door of a grocery store, went in, and came out with fifths of whiskey and cartons of cigarettes. I did not smoke or drink, so it was a kind of amoral diversion. When I was working for wages, I didn't have anything to do with that kind of activity, and now that I had been in trouble, I was even more set on showing myself as a good worker.

On the second day of this short job, I went home for lunch, and my grandfather told me that a man named Harry needed me to work that afternoon, as his almonds were ready and he couldn't wait. Harry was Pat's brother. Their sister, Ann, had just graduated with me. I had worked for Harry picking windfall almonds the year before, I had worked for Pat lining bales, I had worked for Harry hoeing weeds, and I had worked with all of them pouring a concrete slab for their almond shed. Pat mixed the concrete by hand, Ann drove the tractor to pour the wet mix into the forms, and Harry and I worked the mix, tamping and leveling it. I had agreed to go to work in the almonds for a solid month at the best farm wage around, $1.75 an hour, and Harry needed me.

I made my apologies to the old man, whom I had told ahead of time that I had another job to go to, and I went to work for Harry. At twenty-four, he ran the whole farming operation, after the recent death of their father. Pat and I were the knocking crew.

I had worked for a short while the summer before for yet another older man, the father of another girl in my class, who had an old crank-up John Deere and a lightweight sled. He had had a heart attack, so he let me and Robert knock the almonds by hand and drive the tractor. With my more recent employer, the long-since-retired owner of the bakery, my pal and I followed a similar method. It was all hard work, but it was calm and unhurried. With Harry and Pat, all work was efficient and in high gear.

At an earlier time, when I was hoeing weeds, I had asked Harry if I could work more hours. He told me he could get a day's work out of a man in eight hours, and I saw soon enough that both he and Pat could achieve that goal.

Harry had built a wooden step for me right above the power take-off (PTO) of an old Oliver tractor that was in very good condition. I stepped up into the seat and pushed the hand clutch, and the tractor took off, pulling the sled. Pat pulled out a sheet and dropped it flat. I stopped when the edge of the sheet was about to touch the trunk of the tree. I jumped down and pulled out the other sheet while Pat drove the tractor with the shaker to the current tree. He shook, and I poled any of the stubborn almonds, always watchful for hornets and wasps, as when I knocked prunes. I might also have to hit a branch or two with a mallet, then put it in the sled with the poles.

Pat and I tipped the sheets to make a row of almonds in the middle of each canvas, perpendicular to the wooden sled where the edge of the canvas was cleated to the open side. Each of us gathered a sheet and worked it through our encircled arms, like drawing a napkin through a ring, and dumped the almonds into the sled. Then each of us would pull in the sheet, stacking it in folds so that it could be pulled out smooth at the next tree. This was the same work I had done for the other two growers, but our method was vigorous and efficient.

Harry saw to it that we had wooden bins close to where we would need them. Either he or someone else (like Ann) used a forklift tractor to set out empties and take in full ones. The bins were almost twice the size of a peach or prune bins, being square and tall.

When the sled was full, Pat and I would roll or walk a bin into place next to the high back wall of the sled, and each of us would take up a scoop shovel. At that point in my life, I had not settled into shoveling in just one way, so I shoveled left while Pat shoveled right. He was pleased with that compatibility as well.

As with other crops, different varieties (such as the Nonpareil and the Neplus) ripened at different times, so that the grower could harvest them in sequence and not have everything ripen at once. At times, given the nature of the orchard, we needed a third hand. One fellow came to work for a day, told tall tales of stacking hay bales fourteen high on a truck in a hundred-degree heat (as Pat and I exchanged glances), and came back from lunch saying that he didn't have much of an appetite in this heat and had a quart of beer for lunch. I thought he might die that afternoon, and he did not come back.

My brother Bob came, and he did better, but Pat and I were already in shape for this work; and Bob, who was always as good a worker as any employer or coworker ever met, struggled at being thrust into this new exertion in the intense heat.

In another orchard, my brother David came to help. He was small for his age at fourteen, but he picked windfalls and helped with the sheets. At one moment in my fast-paced work, I tossed a mallet head-first into the sled, and the handle slapped straight up, hitting David below the eye as he stood on the other side of the sled.

"You!" he hollered. But he didn't say what. I think that for a moment, he thought I did something deliberate. It gave him a black eye but nothing like the pair he had after the car wreck on the Coast Highway almost five years earlier.

Harry always gave us an hour at lunch. It was part of his method of getting a day's work in eight hours. Most farm jobs in those times had ten-hour days and more, with a half-hour lunch. With an hour, a man could go home and drink a quart of beer. Two boys could go into town, which Bob and I did. Even if we packed our lunch, we could have a cold soda pop and see if there were any girls were around—which, of course, there never were.

One day we had to wait for a train and arrived at the yard a few minutes late. When I told Harry about having to wait for a train, he smiled and said, "One excuse is as good as another." That was a good lesson to carry into the orchard with me. It stayed with me, because it was true. Regardless of the reason, or the excuse, lateness is lateness, and someone may be waiting. Years later, and for many years, I would share the saying with my students, explaining in a positive way, I hope, that the reason is always a good one for the principal person, but it does not change the outcome. And I would remember Harry, the great taskmaster, smiling.

For most of the season, it was Pat and I, working our perfect little industry, drinking coffee from the same plastic thermos cup, enjoying the hard work, and enjoying doing it well. Pat told me stories about running the hurdles in high school, outrunning a cop at a railroad crossing when he was in the Army, and driving his race car. Destruction derbies were just becoming popular in our part of the country, and he told me about attending one of them. Most of the time, we worked. We talked only during the ten-minute breaks. Like all seasons in the fields, this one came to an end when the crop was in.

————

Bob and I needed any money we could earn. With Grandpa's permission, we went to work for a few days in the Chico-Durham area, where almond harvesting was still under way.

Through the labor office, we found a job knocking young trees with rubber mallets. The grower chewed us out for skinning the thin bark. He said, "It's just like gangrene in a man." When we finished knocking, he put us to work raking the almonds into windrows to be picked up by a machine. His son, who was about fourteen, worked with us for a little while. He was one of a couple of fellows I have seen who had big teeth and worked with their mouths open, so that dust settled on their teeth.

Bob and I slept in the car on the river bank for a couple of nights. We ate cold food and behaved ourselves. At the end of the job, he went back to stay with Grandpa and David, and I went off to college.

————

Chico State College had a picturesque campus, with ivy-covered brick buildings, trees and lawns and hedges, and a creek running through with clear water and smooth stones. The college was established in 1887, the year my grandfather was born, so it had an established presence in our area. About fifteen students from my graduating class were attending, plus students from previous classes. I also recognized students from other towns, whom I knew from wrestling or from having lived there.

Among the students from Gridley was a girl I had known in the first grade and eighth grade and who, out of hundreds, had sat straight across from me the fall before when we took the ACT exam in the college gym.

Also among acquaintances from the past was Webb, the brother of Avery, who had been Sandy's ally. I had known that they had gone to Guam to live with their original father and had taken his name, and Webb now confirmed that information. He also told me about his brother beating up a homosexual and spending time in prison for it. He said that Avery was the toughest guy on Guam and suffered when he had to endure the hardships of prison. Webb himself was now following the Lord and had a bit of a sanctimonious air about him, but he was friendly and earnest.

Almost everyone in our area knew the college in some way. I had been on the campus to take the standardized exams and to compete in the math contest. People from the college came to our communities to give choir concerts, guest lectures, career day presentations, and similar talks. The wrestling coach refereed high school matches and tournaments.

I did not feel like a stranger, but there was much that I did not know about college. No one in my family had gone to college, and I did not know any older students well enough to have visited with them when they came home. Some of my fellow students had come for summer orientation, but I had seen that as a great cost at a time when I had to be working.

I did not know what a major was. I thought it was a person's strongest subject, so I declared my major as mathematics and my minor as Spanish. When I acquired a college catalog and looked into it, I was surprised to learn that with time, a person took more and more classes in the major area and few to none in other areas. I had always enjoyed all subjects, and I had thought that college would be four more years of studying all of them every semester. As I looked in the catalog, I became interested in studying beyond a bachelor's degree, but I wondered if I wanted to spend all that much time in mathematics.

I did not understand the idea of general education or breadth requirements. My friends were full of jargon, telling me that they were taking Western Civ and Poli Sci for this and that requirement. I had to read the college catalog to make up for that lack of knowledge.

I met with my advisor, a math professor, who helped me set up a list of classes. I went to a day-long session of arena registration in the gym, where students waited in long lines for computer cards for the respective classes. When a class closed, the student had to rearrange his or her schedule, hand in cards, and stand in line for more.

At the end of this harrowing process, I had my picture taken for the yearbook.

I ended up with a schedule of calculus, history of Western civilization, English, Spanish, and Humanities Honors. I did not know what the humanities were or what honors courses were, but I understood that I was invited into the course on the basis of my entrance exams. In English, my ACT score allowed me to be exempted from the first-year composition course, so I went into a sophomore-level general literature class. I also went out for the wrestling team, which fulfilled a P.E. requirement. I found out soon enough, however, that I was way below the varsity wrestlers in ability. I went to the workouts and practices and became much better, but the grown men were still far superior.

For my living situation, I could not afford to live in a dorm, and I did not want to live among so many people anyway. I found a vacancy at the least expensive boarding house on the list (new students had to live in approved housing unless they had parental consent to do otherwise). The boarding house was about twenty blocks from campus, in a quiet residential area where people burned oak leaves in the gutter. I did not mind the distance. Street parking next to campus was easy, as I had a class at seven-thirty, and walking was always easy as well.

One of the lads in the boarding house was from Gridley and had some of the same friends I had, so we got along well. Another lodger was from Chico, so we knew some of the same people. The fourth boarder was the landlady's grandson, who bragged of getting drunk and having sex with a girl in front of his friends and not remembering it. He said he played the guitar, and I wondered about that as well, until he plugged in his instrument and filled up the room with the first few lines of "Get Off My Cloud."

Living in the boarding house included having plenty to eat. The landlady mixed instant milk with dairy milk, but she fed us full meals. We also had hot showers, which I had not enjoyed at home for a couple of years. I even brushed my teeth with warm water for a while.

Another luxury was the telephone. We had a time limit, but we were allowed social calls. Not having had a phone since Half Moon Bay, I felt as if I was catching up. And there were lots of girls at college. One evening when I was chatting away, I said to the girl, "The old bag isn't here tonight, so I can talk as long as I want."

A few minutes later, I cringed when I saw a light beneath the door that led from our dining area to her part of the house.

The next day, she said, "I heard what you said last night about the old bag not being home. I want to remind you that you have a time limit on the phone whether I'm here or not."

I mumbled something like an apology. I was embarrassed, of course. But I still had that self-protective shell around me that kept me from understanding that I might have hurt her feelings. I am sure she was used to brash young men and didn't mind the opportunity to one-up me, but I wish I had had the capacity then to learn my lesson better. One hopes that even when the regret comes many years later, it contributes to the sum of better sentiments in the world.

————

Being exempt from the composition class and being placed in the honors class made me feel like a smart kid. I wrote an essay for the boarding house student from Chico, and when he received a C on it, he said he would write his own essays. I did not know that writing college essays was on a higher level than in high school. I did not know what a thesis or main idea was, on that level, so being exempted turned out to be a disservice that I did not understand or overcome for quite a while.

In the honors class, we read great works and talked about great ideas. We read *The Iliad*, the Greek tragedies, Dante's *Inferno*, *Hamlet*, and parts of *Paradise Lost*. We learned about polytheism, monotheism, predestination, free will, and all of the related ideas that were useful to an educated person. I received B's on my essay exams and papers, and I did not know what I lacked.

In the English class, we began by reading *The Sound and the Fury* by William Faulkner, so I had my head under water from the beginning. We went on to read short stories, including "That Evening Sun" by Faulkner, "The Lottery" by Shirley Jackson, and "The Jockey" by Carson McCullers. The professor made sense of these stories for us, as he did with a couple of modern plays and a long sequence of poems by Robert Frost. He was a good professor with a wry sense of humor, and he seemed to enjoy letting the more experienced student argue with him about the works we read.

He was in his early thirties, I would guess. He was in good shape, and he worked out in the weight room where we did some of our pre-season conditioning for the wrestling team. He was droll and friendly there. I noticed that he wore hearing aids. He had his office in one of a few buildings that the college rented across the street from campus. When I visited him there, I thought I might have been in the office of an optometrist or an insurance agent, as the light came in through a wall of opaque glass blocks. In the second semester, I saw him once on campus, and he told me to drop by some time before it was all over. I didn't get around to it, and when I came back to school in the fall, I heard from a couple of other students that he had died. I asked what he died of, and the student with the news laughed and said, "He just died, that's all." I thought it was way too bad that a promising young professor would die and then be tossed off in a comment. I wished I had gone to see him. I wondered if he had had a premonition.

Years later, when I would read Frost's "The Road Not Taken" in preparation for class discussion, I would remember this professor's presenting the poem, and Frost in general, as something to be taken with ironic possibilities. His name was Beatty, and I have always been sorry that he was not able to live longer and to be of more benefit to a greater number of students.

My Spanish class that first semester was interesting. I was placed into an intermediate-level class, where we learned terminology and features of phonetics and phonology. Our instructor was a young and pleasant woman from a Central American country, an aspect in itself that helped me become aware of the larger world of Spanish-speaking people.

The history class was a large lecture class in which I kept myself attentive by taking notes in shorthand. Re-reading my notes was an amusement as I reviewed them with friends in the class.

My hardest and least enjoyable class was Calculus, which did not bode well for a math major. The professor was an older man from Czechoslovakia. He did not explain himself well in English, and he did not seem to have the talent of some teachers, like Mrs. Walker, to understand what the student needed to have explained. When I or another student asked a question, he would do the problem on the board. If we asked a second question, he would do the problem again. He did not explain the concepts of differentiation and integration or the applications. He would just say, "This is Zigma," in his accent, and do the problem. As everyone knows, in mathematics, each step builds on the previous one, and a person has to understand everything all along. I could see that I was losing ground, though I was able to salvage a *B* in the class.

About halfway through the semester, I went home one Friday night. I had been out late, so, rather than come in late and wake up my grandfather, I parked my car off to the edge of the driveway, behind some bushes and next to the neighboring cabin. I planned to sleep in my car and to go inside the next morning as if I had just gotten there. That way, I wouldn't have to discuss how late I had stayed out.

At some hour between midnight and sunrise, I woke up to the mutter of voices. Lying still and quiet, I picked up a few scraps of conversation. One voice was my grandfather's, and the other I recognized as belonging to the father of a friend of Bob's named Ray. I peeked out and saw their family car, bronze in the moonlight with its motor running and its headlights shining. I gathered that my brother Bob and his friend had been in a car wreck and were in the hospital in Corning. I did not interpret a need in either my grandfather on in Ray's father to go there that night. So, rather than let my grandfather know that I had been out late and was trying to cover it up, I went back to sleep, or tried.

The next morning, I went in for breakfast and pretended to be hearing the news for the first time. I learned that the wreck had been on the highway in front of two truck stops, that Ray had been driving Bob's car, and that a third fellow, the friend who had gotten into trouble with Bob and me, had been with them. I still did not know how serious any of their injuries were.

I drove my grandfather and David to Corning, and we stopped at the truck stop on the right. An attendant said that the wreck had happened across the highway, as the car was turning left into the other truck stop. I asked if anyone was hurt bad. The attendant laughed and said hell, yes, he guessed at least one of them had got killed, he had his head split wide open.

. It was just a few minutes' drive to the hospital from there, but in those few minutes I didn't know what to think. If someone had died, Ray's father should have known. The cold-hearted truck stop attendant seemed pretty sure. I wondered if I should harbor the selfish hope that if someone did die, it was not my brother but one of our friends. I had to prepare myself for the worst, that my brother might be dead; and then, no matter how I hoped, I felt guilty.

At the hospital we found the room with no trouble, and we walked in, still uncertain. There, seated around a table and playing cards, were all three boys, alive. It was a great relief to have expected the worst, and the next to worst, and then to find out that nothing of the sort had happened. But it hadn't been a false alarm. All three of them had bandages around their heads, had been stitched up, and would have scars. I learned that there had been some cracked heads and a lot of blood.

One aspect that threw me off balance was how cheerful my brother sat there playing cards and telling about the accident, how he had been making out with a girl in the back seat, how he had been her protection, and how she had already visited him that morning and kissed and hugged him in the deepest gratitude and had been run out by the nurses. It was all a jolly story to them.

Later, when I went to check on Bob's car, I saw the crumpled steering wheel and the hole in the windshield on the passenger's side, where our other friend had plunged through. And I saw where my brother had bounced around in the back seat, serving as sort of a cushion for the girl who was with him.

I felt at odds with myself, having felt guilty and uncertain and still not knowing how I should feel.

————

In the semester system of those years, the first semester did not end until late January. I had a research paper to do for the Humanities Honors course, and I had it hanging over me during Christmas vacation.

I worked for part of that vacation for my seasonal employer, Harry, pruning trees and hauling brush. Harry's mother worked with us, and she brought oranges from their tree. Harry, always cheerful, said an orange was not worth his time to peel it, so his mother peeled his. She brought him Snickers candy bars, and those were worth the effort to unwrap. We had a jovial time working and laughing in the cold, wet orchard as Harry would tell me which branches to cut. And his mother always had my check ready, with the wages and deductions written in neat handwriting on the envelope.

————

Back in Chico and the boarding house for the last part of the vacation, I spent long, dreary hours at the library trying to figure out what I should include in my paper on symbolism in Greek tragedy. We had not learned to do anything but borrow sources in high school, and if there were any tutoring sources available in college, I did not know about them. In the end, I put together a paper to hand in, and I received my characteristic B.

————

The Plymouth Valiant began to shudder and tremble, so Bob and I traded it in for a 1954 orange-and-white Pontiac station wagon. Like the Buick and the Cadillac and the Oldsmobile, it was a good, sturdy car. I drove it a hundred miles an hour a couple of times, but I treated it well otherwise. I drove it back and forth to work for Harry until the transmission gave out on me one morning. I was on foot, but I didn't mind it. I knew how to hitchhike.

Our father and Carmen and the little ones were living in Gridley in the government housing we had known of when we lived there in my eighth-grade year. I drove down to Gridley early in the semester when Carmen's sister Patricia was visiting. One day in winter, Bob and I hitchhiked from Chico to Gridley and back. On the return, we rode in the bed of a pickup. A heavy rain began to fall, and we stayed dry by sitting up close to the cab.

For semester break, my roommate from Gridley and I decided we would hitchhike to L.A. It seemed like a large, daring thing to do, and some of our friends raised their eyebrows. We made it to San Jose the first day, where my friend had a family friend who had a young family and an apartment. The fellow put us up for the night and set us out on the freeway early the next morning.

Cars whizzed by like I had never seen, and before long, we each had a citation for being pedestrians on the freeway, and we were confined to on-ramps from then on.

We spent most of the day getting to Santa Cruz, which was not very far. Looking for another place where we could mooch, I found Grandma Christensen's number in the telephone directory. Things had not built up much in six years, and I found our way to Bethany Curve.

I had an enjoyable visit with Grandma Christensen. She fixed us a good meal, had us take baths, and showed us a room where we could spend the night. She told us that Fred and his younger female cousin were still living there and that Fred would be home soon. She showed us pictures of him in his drum major outfit.

Fred came home, driving a grey coupe from the late 1940s. He invited us to go out and cruise with him. He knew where to go, and we ended up hanging around with a couple of sleazy girls who knew Fred from high school. They smoked cigarettes and told us not to sit on cold concrete steps because they gave a person the piles. They went into a liquor store and stole a couple of half-pint bottles of vodka. None of this interested me, but my roommate liked to drink, and Fred was interested in the vodka as well, and one never knew what things might lead to with the girls.

Fred's girlfriend showed up in her car, having seen Fred's, so he went up to her window with a great show of affection to block out her view of the two girls. Fred came back and told us we had to go, as he was going to meet his girlfriend at his grandmother's house. We drove off with one of the bottles of vodka stashed in his coupe.

My friend and I were beginning to run out of steam for going all the way to L.A. and making it back in time for classes, and we did not look forward to seeing more of Fred. So we left Grandma Christensen's that night, on foot, and trudged toward the highway. The air was cold and foggy, so we found a closed-off stretch of asphalt and slept in the same sleeping bag until daybreak.

On the way back to Chico, my friend told me that no one had to pay those tickets for hitchhiking on the freeway. They were like parking tickets, and San Jose was a long way away. I had just turned eighteen and didn't know that much, but I thought I was adventurous, defiant, tough, and wise to the world. We made it back to Chico, admitted to our friends that L.A. was a bad idea, and made ready for the next semester.

———

My friend from Gridley, along with another fellow we both knew from Gridley, plus a classmate of mine from Orland, and I rented an old, two-story house on the southeast side of Chico. A fifth fellow, from Oroville, joined us, as he knew one or both of the fellows from Gridley. My thought was that we could live for less and we could cook our own food. My father even brought a box of groceries, as a gesture of contributing to my education.

I soon discovered what life was like with four other undisciplined young adults. They drank and shouted. My brother Bob came over and drank and shouted with them. The fellow from Oroville put on comedy records for him and others to laugh at. When he got drunk, he disclosed that he hated his father and would like to kill him. My friend from Orland, whose father had died during the summer, became maudlin when he talked about his own father. I did not drink, and the second fellow from Gridley drank only a little. He also went home on weekends, so he put a padlock on his bedroom door. The others were determined to have raging parties, and they did.

I knew things were not going well when a couple of party animals broke the hasp off the absent roommate's door so they could take a girl into the room. I was getting fed up as well, and a general sense of displeasure was spreading among the five housemates. The second fellow from Gridley and I agreed to look for a place of our own.

We found a cottage on the other side of town, off the highway as it came in from Orland and Hamilton City. On the first day that I saw that my other roommate from Gridley was not wearing any of my clothes, the more civil fellow and I made our move.

———

I was close to broke at this point. I sold the motor out of my Pontiac to the girlfriend of my recent roommate from Orland, who did not begrudge us for breaking up the party house. I sold the body of the Pontiac for salvage.

I was trying to keep up my schoolwork and was not always doing well at it. At the beginning of the second semester, I saw that I was too far behind in calculus, so I dropped calculus and took a literature course. In the humanities course, we were reading *Gulliver's Travels,* philosophers like Kierkegaard and Nietzsche, and French writers such as Sartre and Camus as we moved toward existentialism. In the literature course, we were reading *Candide, The Red and the Black, Crime and Punishment, Sanctuary* and *Requiem for a Nun, Metamorphosis* and *The Penal Colony,* and *No Exit* as we moved toward existentialism. Some of my reading was not very thorough.

I still did not know what was missing in my essays. In those days, there was a distance between the professor and the student, as the professor set the graded papers on a table in front of the class and allowed the students to find theirs as they saw the grades on the front pages of the other students' work. Essays not picked up in class were left in a box in the hallway outside the professor's office. For my essay on Kafka, I tried to do something more imaginative, and I received a C. I went to the professor's office to ask what I could do better. I did not know that many people of his rank did not grade their own papers but had a reader or a grader. In my naive way, I thought he knew me and remembered my work, so I asked him what I should do. He shrugged and said, in a confidential way, that I should try something different, something that was not like all the others. One thing impressed me in our meeting. He was dexterous in tipping up his pack of Camels with one hand, letting a single cigarette fall out, taking it between two fingers of the same hand, and holding it as he lit it.

I was struggling in my physics course. I was placed in a course for science, math, and engineering majors, but our physics course in high school had been very soft. I was afraid of the college course, but I kept up a passing grade.

On the bright side, I did well in Spanish. We were reading

plays, poems, and short stories. Along with the humanities course and the literature course, the Spanish course was helping me do something I had always wanted to do, and that was to be well read. I had become an English major, although I did not have an advisor or a plan in that area.

One other class rounded out my course of study. I had enrolled in the second semester of first-year English. That course did not teach principles of composition or essay writing, but the professor had us keep a journal for a few times each week for several weeks. He criticized me for writing short sentences like Hemingway's, to which I took exception, not having read but a couple of stories by him in high school. I tried to follow the professor's suggestions to write in different ways and to explore feelings, but at that point, all of my efforts were rigid exercises. On the more positive side, we also read several short stories from an anthology that I kept and continued to read on my own.

———

I made a good move by renting the cottage with the civil chap from Gridley. However, I gravitated toward hanging out with a couple of other pals from Orland, both of whom were taking classes at Chico State and whose families had moved to Chico. These fellows were living at home, so they had stability, but they thought it was cute to go out and steal things like a coffeepot or a crystal decanter or a bicycle. They knew I had some experience in that area, so they drew upon my knowledge.

I found myself drifting back into petty crime. I was not doing dilettante theft like my friend who would ping his crystal decanter and enjoy the sound. When I needed a pair of shoes or a pair of pants, I knew how to get them. I procured concealable food items such as lunch meat or round steak. Thinking of myself as an honest person, I confessed my transgressions in my probation reports, which I was always diligent about writing. The austere probation officer wrote back a warning.

———

Toward the end of the school year, a police car pulled off the highway and into the driveway by our cottage. One of the two deputies asked for me.

They said they had a warrant for me for failure to appear on a hitchhiking ticket in Santa Clara County. The bail was thirty-six dollars. I had only twenty dollars, as I had just given my rent money to my roommate. He would not lend it back, so I had to use my remaining money to pay a bail bondsman. I had to go to jail either way, but by not paying the bond myself, I would have to go to San Jose during finals week.

———

I hitchhiked to San Jose and stayed in a two-dollar hotel room. In the morning, with a haircut, shirt, and tie to make me presentable, I appeared in court. I spoke in a clear, steady voice and waived my right to an attorney. The judge was courteous. He asked me what the enrollment was at Chico State. I told him it was about 6500. (Later I would learn that his was a common question that professional and business people knew to ask about a college.) I explained the circumstances of not having enough to pay the bond and thus having to appear in person during final exams, all for a citation that had had a two-dollar fine to begin with, which I was sorry not to have taken care of. He asked me how I had traveled to San Jose, and I told him I hitchhiked. He asked me if I would promise to take the bus back if he dismissed the fine, and I said yes.

I took the bus to Chico, finished my final exams and the school year, and got away from petty crime for a while.

FOURTEEN

n the procession of used cars that we went through, Bob's damaged Ford Falcon went the way of many others. A movement had begun in the country, championed by Lady Bird Johnson, to hide the junkyards from the common eye, and the businesses would become auto dismantlers and salvage yards. As a sequel, used cars would become pre-owned vehicles. In early 1969, Bob and I would visit a large auto dismantler in central Los Angeles, in search of a wiring harness for a Plymouth Valiant he had at that time, and the man in charge said no one had time to take the harness out of their specimen, which would be "crushed flat as a bitch" the next day. But in our present world, junk yards were still junk yards, where we could go in and find a part ourselves—a window crank, a piece of carburetor linkage, a hub or axle spindle—disconnect it, bring it to the shack or counter, and pay somewhere between twenty-five cents and five dollars.

With the Falcon and my Pontiac station wagon both gone, we bought a 1953 Plymouth, again in the sixty-dollar range. The car was a dull grey with reddish primer showing through on the worn spots. It had a standard transmission and no power steering, so one day when David went with me to

Paradise to visit one of my more intellectual friends, I put the Plymouth out of gear, shut off the engine, and let it coast for miles downhill toward Chico.

Now at the end of the school year, I packed up my few clothes, books, and kitchen utensils, put them in the Plymouth, and drove to Orland.

Disorder was under way. Grandpa had been taken to the hospital to have the lower part of one leg amputated. He was turning eighty, and he had had diabetes for longer than any of us knew. He had not let anyone know about his toes, and gangrene had set in.

He was going to be in the hospital for a while and would be transferred to a rest home after that. Bob and David were going to have to live somewhere else. The reasonable choice was to stay with Suzi, who had moved with her husband and children to Vista, near Escondido in San Diego County.

Most of these decisions were made in a short while as I was finishing my semester in Chico, without a phone as usual. At this same time, Sandy came home on leave after a cruise on an aircraft carrier to the Philippines and to the edge of the war in Vietnam. He had sent me money during the cruise, having done well at poker and pinochle as well as not being in port very often to spend his pay, and he had told me I was free to use the money for college expenses and to pay him later. I owed him four hundred dollars, which he was not worried about, as he was flush with his more recent earnings. So was his good friend, Magoo, an entertaining fellow from Tennessee.

They were sailors on leave after a long cruise. They had bought a dark-blue 1958 Chevy, and they were cracking twenties, to use Sandy's phrase, to buy gasoline, cigarettes, beer, and hamburgers. Gasoline was about twenty-nine cents a gallon, cigarettes still cost around twenty-five cents a pack, and beer cost a dollar and a half for a six-pack. David and I did not smoke or drink, but we joined in on the hilarity. We heard stories about the girls in Tijuana, the girls in the Philippines, and the "smoker" or boxing match in which Sandy beat Holcomb the Hawk.

Sandy's old friend Avery showed up, saucy as ever, married, and not showing much wear from having been in prison in Guam.

Tommie was out of circulation, having gotten pregnant with someone we didn't know and having had a baby with red hair like hers. Her friend Sue, sister of Walt and Robert, had an older boyfriend named Dennis, who drank Sandy and Magoo's beer and moaned about the martyrdom of having to milk cows twice a day.

While Bob and David finished the school year, Dennis went with Sandy, Magoo, and me to Modesto, where our father and his family were living in a government housing camp. Money ran out, and we hoed weeds for a couple of days. We worked with long-handled hoes, but Dennis ended up on his knees, making small, pitiful strokes with his hoe. The foreman spoke English and was kind to him.

Sandy and Magoo received their most recent paychecks, so we went to the boardwalk in Santa Cruz, as Sandy and I had done in our newspaper days. Sandy met a girl from Turlock, and I met a girl from Walnut Creek.

We went to see our grandfather in the hospital. He was in something of a fog and seemed to be processing the loss of his leg.

Back in Orland, we vacated the rental house. Bob and David would ride with Sandy and Magoo to the San Diego area. The Miramar Naval Air Station was located between Escondido and San Diego. Dennis and I went along as far as Turlock in Dennis's light-blue 1952 Oldsmobile. After Sandy said goodbye to his new girlfriend, I said goodbye to my brothers, and the 1958 Chevy went south.

Dennis and I drove out on a ditchbank to sleep in the car, but we were rousted by deputy sheriffs and were told to move along.

In Orland again, life slowed down. I had the 1953

Plymouth with my few possessions, a couple of cast-iron skillets, and a box with Grandpa's meat saws, cleavers, and butcher knives. I had a job opportunity in Big Sur, but other than that, I did not have a place to live or anyone to answer to in the summer of 1967.

———

My friend who liked to listen to the ring of crystal had an unconventional family. The mother and her five children had all taken the last name of the stepfather, a schoolteacher named Jones. When we were sophomores in high school, I asked my friend how long the parents had been married, and he said, "Oh, they wouldn't make that mistake again." I believe they were independent and free-spirited. The father did not like being pressured to join the teacher's union in Orland, so he took a job in Chico and moved the family into a large house that used to be a fraternity house. On one of my visits there, I noticed the mother's amiable habit of wandering from one room to the next with no clothes on.

They were getting ready to go to Big Sur, where they went every summer to work in the resorts. My friend told me it was easier work than farm work, it paid better, and it was all in a cool, coastal climate. The family invited me to leave my things at their house and to join them in Big Sur in a week, and they would find me a job.

I stored my books and clothes and kitchen things in one of their many rooms. I also had a bicycle there, which I had stored at the end of the school year. I left the box of butcher equipment and the skillets in the back seat of my car.

I went to see my grandfather again, stopped to see Tommie's mother, and parked the Plymouth on the street in Chico where the former fraternity house took up a large corner lot. My host family had told me there wasn't much space at their lodgings for another car, and I in my confident way said I would hitchhike, which I did.

———

Big Sur was new to me, being off the main roads I knew. The narrow coast highway, the towering mountains, the cool air, and the dense vegetation were all a wonder. I was not there long when I saw some hunters showing off a huge wild boar they had killed. There was not much of a visible year-round population, but there was a population of seasonal workers, many of whom knew one another from one year to the next. The place where my friend's family was staying was better than a labor camp, but it was modest and cramped.

My friend had told me they could find me a job as a busboy. I did not know what one was, but I soon became one. First, I had to have a haircut, shave off my sideburns, and find a bow tie. I had brought a white shirt and black pants, as advised.

My friend's mother took me to an expensive-looking gift shop that had a name like Persephone, where a gracious Black lady took us to her work room and sewed me a tie out of black fabric.

At work, I was told I would have to find some black shoes. I said I would do that as soon as I had a day off and could go to Monterey. The next day, I was thrust into the world of polite dining, where I became aware of my place in the hierarchy of waitresses, waiters, hostesses, busboys, dishwashers, the kitchen boy, and the tyrant of the kitchen, the cook.

The work was almost foreign to me. The guests were polite and friendly and conversational, and I tried to be entertaining as I poured coffee and water, delivered desserts, and took away the used dishes and utensils. A waiter a few years older than I took me aside and said, "John, I don't want you to take this wrong, but these people don't come in here to talk to you. They come in to enjoy their meal." I had not worked in such a disciplined setting, and I strove to be more reserved.

I was also not used to being ordered around by waitresses, hostesses, a manager, and anyone else above me. The cook was the worst. He was about fifty-five or sixty, with combed-back white hair that still had some tints of red, and a thin mustache that I associated with the wartime generation and old movies. He made sure we understood that we ate at the employees' table and from the employees' menu, offered by the kitchen boy, Gary, who walked with a limp and had an apologetic smile.

Employees could have sherbet, not ice cream. In a place where food was so abundant, I made the mistake of serving myself a cylindrical scoop. The cook, whose name was Harry, descended upon me.

"Who told you you could have sherbert?" He pronounced it as everyone did.

I said, "No one told me I couldn't."

"Who do you think you are?"

I shrugged, thinking to myself, *To hell with it*. I said, "I won't eat it, then." I tossed it in the trash barrel.

That touched him off. He berated me for wasting food, and I left my lunch break early and went back to work.

Most if not all of the other seasonal employees at the Big Sur Inn lived in a kind of dormitory or barracks, and I was an outsider. I did not realize how breezy or cheeky I came off to others. I had met a couple of other employees who were not refined, but they were dishwashers and did not interact with the public, and I imagine they knew how to steer clear of the cook.

On my first day off, I did not yet have enough to buy a pair of black shoes, but I felt free to hitchhike to Santa Cruz. I invited my friend's fifteen-year-old sister to go along, and her parents gave her permission. On the boardwalk, I saw someone I knew, a long-haired Asian fellow named Allan, who was a friend of my intellectual friend in Paradise. He played in a band. I said hello and introduced Margie, who, I guess, was taking in her own perceptions of the summer of 1967.

We made it back to Big Sur without incident.

———

On my next time off, I had two days, so I decided to hitchhike to Chico to check on my mail at General Delivery and to take a glance at my car. My friend's parents told me how to get into the house without a key and told me I could stay overnight.

In Chico, I discovered that my car was gone. I went to the police station, where I learned that the car had been towed away. It had a flat tire and thus appeared to be abandoned.

With the help of my other friend who lived in Chico, I found the towing yard, which was an adjunct to a wrecking yard. The Plymouth was secured behind a cyclone fence, and the towing and storage bill was more than the car was worth and more than I had. I asked the fellow on duty if I could take some things from the back seat, and he said I could take a couple of things but not all. So I salvaged the cast-iron skillets and had to leave the box of butcher equipment. I felt guilty and disappointed, but there was not much I could do against a system that towed and impounded cars. I had not done anything wrong, but I had left a car on the street, and I had to take the loss.

I spent the night in the large house and hitchhiked to Big Sur the next day.

———

I had not yet made enough money to spare for a pair of black shoes, and I had not been inclined to acquire them by some other means, as I was trying to stay out of trouble, when the manager called me into his office. I stood while he sat at his desk.

"John, we're letting you go."

I nodded. I felt that I had made concessions and had tried but had not fit into this unfamiliar environment.

"Because of your hair, your dress, and your attitude."

I felt my spirit sink. Some of his criticism was justified, but I had cut my hair and shaved my sideburns, and I had worn a bowtie and white shirt and black pants. I thought he might have been looking for more reasons and cited my appearance. As for the attitude, I knew I had not conformed well enough, but I also thought I had the cook to thank for some of the manager's assessment.

———

I did what I knew how to do. I went back to Orland, rented a small trailer at Shady Oaks on the highway north of town, and looked for work. I fetched my bicycle, so I could ride into town. On one hot afternoon, a woman stopped me on the street and asked me if I would help lift a camper onto a pickup. I said I would but I had to go home and put on some shoes. I was in my Bohemian attire, in the spirit of that summer, wearing a T-shirt, cut-offs, and no shoes. I cycled out to the trailer park, put on some shoes, and met the group at the designated address. The lady paid me five dollars.

———

With no work at the moment, I hitchhiked down to Berkeley, where my intellectual friend was taking summer classes in Near Eastern languages, one of his many inspired ideas and false starts. His girlfriend, from our humanities class, was working as a waitress and paying her own way in her own apartment, and I thought she might have been paying some of his expenses, as I had not known him to work.

We went to a concert at the Fillmore Auditorium, where we saw Mike Bloomfield and the Electric Flag, the Steve Miller Blues Band, and someone else.

Back at my trailer, my ears echoed for two nights as I went to sleep.

———

I had a hard time making my rent money, and one of the proprietors at the trailer park took my swamp cooler when I was gone. I did not appreciate the gesture, so I moved my few things into town, where Tommie's mother had a couple of unoccupied rooms. I stayed in the room of Tommie's brother who was in the Army, and I helped their mother, who was a bit ungainly with weight, to scrub the kitchen walls and paint them.

I had inquired around for work, and some came my way. Harry, the almond grower, needed someone to hoe weeds around the trees in one orchard. He said he had gone out to see what the work was worth, and he had hoed twenty-one trees in an hour. A worker like myself should be able to hoe twenty an hour, and his wage for that kind of work was $1.60, so he could offer me the work at eight cents a tree. I took it.

He picked me up in the morning and took me into town in the evening, smiling as always. He was efficient but not stingy, and he knew that things were not always easy for me.

Some of the trees had dense patches of weeds and took ten or fifteen minutes, while others took three or four minutes. When I was doing well, I was making $1.40 to $1.60 per hour, but I saw a stretch of lighter weeds ahead.

At that point, Walt came back. He had calluses on his hands. He said he had been stationed in the Bay Area and had been scrubbing ships to be painted the well-known battleship grey, and now he was on leave. He was going to marry Tommie and become a father to her little boy.

Tommie's mother had told me some of this, but I still had to digest it. Walt's brother Robert and my brother Bob had been crazy about Tommie but to no avail. When Sandy came home from boot camp a couple of years earlier, he told me he had sex with Tommie. I don't think he told Bob, because Bob had been jealous of Sandy's flirtation with Tommie the year before. Now, Tommie had hooked up with someone else and was going to marry Walt.

He said he needed work, and he asked me if I could help him out. I checked with Harry to be sure, and I invited Walt to share my contracted hoeing job. He helped me take advantage of all the easier, better-paying work, and he went off to where he and Tommie were staying.

———

I was on the lookout for my next job when a large, light-blue Rambler Ambassador with a white roof pulled up in front of Tommie's mother's house. Bob and David were in the back seat, and I soon became reacquainted with Uncle Chuck and Aunt Anne.

Bob and David had written to me and had told me that things had not worked out at all with Suzi. As they told it, she was an obsessed disciplinarian with her children and tried some of the same methods with them. They had gone from her house in Vista to Chuck and Anne's in Escondido. Now the four of them had come north to take care of custody matters at the courthouse. They had visited Grandpa. They invited me to ride back to Southern California with them. Uncle Chuck would even have some work for me.

Leaving my bicycle and a few items with Tommie's mother, I went off to spend some time with my brothers.

———

Uncle Chuck was a building superintendent for a contractor who built homes for clients and on speculation. At the end of a job, there were always several details and pick-up tasks to tend to, so I spent a few days cleaning up concrete rubble, picking up lumber scraps, and moving dirt.

When I tipped the wheelbarrow up and it got away from me, flopping into the hole where I was pouring the dirt, Chuck said, "I can see you've never used a wheelbarrow before."

The old farm worker rose up in me. "I have used one before," I said. "I just haven't moved dirt this way."

Chuck and Anne were hospitable. They lived in a comfortable home in a subdivision. Their daughter Kathy, who was my age, was shiny and smiling, while their daughter Barbara, a year behind David in school, was also pleasant but more reserved. The two older daughters, Dixie Jean and Maryanne, were out of the house and married. I made Barbara a necklace out of watermelon seeds, perhaps to prove that I had been to Berkeley and Haight Ashbury.

Chuck took Bob, David, and me to the Navy base to visit Sandy. As a daring little adventure in itself, I stayed overnight in the barracks, wore dungarees, and went to mid-rats (midnight rations) to eat military fare. The next day, a pal of Sandy's gave me a ride to Escondido in his Dodge Charger, turning up the volume as Bill Cosby sang his song about the little old man, in which everything was all right, up tight, and out of sight.

Time came for me to go north. I assured Chuck and Anne I could hitchhike. I insisted. Anne drove me to the freeway on-ramp in Oceanside, kissed me on the cheek, and gave me ten dollars. In an admonishing tone, she told me to be careful, and I said I would.

Undaunted, I hitchhiked the seven hundred miles back to Orland.

I rented a room on Cherry Street in Chico, in a court of rooms with kitchenettes. The place was set up for working men, with public bathrooms in the middle between the two rows of rooms. My rent was twenty-eight dollars a month.

Walt came to stay with me for a few days. He told me that he had not really been scrubbing decks in the shipyard. He had gone AWOL and had gotten the calluses by digging holes to inspect telephone poles. Now he was doing some small odd job and was going to go back to Tommie.

I wondered why he hadn't told me the truth to begin with, but I didn't worry about it for long. He moved on, and I enrolled in fall classes at Chico State.

I found a job washing dishes at a restaurant on the old highway on the north side of town, where I would sit on the back step in my free moments and think about how nice it was to work outside. Later on in the evening, a grubby man came in to exchange barrels for scraps to feed his hogs. The woman who ran the kitchen, Vera, told me I could have anything I wanted to eat except steak. That was all right with me. This was more my kind of kitchen work, even if it entailed vacuuming the dining area at night and cleaning the restrooms.

———

The summer of 1967 had not been good for self-discipline, and I had not saved any money. I had stayed out of trouble, but I did not feel that I had a clear direction as I went to my classes. I had a Shakespeare class that I enjoyed, but the others were nondescript.

———

About two weeks into the semester, on a Saturday, I returned to my room after a day of work, and I found a suitcase and a note. I recognized my brother Sandy's handwriting. The note said he would be back. A friend had left a bicycle at my place, and it was gone.

After a while, Sandy returned, riding the bicycle into my room and spilling over. He had had a few beers.

When things settled down, he told me he was AWOL from the Navy. He had been thrown in jail in Tijuana for being drunk and urinating in the street in back of the bar, typical behavior of sailors. When he returned to the base, he was cited for being absent without leave. He thought it was unfair, and if he was going to be charged with being AWOL, he would do it. So he packed his bag and hitchhiked up to see me. He was twenty years old but had an extra I.D. of Magoo's, so he could pass as someone else and go into bars, which he had done. We stayed up and talked into the night.

On Monday, I dropped out of school. I had not started the semester with good motivation, and it sounded like good adventure to knock around with my brother for a while. I also decided to keep a journal. I had written a few times a week for a couple of months as part of my English classwork the semester before, and I thought I might record some interesting experiences. I had read a few modern novels such as Pynchon's *The Crying of Lot 49*, Vonnegut's *The Sirens of Titan*, and Burgess's *A Clockwork Orange*, plus a more pedestrian but risqué work by Erskine Caldwell entitled *Tragic Ground*, so I had a borrowed sense of style to go along with my more traditional readings from the last year or so.

We picked up a little bit of work in Chico and Orland, as there was still some almond knocking, and olive picking had begun. We were referred to a job in Live Oak, so we hitchhiked down there, slept in a cold field under a blanket, and rented a room the next day. Our work, which lasted a few days, was called vine seed harvest. It was new to me. It consisted of picking up overripe melons, putting them into plastic five-gallon buckets, and dumping the contents into a machine that had a large cylindrical screen. The machine separated the seeds from the pulp. "Vine seed harvest" seemed like an elevated term for work in which a person crawled along and had his hands caked with juice and dirt, but I learned that the same process was used for cucumbers, which also grew on vines.

We worked with a mixed crew containing a couple of older Black men and a few younger Mexicans. Our boss was an informal contractor named Luis García. We finished one field and had to wait a couple of hours for Luis, which I thought was an inconsiderate waste of our time. But he showed up, nonchalant and smiling, with a twelve-pack of Olympia in cans. I did not drink, and the two older Black men did not partake, but I saw how well beer placated some people.

We soon saw that we would have to keep moving to stay employed, so we left our room in Live Oak. I gave up my room in Chico and stored my things with friends. We took along good shirts and neckties as well as outdoor work clothes. A day's hitchhiking took us to Modesto, where we found a cheap hotel room. The atmosphere was relaxed all the way. It seemed that wherever we went and every car we got into, The Stone Poneys were singing "Different Drum."

We visited our father, who was now staying in a government housing camp near Modesto. Carmen's sister Tencha was living in an adjacent fiberglass hut and taking care of the kids. Our father had two cars, so he lent us a 1960 Ford station wagon.

Our first job took us to the bell pepper fields, for more stoop labor. We picked peppers and stayed in sleeping quarters that were not rooms but cubicles made of plywood partitioning in a barn. The sleeping areas had two levels of bunk beds made of construction-grade lumber, and there were no ceilings.

Sandy and I were lodged in an area with three other Anglos, older than we were. As the four of them drank and played cards, I launched into an imitation of an evangelical preacher, which, out of context, offended someone in a nearby cubicle. My chastisement came back across the rafters of the barn.

After a couple of days of bell peppers, we picked tomatoes

at thirty-five cents a box for the same contractor. Together, Sandy and I picked seventy-five boxes one day and sixty-seven another. The boss moved us from picking to stacking full boxes onto trucks.

During this time, the other three men were telling us stories of making more money in other places like Alaska, Texas, and Bakersfield. They said they could find work in the oil fields for a couple of good workers like us and make five times the money we were making here.

Early in our acquaintances with these fellows, we went to a service station together. They had a 1960 Cadillac, sea-blue with a pale white top, with Florida plates. It belonged to Paul, the oldest of the three, who was about fifty, bald, and paunchy. He did not dress or look as if he had done much physical work. He also had a small white poodle.

The next fellow, in his mid-thirties, was large and burly with reddish-blond hair and one eye that did not track with the other. He gave his name as Julius. At the service station, he proposed to fill our tank on his credit card, and we could give him the money. It was all the same to us, so we went along with it. As he was paying with his card, he told the attendant to put the Cadillac's license number on both credit card purchases so that his wife wouldn't think he was f-ing around somewhere.

When he had his wallet out, he said, "You wanna see what I caught my wife doin' when I came home from work early the other day?" He pulled out a photo and showed it to the attendant, who smiled and laughed. He showed the same picture to my father when he met him, but he had less reason to distract my father. He liked to talk. He told us how he would "trow a chot" into his friend's wife, Patty, and how he did not appreciate Paul's comment that he was the only person Paul knew who could shoot pool with one eye and watch the bar T.V. with the other.

The third man, Jim, was a few years younger than the

bruiser. He had an average build, straight brown hair, shifty brown eyes, a prominent nose, and a quiet demeanor.

When Sandy and I had enough money to hit the road, our father said we could take the station wagon and pay him four hundred dollars later. So we were all set to travel with our new pals to Bakersfield.

We rented two rooms at the Tower Motel for seven dollars a week per person. By now, Sandy and I had learned that Julius's real name was George, while Julius (with a Greek last name I had seen on the card) was someone in Florida. We also learned that George and Jim were brothers, which they seemed to be, in spite of their outward differences.

Sandy held his own at gin rummy with Paul and at arm wrestling with George, but those fellows were in another league at hustling. Paul was a pool shark. George and Jim could shoot a good stick, but Paul could do anything he wanted. One routine they had was to go into a bar but not together, pretend to meet over a game of pool, let George win, have George lose to the next patron who had a quarter on the table, and let Paul come back to take the new patron to the cleaners. George might make money on side bets in the meanwhile.

We found a bar named Guthrie's, about a mile and a half away. (Both it and the Tower Motel were still in business fifty-five years later when I looked them up online.) No one checked our I.D.'s, and Sandy was right in his element with our three companions. I tried to remain inconspicuous. A middle-aged, well-dressed Hispanic patron named Sal, who was shooting pool, offered to buy me a drink. I accepted and had my first alcoholic drink in a bar, a whiskey and Seven-Up.

I didn't care for the carousing, so I went back to the motel. The others went from one bar to another, and at some point, Paul stranded the others. They came back to the motel and routed me to drive the station wagon so they could look for Paul. George took Paul's poodle along, and he had the dog riding on the window ledge. He told me to cut the car one way and the other, so I did. At first I thought he wanted to let the dog fall out, but then I found out he was holding onto it. I didn't know what he was up to, but in another moment, I had something else to worry about as a red light appeared in the mirror. The cop wrote me up for exhibition of speed, which was a very punitive charge for young hot-rodders. I was just a malleable kid in a station wagon, but now I had a ticket that was going to be expensive.

We went back to the motel, and after a while, Paul showed up. George began ragging on him for leaving him in a bar and making a fool of him. Paul was drunk and made a sullen comment to the effect that it wasn't any big deal. George punched him. Paul drew into himself, and it was evident that he knew better than to hit back. Later, George would say to us, "That was a pretty good chot I gave him, wasn't it?" At the moment, however, the tension suppressed the comedy.

The next day was Sunday. We were able to cook in our rooms, so I fixed some noodles and salad. After a gallon of wine and some card playing, the others went out to look for opportunities in the bars. I went to sleep.

The next morning, I learned that Sandy and George had brought a middle-aged woman to the motel. If they did anything, it was in the other room. As Sandy told the story afterward, George took her pocketbook and left her in a doorway uptown.

George had scored about forty dollars in cash, nine traveler's cheques for twenty dollars each, a checkbook, and a Master Charge Card. He gave Paul the traveler's cheques to cash, and he gave Sandy and me the checkbook and the credit card. He told us to go out and see what we could do with them. By now it was Monday, and the stores were open. We left at about the same time that Paul did, around noon.

I had never used a checkbook or a credit card, and Sandy did not know much about them, either. The first thing we tried was to buy clothes in a department store, where the manager took the checkbook from us and told us not to get into trouble like that.

Next, we went to a music store. I had been to one in Chico with my intellectual friend and his girlfriend. We had gone into a listening room and had heard Judy Collins sing "Suzanne," a very memorable aesthetic experience that I wrote about in my journal that semester. On this day, a young Black girl took a record into one of the listening booths, put it on, and danced and gyrated in silence but in full view beyond the plate-glass door. I picked out four Rolling Stones albums and paid for them with the credit card.

With a little confidence now, I went into a clothing store. Sandy waited across the street in the car. I picked out a pair of Levi's and a pair of rough-out Wellington boots, but when I gave the card to the old lady at the counter, she glanced at the card and gave me a suspicious look. I had signed in the music store as if I were the woman's son, and I was ready to do so again. The woman asked me for some I.D., and I said it was back at the hotel and I would go get it. I turned to walk away and thought I should try to get the card back. I returned to the counter and said, "Now that I think of it, my mother wouldn't want me to buy the boots." But the woman was already on the phone.

I walked out of the store at a fast pace, and instead of walking across the street to the car, I turned left. I was wearing a red wool overshirt, and I took it off and bunched it in my hands. I kept walking fast. I looked back, and I saw two Black kids following me. I took off running, crossed the street, and paused for a second as Sandy came up in the station wagon, reached over, and opened the door so that it swung out toward me. I jumped in, and we took off. I looked back and saw the two boys in the middle of the street. I did not know if they had caught our license plate number.

We drove south out of town about thirty miles to a place named Mettler, where we called the Tower Motel. George said

Paul had not come back yet. We gave a brief explanation of our difficulty and decided to return to the motel.

Not long after we arrived, Paul made his appearance. He had been out all afternoon and into the evening, and he was wearing a white western straw hat. He was drunk but proud that he had cashed every damn one of those traveler's cheques, by God, every damn one of 'em, and he had most of the money.

George said that was fine, but these kids had some trouble.

Paul opened his eyes and said, what was that?

We gave our explanation, and a brief discussion followed. We all agreed that we needed to leave Bakersfield, even though we had our rent paid for a week and had not looked for any work in the oil fields.

We drove our two cars south to Mettler, where we checked into a two-story motel with a restaurant and a good parking lot.

———

The next morning, Paul was gone. He had taken his poodle and his Cadillac, his proceeds from the traveler's cheques, and most of George and Jim's clothes. He had also gotten into the station wagon and had taken all of the good shirts and sweaters that Sandy and I had on hangers.

Now we were stuck with the two grifters, and we needed to move along. We looked for oil work in Fillmore and Piru but found none, so we drove on down to Long Beach.

We found a kind of flophouse or tenement in which people rented rooms in the same old house. We paid a week's rent and checked out a few bars.

The next day, George and I went to the offices of an oil company down by the harbor. It was a clean place with nice office furniture. George introduced me as his nephew, and the man nodded as he looked us over. He said we would have to fill out an employment application, complete with references and phone numbers. George said sure, and we took two applications with us.

Back at the car, George said there was no way he was going to fill out that paperwork. He never had to do that for a rough-necking job. I suspected that the references were a sticking point. He and Sandy and Jim had drunk up most of our money the night before, so they went out to sell blood.

We were at odds about what to do next. We had met and chatted with some of the other lodgers in the tenement, and it seemed as if we were in a low-class place. Opportunities for work did not seem to be abundant.

By now it was late afternoon, and a complaint came forward. Jim had made unwelcome advances on one of the women living there. Whatever he had done, it was enough for her to threaten to call the police. In those days, such an offense would have been more than inappropriate touching; it would have been something more like attempted rape. We had to leave.

George and Jim and Sandy were all for leaving the state and going as far away as New York. George still had his credit card for gasoline. They might look for Paul in Ohio on the way, as that was where he was from.

I was fed up. By my count, it was the fifth time in a month that I had moved out before the rent was up. I was tired of hearing that there was better work somewhere else. And I was not fond of these two men who on a good day could be called criminal-prone.

I called my intellectual friend in Chico to get my bearings, and I decided to go north while the others went east. I made a deal with Sandy that I would pay the old man the four hundred dollars for the Ford station wagon in return for the money that Sandy had lent me earlier in the year. He could have the car.

We drove out of Long Beach to Interstate 5, then north to the place where Interstate 5 and Interstate 10 crossed. The first chapter of my new journal ends with these words:

I bid farewell to Jim and George Novak and took leave of my illustrious brother Sandy. He gave me a $1 bill, one of the $4 he got for a malenky pint of blood. His hand was too swollen to shake. Fighting back tears and a lump in my throat, as when I write these words, I said, "So long, keep in touch," and grabbed the green, $2.98 duffle bag, 3/4 full, and walked the ten yards from Interstate 10 to Interstate 5. The horde of cars approached me on Interstate 5 at 5:45 p.m., the Ford took off, and I put out my thumb.

FIFTEEN

My third ride out of L.A. was with a fellow about fifty who drove a dull-green International Scout. He stopped at a restaurant off the freeway and offered to buy me something to eat. I ordered a cheeseburger. After the meal, he asked me if I wanted to drive, and I said I would.

As I drove up into the mountains north of Los Angeles, he stretched one way and another in the seat, saying he wanted to catch some sleep.

His voice was rough. He said, "There's not much room in here for a long-legged son of a bitch like me."

I paid attention to my driving, going up the grade in the dark. After a while, I became aware of his head touching the side of my upper leg. He shifted in his seat and pushed his head farther. I moved away, nudged with my elbow, put my hand on the floor shift, and tried to push him with my forearm.

This maneuvering and fending off lasted for a few miles until he had his head up onto my right thigh, and I was digging at him with my elbow.

He sat up, and in his coarse voice, he said, "Next wide spot in the road, pull over."

I gripped the steering wheel. I didn't know what he might do to me out on this mountain highway in the dark.

My voice had a quaver. "Just don't do anything to me."

"Look here," he said, "I don't do anything to anyone."

I pulled over, yanked my duffle bag out of the area behind the seats, and took off. The engine gunned, and the headlights moved. I thought he might try to run me down, so I kept a lookout as I clutched my bag and ran.

The Scout pulled out onto the highway and drove away.

———

A couple of years later, when I was hitchhiking through the San Fernando area where this driver had picked me up, I wandered over to a street vendor to buy a sandwich. As the fellow made change out of the coin dispenser on his waist, I thought he resembled the would-be opportunist. I wasn't sure. It was daylight, time had passed, and I was taken by surprise by the coincidence. He went on to another customer and made a crass comment about a woman walking down the street. His voice and his tone made me think it was the same guy. I wondered if an International Scout was parked somewhere near. I walked to the freeway on-ramp and continued on my way.

———

I trudged on in the dark along the mountain highway. Now and then a car went by. I came to a turnout at the crest of a hill, and I saw a truck pulled off in front of a café.

I ran the rest of the way up the hill, lugging my duffle bag. The truck driver was out checking his tires and lights, as I thought all good truck drivers were supposed to do.

"Can I get a ride with you?" I asked, catching my breath.

"Where you headed?"

"Chico. Up above Sacramento." I did not have my usual repose. "I had a ride," I blurted out. "But the guy got forward with me, so I made him let me out. I thought he was gonna run me over."

"Just put your bag in the cab here," he said. "I'm going in for some coffee, and then we'll go. Come on in."

I asked him where he was going, and he said Manteca.

Inside, as I calmed down, I noticed a few details. He was an average truck driver, self-assured and a bit paunchy, maybe in his late thirties. The waitress was the kind I had seen in truck stops. She poured coffee, asked him how far he was headed this evening, brandished her bosom. I imagine she was his age or a little younger. They knew each other by name.

He looked at the menu and asked me if I'd like a hamburger or something.

"No thanks," I said. "My friend bought me a cheeseburger a ways back."

He laughed. He said to the waitress, "Junior here got picked up by a real friendly guy."

She smiled at me, not in a motherly way, but in an older woman way. I smiled into my coffee and felt stupid. He ordered pie.

There was a little world shared between the truck driver and the waitress, like a bubble that I sat on the outside of, brooding. He ate his pie and made small talk with her as she leaned against the coffee machine and smoked a cigarette. Earlier in the day, her full body might have sparked a fire in me, but now I was cooled. They were grownups, and I was Junior.

I was not as tough as I thought an hour earlier.

When the truck driver had finished his pie, paid for our order, and made his parting sally to the waitress, he gestured to me and said, "Come on, Junior." My little crisis had passed.

———

The truck driver took me more than two hundred fifty miles to Manteca, fourth in the sequence of Madera, Merced, Modesto, and Manteca, all Spanish names. The fruit tramps said, "Mann-teeka." In Spanish, *manteca* is lard. As I walked out into the cold early morning, I was glad to be far away from L.A. and Bakersfield.

I kept going north, through Sacramento and on to Chico. I had two ideas. I was going to work, and I was going to go back to school.

In Chico, I retrieved my belongings from my amoral pals who lifted things like crystal decanters, and I moved into an apartment with a friend of my intellectual friend. He had been sharing an apartment with a pal but now had it to himself. He was a couple of years older than I was, very bright, cheerful, and a bit indolent. My intellectual friend and I made jokes about him being a sensualist, as he smoked an occasional cigarette, drank a little now and then, smoked a join to indulge his Byronic sorrows, and had various girlfriends. He was one of a wide group of Chico State students consisting of literature majors, aspiring writers, budding existentialists, aesthetes, cynics, and free spirits. His name was Mike. He was from the San Fernando Valley, where he grew up in a two-parent household and worked on vacations in a stamp-and-coin store.

He and our intellectual friend and I planned to share the apartment during the coming semester. In the meanwhile, I had it for a base as I looked for work.

I did not find work in the Chico area, so I hitchhiked down to the Modesto area where my father was staying, in Westley. I helped him move to another government housing location in Vernalis, not far from Tracy and closer to his current work.

Through a friend of his, I went to work for a few days in the cauliflower fields. I rode back and forth with the friend, speaking Spanish. At work, he went to the crew that cut and loaded the cauliflower, while I went to the crew that tied the heads while they were still on the stalk.

Tying cauliflower was clumsy work. I wore rubber boots, yellow rubber pants, and a yellow raincoat with a hood. The weather was foggy and clammy, the ground was soggy, and all the huge-leafed foliage had beads and runnels of water. At each plant that had a large enough head of cauliflower, I was to draw a length of burlap or jute twine from a sash at my waist, encircle the leaves with my arms, and tie the leaves at the top. The other crew would come next to cut the head from the stalk, trim the leaves across the top, and toss the heads up to the truck.

I was with a crew of about fifteen Mexican men. I thought I might amuse myself by not letting on that I knew Spanish, so I just slogged along, drenching myself as I embraced and tied leaves. Once in a while, I would straighten my back, take a breather, and look around to smile like a dunce at my fellow workers.

Before long, they started making fun of me, as I thought they would. One of them said something like, "Hey, is that guy your brother-in-law?" This good-natured insult in Spanish implies that the fool referred to is married to the sister of the person being addressed. The witty response goes something like, "Yes, he's my brother-in-law because I've been screwing his sister. But isn't he married to your sister?"

This sort of banter went on all day, and it took me some effort not to laugh or otherwise show any awareness of what they were up to.

Sometimes they called out to me in Spanish. "Hey, dipshit, how did you get to look so stupid?"

They would say to one another:

"Did you ever see such a stupid-looking fool?"

"Are you sure he isn't your brother-in-law?"

"He looks like he might be your brother."

Their line of humor lasted through the first day and into the second day, when we finished the field in the middle of the afternoon. We had to sit around and wait awhile for the boss to pay us, and my father's friend came to join us. He did not know of the little game I was playing, so he started speaking to me in Spanish. I rattled back, acting as if nothing had happened in the past day and a half. My fellow workers looked at one another, wide-eyed and, I hoped, mortified. I gave no indication of triumph or ill will or any emotion at all. It seemed like the best way to get the last laugh, and I had not felt any malice on their part, just a bit of crude humor to get through the day at a crummy job.

With a little money in my pocket, I hitchhiked to Escondido. Bob was doing well in school, having received an award in Industrial Arts, and he was back on track to graduate after a dubious junior year in Orland. David was not as happy in his new environment. I imagined he missed Grandpa. He told me he didn't like to have to try to prove himself. But he was getting along, and I encouraged him to try his best. Among other things, I urged him to practice Spanish and learn verb conjugations. He said, yeah, yeah, with not much enthusiasm.

Bob drove me up to Los Angeles for a day, with the purpose of my obtaining application forms for financial aid and admission to UCLA. I felt that I needed a more motivating academic atmosphere, and my aesthete friends (the intellectual and the hedonist) and I had formed the fanciful idea of going to UCLA, enrolling in the film studies program, and becoming writers.

I stayed in Escondido long enough to enjoy Thanksgiving and to see *To Sir, With Love*. My aunt and uncle's house was full with my two brothers and my two female cousins, and I could see that I was upsetting the balance, so I went back to the north.

The superintendent at Mills Orchards had told me to come back after Thanksgiving, which was the time when orange season began. I went there, was hired, and moved into the bunkhouse where Sandy had stayed, in the same large company-owned community where my father and his family had stayed. I had an explicit sense, as I recorded it in my journal, of wanting to settle down, pay my debts, go to school, and take on responsibility.

I began by pruning trees. The row boss was a Hispanic man I knew from before, a company man who had grown up at Mills Orchards, who lived in company housing, who shaved every day, and who wore clean clothes. One of my coworkers was a galoot named Chester, a garrulous fellow with decayed teeth, a puffed-out chest, and a thermos bottle on his belt. He asked me if he had seen me before. I said yes. He asked if I had ever picked oranges. I said, "Yes, you ran over my ladder one time."

Life in the bunkhouse gave me material to ponder. One fellow moved in with nothing but the clothes he was wearing. I gave him a towel. Most of the men were middle-aged. In my journal, I wrote, "I recognize some of them from years past, and I recognize all of them as the types I've seen all my life in all the fields and skid rows and highways and labor offices and bars and restaurants and cabins that I've been at...I see traces of my father in most of them. I guess I'm at the same elevation on the up side of the curve as they are on the down side." I sensed a defeated spirit in many of them. "They just give up. I swear I won't. If I do, I hope I still have this to read."

I earned $1.50 per hour at pruning trees and 16¢ a bag at picking oranges. On many days, I made more than $20 at picking, and I got back into shape after loafing around on the road. During this time, I read *The Sirens of Titan* again, a notable contrast with the run of conversation in the bunkhouse.

After two weeks at Mills Orchards, I drew my pay and

went back to Chico. I worked off and on in a pool hall, where the proprietor, a Lebanese fellow named Frank, paid me with sandwiches, coffee, time on a pool table, and an occasional dollar or two. I brushed tables, washed the pinball machines and the jukebox, vacuumed the carpet, emptied the garbage, swept the sidewalk, cleaned the windows and the glass doors, and even washed the aprons of Frank and his wife, Judy.

———

By this time, Grandpa had been released from the rest home and was living in a one-bedroom apartment in Orland. I had visited him through the summer and the fall, sometimes once a week, so I had kept up with his progress. Now he had a prosthetic lower leg, a much-reduced girth, and a clear mind. He had a telephone to order groceries.

I stayed with him for more than a week, picking up brush and pruning trees for my old employer Harry, who picked me up in the morning and left me off in the evening.

David came on the bus to visit Grandpa, and the two of them went to spend Christmas with our father. I finished my work with Harry and hitchhiked down to join the family. At a layover in the seedy Modesto bus depot, I read *Cat's Cradle*, by Vonnegut, another nice contrast with my surroundings.

David was to take the bus back to Escondido on his return ticket, and Grandpa was going to stay a little while with our father, so David and I hitchhiked to San Francisco and took the bus to Orland. We had a hundred laughs on the streets in San Francisco.

Back in Chico, I pruned almond trees for an eccentric farmer and did more of my sporadic work at the pool hall. I read Kerouac's *On the Road*, which seemed imperative. I was not back in school yet, so I yielded to invitations to visit members of my mother's family, beginning with Chuck and Anne and my brothers, on to my grandmother, aunt, and uncle in Lompoc, and then to my Uncle Jim's place in Sacramento. I had met him the year before when Suzi still lived in Sacramento and Bob and I had gone down during spring break. He had told me his version of hoeing beans for my father, all in good humor. On this current visit, he gave me a few hours' work at running a roto-hammer to take out a bulge in a concrete basement wall. My ears rang for a while.

Meanwhile, my grandmother had given me two hundred dollars to help with my college expenses, which I appreciated very much.

———

In Chico again, I was ready to go to school, even though I was not excited about my classes. I had applied to UCLA, and I needed to complete the current semester. I told myself I had to stick with it and not run like George and Jim and Paul. I had heard from my brother Sandy, who had been picked up in Wheeling, West Virginia, along with George and Jim. Sandy had wrecked the Ford after the three of them left a bar, and now he was in a Navy restriction barracks. The last he had seen of George and Jim, they were still in jail, worried about whether anything would come up on their background check.

Many times I have looked back upon that episode with the criminals and the streets of Bakersfield as a turning point in my life, with the crossroads of Interstate 10 and Interstate 5 as a poetic correlative. During the time that I returned to Chico, I was working my way through needs and demands of each day, so I did not have that larger awareness. But I was trying to look ahead as I also had to look over my shoulder.

I knew that I had set out to get a college education and so I had to do it. I knew that I wanted to have a career based on my education, that I wanted to have stability in my life and to be able to work and live in one place for as long as I chose.

I also knew, as I resumed my life in the college town in the farm country, that I had been on the verge of serious crime and was old enough to go to prison. The attempted credit card fraud in itself was enough to ruin my career as an educator, and if those boys in the street had gotten the license plate number of the station wagon, and if anyone collated it with the license number on the traffic violation, I could be implicated not only with the credit card but with whatever may have happened to the woman.

My change in thinking did not take place all in one day, or even in a semester, but little by little, I went from not wanting to be in trouble to developing broader, more mature ideas of why that kind of behavior was wrong. For the present, I was starting over by returning to school and working when I could. And I was done with crime. I had no interest in any of it.

Mindful of working toward a degree, I enrolled in psychology, cultural geography, U.S. history, biology, survey of British literature, and historical and aesthetic development of film. My classes were not inspiring, and although I had the motivation to succeed and not fail, I struggled with self-discipline. My roommates and I spent a great deal of time playing cards, shooting pool, and listening to music. We stayed up late. I slept through classes. I had a constant sense of what I should be doing, but I often did not have the fortitude to do it. And so I felt guilty. I was also broke most of the time, but I was used to that.

The casual academic atmosphere did not keep me up to the mark, either. On days when I did go to class, I would find class canceled, or the professor just didn't show up. Exams were postponed. More than once, I went to a professor's office to make up an exam or assignment, and the professor did not make it for the appointment. I knew that many students were diligent and did their work all along, but I had not learned to set standards for myself and to make my own challenges.

On the other hand, my experience would prove to be valuable. It would help me understand my own students, years later, when they drifted in seas of low motivation and a low power to act against the large, impersonal forces that seemed to press in on all sides.

———

I worked for a short while at a drive-in called Sno-White's, which specialized in hamburgers and ice cream but also produced donuts in the morning. One of my duties was to clean the greasy donut area with lime, which gave me a blister on my fingertip. I went to the student health center, which had a reputation for mediocre treatment. When I complained about the pain, the doctor who jabbed my finger told me I could do it myself the next time.

———

At the theater, I saw a movie called *Elvira Madigan*. It became an interesting addition to better-known movies I saw in the films class, such as *Orphans of the Storm*, *The Big Sleep*, *Duel in the Sun*, and *On the Waterfront*, as well as *Un Chien Andalou*. All of these were more enlightening than movies I had seen at the Orland theater after a Friday shift at Sprouse-Reitz, such as *Ten Little Indians* and *Castle of Blood*, or on a rare occasion, *A Shot in the Dark*. Even *Doctor Strangelove*, which we had seen at the drive-in in Chico at that time, was more thought-provoking than movies that came through Orland.

———

One day in early spring, I hitchhiked to Orland to see Grandpa. On my way back, I had a ride for a while on the back of a farmer's tractor. After that, I walked along the highway and passed a stack of hay bales that had new green grass growing out of the top. That afternoon remained with me as a moment of time in a simple past that would recede but always live.

I went to Escondido for Easter Break. Suzi took me to my mother's grave, the only time I was ever there.

Sandy had been released from the Navy on an undesirable discharge and was working at the service station where Bob worked.

On the way back, I stopped in Lompoc to visit my mother's family. I met a cousin of my mother, Sylvia, who had been a good friend. She told me of letters my mother had written from the cold, distant ranch in Oregon.

With farm work coming up, I bought a 1952 Chevrolet with 93,360 miles—quite a bit of mileage for a car of that vintage. I saw it advertised in the paper for $65 and bought it for $60, as the man selling it admitted that it used a little oil. It also had worn tires, so I had to change a few flats and buy used tires for replacement.

I went to work for Harry on weekends, shoveling levees, or borders, for irrigation in his almond orchards. I slept in the back seat of my car at a turnout along the highway, not far from where my father and I drove past Sandy when he was hitchhiking.

In Chico, at the house of some girls who were somewhat hip and had played "White Rabbit" every time I went there in the fall, I heard a band called Big Brother and the Holding Company. I had heard them during the summer, booming on the radio with "Blind Man."

Pioneer Week came to Chico State. I went to an outdoor concert with Big Brother, making it just in time to hear their opening song, "Down on Me," and to see Janis Joplin, who was said to have drunk a bottle of Southern Comfort on stage.

My friend from Orland who had shared the party house with us the year before was in a band with his older brother. The first year, they called themselves the Lords, Ltd., wore matching outfits, and did songs by all the British groups. Now they called themselves Cranberry Frost, dressed like hippies, and played songs like "Purple Haze," a throbbing version of "Mona," and an updated version of "Wabash Cannonball."

A week later, I heard a group called Olduvai Groove.

Two weeks later, as I was finishing a workout at the gym, I heard Eddy Arnold rehearsing for his concert that evening. Chico State had a little of both worlds.

———

I crossed paths with Sandy's old pal Avery, who said he was getting ready to go to college. He coaxed me into agreeing to take the ACT for him, but when I was left to myself, I pulled together my principles and had my roommate leave a message to say I wouldn't do it.

———

About a month after visiting my mother's grave and meeting Sylvia, I dreamed about my mother. It was the only time I could recall that I ever dreamed of her, and in my dream, she was a good mother who cared about me.

———

I made it through the end of the semester and passed all my classes. I wished I had done better, but at least I was not failing myself in my plan to get back into school and to go straight.

My immediate plan was to work about a week for Harry and to drive my Chevy south to be near my brothers and to work for the summer. On my first day of this sequence with Harry, which was the new Memorial Day falling on a Thursday, we were delivering hay in Corning when my hay hook slipped as I was pulling a bale out of the middle of the load. I cut my right index finger close to the knuckle, severing muscle, a nerve, and a blood vessel. A doctor named McGee stitched me up.

———

With my hand in a bandage, I drove south, picking up hitchhikers all along the way. I made it in time for Bob's graduation.

I was talking him into going to Santa Monica City College and had stopped there on my through the L.A. area. Now we took a day to drive up to UCLA and the city college. We drove along Highway 1, just to see it, and stopped for coffee at a truck stop in Long Beach. At our table, I selected a song on the jukebox called "Folsom Prison Blues" by Johnny Cash. We had not heard it before. I said to Bob, "That one's going to be a hit."

———

I worked the summer in Escondido. My uncle Chuck obliged me to cut my hair and sideburns so that I could work for him. I nailed two-inch roof decking by hand, getting a terrible sunburn on my ears and neck as I learned to drive sixteen-penny nails. I did a variety of other jobs for him.

I also found work at the employment office. I did yard renovation. David and I picked potatoes into small bags for nine cents a bag. I worked for a few weeks on a hay lot, stacking bales and delivering bales and cubes.

My main job in the second part of the summer was with Paxton Masonry, where I made good money (three dollars an hour) and learned about the hierarchy and bullying in the construction world. A bricklayer from Texas, who had stayed in San Diego County after his service in the Marine Corps, berated me for not having learned anything in college, for not cutting the re-bar with precision, for not stacking the block far enough from the wall under construction, and for any other fault he could find. A bricklayer of Italian descent, proficient with the "f" word, also chewed me out. The head laborer bossed me around, and even Mr. Paxton himself came down to pick on me at my job level. But I learned to mix mortar and cement, operate a big wheelbarrow, shovel mortar up onto a scaffold, strike the joints between courses of block, brush away crumbs of mortar with a wire brush, look out for my knuckles, and not stick my hand in any of the wet mix.

On weekends, I washed dishes at a truck stop. One of my fellow laborers on the masonry crew said, "Man, you must really want the money." I said I needed it. I didn't tell him the details, but I sent a money order every week to my hedonist roommate, paying him for past living expenses. When we met in the fall at UCLA, he told me that his mother and his friends at work said I would never pay him, and he was happy to tell him that I did. It gave me a decent feeling about myself as well.

———

At the end of the summer, I sold my smoking 1952 Chevrolet for $35. A good friend from Orland who now lived in the L.A. area helped me move my clothes and books to Los Angeles. I rented a room at the Pico Motel, in a Black section of town, for $22.50 per week. I was now in the city.

SIXTEEN

Less than a year earlier, when I had stood at the intersection of Interstate 5 and Interstate 10 and had said goodbye to my brother Sandy and our two criminal companions, I was making a conscious decision to try to get away from the low life and to go back to school. Now, not many miles away, on a hill in West Los Angeles, in the presence of Royce Hall, the majestic brick building with non-identical towers, where I would have many classes, I was getting my life on track.

It was not easy. For many more years, I would struggle with self-discipline, romantic relationships, and my place in the world. But I was on track. Education was my salvation. My three years at UCLA added to the preparation I had accumulated all along, and they helped me develop a moral sense that had been incomplete. Course by course, term by term, in my readings, in the class discussions, in conversations with fellow students, and in the examples of my educators in languages and literature, I became aware of and considered ideas about ethics, morality, integrity, social responsibility, and consideration of others—concerns larger than just my own survival. What had been missing in my life earlier, which was offered to many people through family or church or social groups and may have been offered to me but not recognized, came to me in this period of my education.

Again, it did not happen all at once. Not long after I arrived at UCLA, I felt out of place. I did not like the impersonality of the city and of the campus. I was not homesick as many students are, for I did not have a home. But I had a place, and that was the country. I was living proof of a saying I had not yet heard, that you can take the boy from the country, but you can't take the country from the boy.

I was renting an apartment with my Chico State roommate from the San Fernando area. Our intellectual friend had married and was attending Westmont College, a small Christian school near Santa Barbara. I derived the idea that I wanted to transfer to UC Santa Barbara, a more bucolic place. I went to confer with a financial aid advisor, who talked sense into me. We spoke Spanish for sociability, but he told me in plain English that I had a good financial aid package at UCLA, was in a good program, and should take advantage and stick with it. I found myself capable of taking advice.

I took French classes almost every term I was there. I knew that I would need more than Spanish for a graduate degree, and I had wanted to learn French for a while. These courses were good for me as a student as well, because they required me to study and prepare every day. Moreover, the quarter system started up fast and kept a brisk pace, unlike the casual semester system at Chico.

I took a chemistry course the first quarter, and I applied myself well. I misread the instructions on the final exam, however, and I received a final grade of C, the only C on my transcript at UCLA. It was a good lesson to share with my own students in later years.

In the second quarter, I took survey of British literature

with Walter Anderson, who would become my mentor. I also took a great course in Greek literature in translation. From then on, I was a real student, meeting the challenges in a higher-level system.

In the third quarter, I rented a room with kitchen privileges from an eccentric elementary school teacher named Estelle. I settled into my studies even better, with no roommates and no influences. I had quit watching television in high school, hearing all the comedies from the living room where Grandpa had the set turned up loud. Now I read Restoration plays and Victorian novels, and practiced French, with no interruption except Estelle's cats.

Between the first and second quarter, David and I were walking into a restaurant when we saw a newspaper telling that John Steinbeck had died. David and I had both read Steinbeck in high school, and I would read him many times more. He wrote about the world we grew up in. My valedictorian friend, encouraging me to pursue my ambitions, told me, in a generous moment, that I could be another Steinbeck. I did not want to be someone else, but Steinbeck was an inspiration.

Bob stayed with Mike and me for a while during the second quarter, trying out classes at Santa Monica City College and working at night jobs, but he went back to Escondido to spend time with a girl he had met.

On a sunny afternoon in the spring quarter, after I had toured the arboretum and had written in my journal, I sat on a bench on Westwood Boulevard to wait for a bus to take me to the part of West L.A. where I lived at Estelle's. As I sat there, I saw a woman approaching. Time seemed to stand still in the quiet way of dreams or *déjà vu* as I noticed the dark glasses, the white cane, the dark purple jacket and skirt, and the proper posture of a person with her head lifted and her mouth set. I was quite sure it was Miss Gurrola, the Spanish teacher during my first two years in Orland. I never had an idea that she had anything to do with Los Angeles, and so my seeing her had the disorienting effect that it did. I was reluctant to speak. I watched her as she stood nearby, opened her purse, and reached inside, perhaps for her bus pass. I saw her checkbook with her name stamped on the cover: *Vera Gurrola*.

Now that I was sure, I introduced myself. She remembered me, my brother Sandy, my father, my stepmother, and some of the faculty at Orland High. She said she was doing well, had been teaching for the L.A. city schools, and sometimes took classes at UCLA herself. Then in a moment my bus arrived, I said goodbye, and our meeting ended. I thought I would see her again, but L.A. was a big city, and I did not.

More than fifty years later, as I wrote up a reminiscence of this meeting for my blog, I had the good fortune of finding a paragraph in my journal on Friday, May 2, 1969, the day I saw her at the bus stop.

As I looked up a few details online, I found out that at that time, Miss Gurrola lived not too far away from where I saw her that day. I discovered that she had gone to high school in the L.A. area, in Sun Valley, which is in the San Fernando Valley, not far from Hollywood. She graduated from John H. Francis Polytechnic High School with the class of 1949, she attended UCLA on a scholarship, and she graduated in 1953 with a bachelor's degree in Spanish. It occurred to me that I might have sat in some of the same classrooms.

Also in my research, I found a photograph of two students in a beauty class in Hollywood in 1946. One is sitting in a chair, touching a mannequin head. The other is standing, working on the hair of the student sitting. The one standing has dark glasses and long, dark hair, and she is smiling. Her name is Vera Gurrola. The caption tells that the other student is Miss Helen Lopez, and both students have been blind for two and a half years. It was very touching to see her again in that photo.

———

On Memorial Day weekend, Sandy, Bob, David, and I took a barnstorming trip to Orland, where we had a family portrait taken, the only one of its kind in our family, with the four of us brothers, our father, our grandfather, Carmen, the two little girls (Carmen and Irene), and the dachshund. We went in Bob's red Chevy convertible, which had a wolf whistle. "Bad Moon Rising" played on the radio. On the way north, David and I bought hats in a general store in Dunnigan, next to Bill and Kathy's. When we stopped in Woodland on the return trip, our old friend Robert came skulking out of the little shack at the service station.

———

David graduated from high school in June. Later that summer, he and I were about to take a trip north in a 1950 Chevrolet I had bought, and the engine blew up. We had a hilarious hitch-hiking trip, singing "Harper Valley PTA" and "A Boy Named Sue" at freeway on-ramps where longhairs beat tambourines, asked, "What's happenin'?" and answered, "Jesus."

———

Bob married Dianne at the end of the summer. David enrolled at UC Santa Barbara. Sandy was stocking sheetrock, making good money, and spending it in the bars. He was on his way to become the best fighter, shuffleboard player, and poker player (and not bad at pool) in the bars in Escondido.

———

I spent the next school year at Estelle's, taking more French and literature courses. In the middle of the year, I had a breakthrough. Up until then, I had received B's on my literature papers, and I did not know why. I had amassed enough graded papers at my new school that I was able to set them out together and compare the comments. From that application, I formed an understanding of what a real thesis or main idea was and how it should govern an essay. It was one of those things that professors did not dwell upon; they nodded and said they assumed we had learned it, and we nodded in return. I had even had to take the composition course I was exempted from at Chico, and I had missed it there. Now I had it.

———

Bunche Hall, at twelve stories, was the tallest building on campus at the time. It had an observation deck on top, where a person could see quite a bit of the L.A. basin on a clear day and quite a bit of smog on a regular day. One afternoon, I stood in the elevator in Bunche Hall and was joined by Lew Alcindor, later Kareem Abdul-Jabbar. He was polite and modest, as he has always been known to be.

———

Bob and I had put another engine in my 1950 Chevy, so I spent weekends going up to UCSB for a lark with David or picking him up at the bus station in Santa Monica. In one of my stays at UCSB, I left my car unlocked, and someone took my black western hat that I had bought on the barnstorming trip. All our lives, we had left our cars unlocked, and now, in a place inhabited by people better off than I was, someone had stolen from me.

During my stay at Estelle's, she told me a story about a friend with whom she played tennis and exchanged intellectual ideas. He was enrolled in the graduate program in Near Eastern Studies, preparing for a possible career in diplomacy. He was office assistant to his major professor, and he took it upon himself to request a new parking sticker, with the explanation that the professor had bought a new car. Parking was very expensive on the UCLA campus, with multi-level parking structures. A few months later, the professor did buy a new car, and she requested the new parking sticker herself. The student was called in and was told that he was going only as far as a master's, wasn't he? It was left to be assumed that anywhere else he went, people would check his references where he had studied and had a position of trust. This was a good story for me to hear and remember.

Also during my second stay at Estelle's, I went out on walks at night when I had finished studying. I had time and the peace of mind to think about what I hoped to have in the future. I envisioned a teaching position with my own office in a small college where I could live in the country, and it became a recurring thought or image for me as I walked the city streets at night.

Across the quad from Royce Hall sat the majestic Powell Library, where I sat amidst venerable books and did my reading and writing. On the lawn between the two buildings in the spring of 1970, students protested the killings at Kent State. National Guardsmen stood on top of the library, armed, as students on the ground formed the seven-letter insult with their bodies.

My French professor that term, a man who had contracted malaria while serving with France in World War II, stood with patience and dignity while an insolent protestor interrupted our exam and cursed at the instructor.

———

In the summer of 1970, I convinced Bob to move with David and me to the Sacramento Valley, where Grandpa was now living with our father, Carmen, and the girls. Bob and Dianne had a baby girl, Michelle, but they went along with the plan.

In midsummer, Bob and I went to work in the peaches for Monte, whom I remembered from five years earlier. He put us to work driving the tractors that hauled the bin trailers, and when the peaches needed time to ripen, we mowed weeds in a big orchard of young walnut trees.

Bob hurt his shoulder, so David took his place hauling peaches. We met each other on the road as we hauled full bins to the loading area and empties to the orchard. I drove an old, low-slung orchard tractor, a dull red International Harvester that I had to crank in the morning. It puttered all day, louder when I had the throttle open on the bouncy road, as I drove standing up, singing "The Wabash Cannonball."

———

Bob went into an informal auto repair business with Walt, who had visited (along with Tommie) in Escondido. I left my car with them to have a couple of repairs done.

———

I rented a room with kitchen privileges from a woman named Cecile, a community college English instructor who happened to live on the same street as Estelle but a couple of miles closer to campus. I resumed my studies. We had three-hour final exams, and at the end of the quarter, I took my Milton final and my Shakespeare final back-to-back.

David had stayed in Orland. I arranged for him to use my car, but Bob and Walt had taken it upon themselves to pull the engine (which had come out of a 1956 Chevy) and to put it into the body of a 1957 Chevy that Walt had. They considered it a favor, but I was furious. My beloved 1950 had gone to the junkyard, and the 1957 had a sprung frame that wore tires down in no time. I did without a car and tried to concentrate on my schoolwork.

I was enrolled in a course called The Comic Spirit for a couple of days before I changed my schedule, and I had the privilege of hearing Joseph Heller, the author of *Catch-22*, as the guest speaker. I had not read the book yet, so many of his comments went past me.

Near Royce Hall, a long and wide set of steps named Janss Steps led down the hill toward the west. Guest speakers and free entertainers often appeared there at noontime. I heard things as diverse as the cartoonist Al Capp (expressing his political views) and an edgy band called the Hook. One day, I saw an entertaining group of hip/folk/country musicians. I told David about them. A few months later, I was with him at his girlfriend's house, and a band came on the television. I recognized them. They were called the Nitty Gritty Dirt Band.

I earned my bachelor's degree in English in the spring of 1971. I graduated Magna Cum Laude with Highest Departmental Honors in English, and I was inducted into Phi Beta Kappa. I had chosen UC Davis for my graduate program, so I went north again.

I went to work for Monte in the spring. I was row boss for the peach-thinning crew, who had the job of thinning the small, green peaches so that the ones remaining would grow well. Later, I was the tractor driver and row boss for the peach picking. In between, I hoed weeds, irrigated peaches, mowed weeds in the walnut orchard, and moved sprinklers. David came to work with me.

One day I caught up an irrigation hose in the mower, and I jacked up the heavy mower and tried to pull the hose loose. Another worker and I crawled underneath and tried to cut the hose. As three Mexican workers and my brother looked on, I pulled my head out from beneath the mower just before it fell off the jack. The edge of the deck hit the ground like a guillotine.

———

During our drives to work that summer, we heard a new song by Dolly Parton called "Coat of Many Colors." I knew who she was, as I had heard her sing "Mule Skinner Blues" on the same drive the year before. This new song spoke to me as few songs ever have, and it continues to do so.

———

By now I had a girlfriend. At the end of the summer, we moved to Davis, where I rented a one-bedroom apartment for $135 a month. I had a week before classes began, so I worked at a fruit-drying yard in Winters, and I read *The Great Gatsby* and *The Sun Also Rises*, plus a novel by Faulkner, as preparation for an upcoming class in American fiction.

———

Circumstances compelled me to open a checking account and pay for telephone service. I had an oil company credit card. I was in a new phase of life, in a serious doctoral program.

My girlfriend disclosed that she did not want to live with me forever, so she moved out. My brother David, who had taken a few classes at Butte College near Chico, moved in and enrolled at UC Davis.

We were college pals again. We shared our interests and read each other's papers before we handed them in. He changed his major from Environmental Horticulture to Art History. I talked him into taking French.

———

In the summer, we worked for our Uncle Jim in Sacramento until we had a falling out. David and I moved to an asparagus laborers' shack near the river, and we returned to farm work. We picked peaches in Esparto and worked in the vast tomato fields north of Woodland. He sorted tomatoes on a large harvesting machine, and I drove a Caterpillar pulling a set of huge trailers for the tomatoes to fall into.

Grandpa was in the rest home in Willows, and we went to see him almost every week.

My father was drawing disability and wanted to make money running a card room. He put the business in Carmen's name and mine. I had professional poker chips made up with my initials, and I took out a beer license. The business, south of Orland on the old highway, lasted but a few months. As I wrote in my report the Alcoholic Beverage Commission, I drank the remaining six-pack of my inventory in elegy to the business.

David and I were living in an apartment in Davis in January of 1973. We had been driven into town by the cold, and we did not yet have a telephone. I was teaching one class per term and was enthralled with my new work. One Saturday afternoon while I was reading Thomas DeQuincey in preparation for my class, my cousin Barbara, who happened to be living in Davis with her husband, who was in veterinary school, came by with a phone message. Our grandfather (David's and mine, not hers) had died. He was eighty-five. When David came home, I told him the news from the next room.

It was a very sad time for us, the first death in the family in more than fourteen years. My father had a strange, reserved air about him. I expected him to be broken up and sobbing, but he was on the outs with Carmen and was, I believe, absorbed in his own preoccupations.

Sandy and Bob came to the funeral. They had driven north a few months before, for David's twenty-first birthday. We all pulled ourselves together. Carmen and the little girls joined us on a bleak January day, and a preacher came from town to the cemetery.

Afterwards, my ex-girlfriend told us that LBJ had died that day. It was a Monday. It was also the day of the *Roe v. Wade* decision, but we had no awareness of something like that, so far away.

In the fall of 1973, I met a girl named Laura. She was an English major, and she came from a solid family with a farming background. She was intelligent, athletic, and upbeat. She was a few years younger than I was, which was normal for me because girls and now women my age were often ahead of me in emotional and social maturity. Her family was very civil and cordial, and they treated me with equality, which I will always appreciate.

———

Bob had been on uneasy terms with Dianne for a while, so he came to Davis to stay with David and me. He and David formed a landscaping company, and I worked for them. I dug miles of trench, shoveled mountains of dirt, and wheeled tons and tons of gravel. We rented a house in the country on a few acres with old almond trees and an open area for a garden. I nicknamed the place Radio Ranch, after Gene Autry's base in a hokey matinee series about the Phantom Empire.

———

Student groups at UC Davis put on film series, where for a dollar I enjoyed the Marx Brothers, Humphrey Bogart, and more recent classics such as *Doctor Zhivago* and *The Go-Between*.

Davis was also good for concerts. At the coffee house, we saw Bill Monroe, Doc Watson, Ramblin' Jack Elliott, and many others. In larger halls, we saw entertainers such as John Sebastian and Linda Ronstadt.

I saw and shook the hand of Ernest Tubb in Sacramento, where I also heard Merle Haggard. I saw him in Reno and Lake Tahoe as well. We went to the Detour Inn in North Sacramento and saw Okie Paul Westmoreland of "Detour" fame, whom I had heard on the radio in my childhood. I met his wife, Ola Louise, who showed great friendliness and courtesy to the patrons of their bar.

———

My father had begun to receive warnings about his health as early as 1970 or so. In March of 1972, he and I went to a lawyer in Willows, who advised us to draft a letter in which my father designated me as his heir and as the testamentary guardian of my two younger sisters, Carmen and Irene. My stepmother Carmen became so worn out by his rants that she left him a couple of times. He spent more than a month with David and me in our apartment after our grandfather died. He went back to stay with Carmen, where he camped out on the couch, drank Gallo Port, smoked cigarettes, and hollered.

At Christmas time in 1973, he went to the hospital. I conferred with his doctor, a Korean man who spoke English very well. He explained the test results and said, in polite terms, that if my father quit drinking, he might be able to go home and enjoy six months of family life. I mastered my reaction and nodded.

My father got out of the hospital and went to stay again with Carmen and the girls. He left a few of his belongings with me, at Radio Ranch.

At Easter, he was in the hospital again. I visited him and told him, for the only time that I could recall, that I loved him. I waved at him through the window of his ground-floor room as I walked away.

I called him in the evening on Monday and Tuesday, and on Wednesday night, he died, at the age of fifty-five. I went back to Orland and made the funeral arrangements. He did not want to be buried by the county, so I picked out an inexpensive casket. In consideration for the way he had always treated Bob and David, I insisted on taking on the bill myself. It was $500, a great deal for me at that time. I made an agreement with the mortuary to pay it off at ten dollars a month.

Bob and David came for the funeral. The gathering was very small. I had asked the same minister who had officiated at my grandfather's service a little over a year before, a good man named Reverend Hoppe, to come to the cemetery. I did not know I should have offered him an honorarium. In retrospect, I appreciated his dedication and his repose in the presence of what must have seemed like three godless boys, who, after the brief service, each took a drink from a half-pint of Ten

High, the old man's brand, and put the remainder in his casket.

I helped Carmen file for Social Security, and I assured her that I was ready in my new role to help her do whatever was best for my two sisters. I went through the few belongings my father had left with me, work items that did not fit in Carmen's apartment. The main items in my inheritance were a toolbox and a picking bucket.

Sandy had been on the road and working in places like Pennsylvania and Florida. He came to stay with us at Radio Ranch, and the four of us lived together until David left on the first of his many world travels.

I raised rabbits and goats, and we had famous parties where we barbecued whole pigs.

I was not as efficient a grad student as some of my friends were. I took French courses after I had satisfied my two language requirements. I took creative writing. I did not pick seminars or paper topics that would feed into a dissertation. I had gone to UC Davis to study under Gwendolyn Needham in eighteenth-century literature, but I did not tell her, as I did not want to commit to something and find myself stuck. As it turned out, I took three courses with her, and she retired at the end of my second year.

My general area of study was the history and traditions of fiction. After several courses, I found compatibility with James Woodress, an American literature scholar with a national reputation. With true academic spirit, he agreed to oversee my dissertation on the classic western novel.

———

I made it through my big exams in 1976. I faced the vast wasteland of the dissertation, for which I had not trained myself. The largeness of the project intimidated me. I was still inspired with teaching, and my teaching appointments were renewed for the next year. I hid from my dissertation and focused on teaching and writing.

Laura's father showed me how to shoot a rifle, and I bought a .22 Remington. David and I took the hunter's safety course along with a group of youngsters, and I ventured out to hunt without success.

———

I worked with Bob and David in the summer of 1977, and then I worked with Sandy at hanging sheetrock. I was engaged to be married to Laura, and sheetrocking paid well. For about a month, Sandy and I drove back and forth to Fairfield, west of Davis on Interstate 80. I acquired an inside view of another construction trade, and I learned a little about doing precise work, though I was not good at the trade. My most memorable moment came one day after work when we were crossing the railroad tracks in Davis in Sandy's red Oldsmobile convertible. News came on the radio that Elvis Presley had died.

———

Laura and I were married in September of 1977. Her father, one of the best men I ever knew, was killed in a terrible highway accident on December 7, not long after both of Laura's grandfathers had passed away.

We carried on with our lives. My teaching appointment ran

out, and I worked on my dissertation. Thanks to my education, I did not have to go back to work in the fields or at other manual labor. I found a job as a bilingual math instructor with a government-funded program that helped people improve their work skills. I taught arithmetic with smatterings of algebra, geometry, and trigonometry, along with consumer skills such as how to figure gas mileage, how to compare grocery prices, and how to know the difference in content between a quart and a fifth of whiskey.

In addition to working on my dissertation, I wrote a scholarly article that was accepted for publication and a short story that paid me $250.

I went hunting with Laura's family on some friends' ranch in Mendocino County, which was a great privilege in itself. On one trip, we stopped to fuel up at a Seven-Eleven in Laytonville, and when I walked inside to pay, I saw a copy of *Far West* on the magazine rack with my name and story title on the cover.

Not long after that, though prior to it in publication date, my article on Louis L'Amour appeared in *Western American Literature*, the main journal in my academic area. Both of these achievements took place in the months before my thirtieth birthday.

Under Laura's good influence, I stayed on track. After one term of teaching two sections of basic English for academically underprepared and financially disadvantaged students, as they were called (they were ethnic minorities and poor whites), I worked more on my dissertation.

In the winter when job prospects were grim, I found work with another government-funded agency that improved employment skills. It was in Woodland. This time I was a bilingual outreach worker, helping farm workers with basic math, weights and measures, and some job skills. My brother Bob worked with us for a while, giving classes in tractor driving.

Most of the program participants were Hispanic, but three were from Pakistan. When I learned that one of their languages was Urdu, I tried out a phrase I had learned in the peach orchard. Speaking with good humor to a young fellow of nineteen, I told him not to pick green peaches. He gave me a curious expression and said, "Spanish?" I tried a simpler phrase with an older fellow, offering him a drink of water. He smiled, nodded, and repeated part of it. *"Pani pio.* Drink water."

––––––

I received my first literary award in the spring of 1979, for a modern short story published in *Carolina Quarterly.* I continued to work on my own writing as I did my academic work.

––––––

Toward the end of my time working for the government-funded agency in Woodland, I went home one day to find the front door ajar. Our house had been burglarized. The thieves took the television, the stereo system, a smaller recorder, the toolbox my father had left me, and a couple of power tools. I wondered if one of the culprits might have been a program participant, as there was one fellow who was regarded as shady by some of the others in the program, but we never found out anything. The incident was unsettling, as it gave us a sinister sense of people prowling through our living space. News of the event spread through the program, and in the course of conversation, I asked one of the participants what he would do if something like that happened to him and he found out who did it. He said he would beat the shit out of him. The crime remained strange to me, strange in the sense that it came from a world of experience that I did not know, from an attitude of calloused disregard. Whatever crime I had dabbled in had come at an earlier period in life, before what I might call my awareness, when the wrong was not real to me. It was very real now.

With the help of a loan from my mother-in-law, I flew to Terre Haute, Indiana, in the summer of 1979, for a job interview to teach composition. I thought the town and the campus were dismal, and I winced as I was told that the polluted Wabash River sometimes caught fire. The people there were courteous, and they helped me understand that theirs was an average college that had the current honor of having Larry Bird play basketball for them. I changed flights in Denver on my way home, and I could feel the difference between the Midwest and the West. I felt at home in the West.

I applied for and received an appointment to teach Subject A, or remedial composition, at UC Santa Barbara. In the fall, I returned to the campus where someone had stolen my hat ten years earlier and where I had eaten insipid dorm food with David. I spent one quarter there, driving the four hundred miles and back each week, all as part of building a career.

At the turn of the year, I took a part-time job closer to home at Solano College. I had acquired some community college experience at Yuba College, Woodland Center. Now I was gaining more in an area where I thought I had the best chance of finding full-time work. I taught on campus and at Mare Island Naval Shipyard.

I kept working on my dissertation. I completed it in the spring of 1980. I wished I had finished the project and the Ph.D. program sooner, but I was glad for the larger lessons I learned. I now knew how to set up my own projects, and I knew how to work on a project and complete it rather than keep it at arm's length and avoid it. Many people I knew in the program dropped out along the way, and I knew that if I did, I would be very unhappy with myself. I felt as if I had gone through a long ordeal and had come out complete.

As a reward for myself, I took horseback riding lessons.

———

I had been sending out job applications to colleges in the western states, and I continued to do so. Meanwhile, I had plenty of part-time and limited-term work at home. With my dissertation complete, I was offered a full-time lectureship at UC Davis. I found part-time work at Sacramento State, to the east, and I had more work at Solano College, to the west. I was teaching at all three levels of college at the same time.

At Solano College, I taught one night a week at California Medical Facility in Vacaville, near Fairfield. At that time, it housed Sirhan Sirhan and Charles Manson. They were locked up and far away from my classes, which were attended by robbers, murderers, and committers of crimes I did not learn of. I had classes there for the whole school year, and the experience made a lasting impression. The inmates wore denim, so I was always sure to wear corduroys of brown, tan, or grey so that the officers would let me through. I went in and out through security and heard doors unlock and lock. After a thirty-five minute drive home, in the comfort of my own bungalow and the company of my sweet wife, I often had a whiskey and water and worked on a short story. The inmates who stayed behind bars, and who wrote about their lives in some of their essays, lingered in my thoughts.

For years afterwards, I had dreams in which I was locked up in a similar place, most of the time for a crime I could not remember but that I knew I had committed.

Also for many years, I kept my eye on my pen whenever I lent it to students to put headings on their papers or to sign a sheet for reports or office conferences. When I first went to CMF Vacaville for orientation, among the questions I had for the supervisor was the question of whether someone would steal my pen. The supervisor laughed in his jolting way and said, in his very nasal voice, "If you let 'em."

———

I went to a conference in Stillwater, Oklahoma, to present a paper on Louis L'Amour, and I went to a convention in Dallas, Texas, to look for job opportunities at community colleges. I saw a last-minute posting on a bulletin board for a place called Eastern Wyoming College. I did not have time or any way to look up the institution, and the representative was meeting people without appointments, so I went to his desk.

The person was a fellow about my age who was giving up the position in order to go to the University of Nebraska in Lincoln, to work on a doctorate. He told me a little about the college and how to apply.

———

I was invited to an interview in early May of 1981. I flew to Denver and on to Scottsbluff, Nebraska, where I was met by the dean of instruction and two faculty members. My luggage was delayed, so we went for lunch. One of the faculty members spoke to me in Spanish, and I answered.

After several interviews for teaching and non-teaching jobs in academia, I had the interview that Laura told me I would have, one in which I would not think of all the better answers on the way home.

———

The dean of instruction had told me they were going to interview one other candidate and would let me know in a little more than a week. Back home, I was helping my friend José, a Basque man who had a yard care service, with his monthly statements for his customers when the phone rang. The caller was Guido Smith, the dean of instruction, calling several days sooner than I expected. He said they had reached a decision and would like to invite me to join their faculty. I told him I would have to talk to my wife, but I was sure I would accept.

I felt washed out. José said I was white. The dream of my lifetime had caught me off guard. But it was real.

———

Laura and I bought a 1977 Chevrolet short-box, stepside pickup with 38,000 miles on it. It was black and sporty with big tires and a lift kit, which were not my style, but it was a good deal at $4500, and we knew the owner.

I invited Sandy to go with me on a trip to Wyoming to look for housing, and we invited Manuel, who had just turned twenty-one, to go along. He had been in foster homes when our father was alive, had returned to live with his mother, and had worked with Sandy and Bob. He went with Sandy and me in the black pickup.

———

I had come to rent, but all I could find was houses for sale. Interest rates were at 14¾%, plus more for first-time borrowers. I found a house near the center of town, with two bedrooms on the ground floor and a two-bedroom basement apartment, built in 1920, and all in need of a little work.

I did not know how to buy a house, but I called Laura, and she arranged with her mother to help us with the down payment. Laura was not going to move with me for the first year, as she had finished her master's and had career opportunities in Davis. I had a sense that I was looking at a place where I would live alone. I bought it for $29,000, which was more than my annual salary.

———

Laura and I went to Alaska to visit some grad school friends who had lived there. She was out of sorts the whole time, and my friend asked me what the hell was wrong. I told him that things were not going well. We enjoyed seeing Alaska, though.

———

In spite of our difficulties, Laura was always the best. She helped me drive the black pickup, with a U-Haul trailer, to Wyoming. With the help of my new colleague who spoke Spanish, whom I happened to see on the street, I moved my belongings, including the 1910 oak desk I had bought nine years earlier, into the house. The house was still almost empty. The kitchen stove, which I had spoken for, was gone, and I had to use my Coleman.

Laura stayed long enough to meet a few of my colleagues and their wives at a little welcoming party for me and another new faculty member. It was a step back in time for Laura. The men gathered and talked in the living room, and the women gathered in the kitchen and talked about children.

I took Laura to the airport in Scottsbluff and returned to live in the house alone. As I wrote to a friend, I felt as if I was camped on the edge of the Great Plains.

SEVENTEEN

Torrington, Wyoming, was very much like Orland and Gridley and other towns I had known fifteen to twenty years earlier, right down to the JC Penney store on Main Street. Many of the same crops, including beans, sugar beets, and grain, grew in the valley. Torrington also had the largest livestock sale in Wyoming. In spite of the occasional feeling that I had been sent into exile, I felt at home.

I had declared that I wanted to live in a place where the cows outnumbered the people, and the dean of instruction said Wyoming was likely to be that way for a while longer. A small herd of cattle grazed in a pasture just west of the college. People asked me how I liked it in the West. I said I traveled three days east to get here, and I liked it mighty fine.

Most of my students came from farms, ranches, and small towns, so they were familiar to me even as there was more of a sameness among them than I was used to. Time and again I told people that I had grown up in small towns like Torrington, but some students and coworkers persisted in making comments about my coming from California and the city.

In the fields and in graduate school, I had met a great many people who came from other places and complained about how things were done in California, in contrast with Texas or Ohio or Minnesota. I also had heard from my father that my grandfather did not complain, that he had made his living here and was satisfied with it. I resolved to do the same, to take my new country on its own terms and not to tire people with remarks about how we did things in California. In personal conversations, I referred to my native land as the old country.

At that time in academia, the standard practice was to give a job three years. By then, the employee would form an idea of whether the position was a good one to stay at and whether the administration wanted the employee to stay. Eastern Wyoming College was a very traditional place, behind the times in some ways such as gender equity (the male administrators referred to the secretaries as "the gals") and ethnic diversity (I saw my first all-white basketball game since fifteen years earlier in the small town of Biggs), but humane and welcoming.

The dean of instruction found out that I was interested in hunting, so he bought an antelope permit for the first time in several years and obtained permission for us to hunt on another employee's ranch. I had my antelope at ten minutes after sunrise, and he had his by noon. Later in the fall, he introduced me to some of the local pheasant hunting. I was glad to introduce him to my Brittany Spaniel, Fred, who had come with me from the old country.

———

Sandy came and visited in late September. He traveled on the train and brought a foot locker of tools. He worked on my house while I was at school. We went out and got him an antelope.

———

I received the news I had been dreading, that Laura would not join me. The letter came on my birthday, in December. I did as I had done in various ways in my life, and that was to find stability in my academic environment. When my sprits were lowest, I reminded myself of what I had to be thankful for—a house, a vehicle, and a secure job in a career.

————

I lived in the large house alone. Sometimes I felt guilty about having so much to myself. I wondered if I should share it, but I did not want to deal with a roommate. Without intending to do so, I did share the house. I had more than one tenant in the basement apartment who moved out owing me rent.

————

My sister Carmen visited in the spring. She was about to graduate from high school, and Wyoming offered an adventure. She and Irene had become good athletes and good students. Carmen's best sport was basketball, but in the tryouts, she had better results in volleyball and was offered a scholarship.

————

David came out on the train at the end of the school year. He had made three trips to Europe and was ready to see more of the American West. We traveled and camped in the black pickup on a tour of the Black Hills, Yellowstone, the Tetons, southern Idaho, and the Snake River. In California, he showed me Yosemite. I attended Sandy's wedding on June 12, Suzi's birthday, and drove back to work on my house.

————

Carmen spent one school year at Eastern Wyoming College. During that year, I became friends with Casey Fortune, a hell-raising cowboy from South Dakota who was my advisee but who, on my advice, did not take any classes with me. Irene came out for a visit, and at one party at my house, she and Carmen asked me if Casey was like Bob at that age. I said, pretty close.

———

By the end of my third year, I was ready to move to the country. The school had changed its policy from granting tenure in the third year to granting it in the fifth year. I went to see the dean of instruction. He told me that tenure didn't mean much anyway, as the school could always fire someone out of financial exigency. He said I should make whatever real estate decisions I wanted to.

By then I had a girlfriend, a young woman who worked at the college as a recruiter. After a third summer of working on my house, and a forceful hailstorm that earned me a new roof, I sold the house and bought a parcel of land a few miles out of town. The previous owner had lived there in a double-wide mobile home, so the property had a well, a septic tank, electricity, and phone service. The price was $20,000, which many people considered to be too much for a small acreage, but the existing amenities made it a good deal for me, even though it took all the money I cleared on the house.

My girlfriend arranged to buy a single-wide mobile home. From one realtor, we had heard the term "tour home," which was irresistible. I went to work with my field hoe, clearing Russian thistles from the driveway and the site for the tour home.

My 12.46-acre parcel had a great deal of the original short-grass prairie sod, with sagebrush and prickly pear. Two little trees had survived the unoccupied period. The rest was as bare as the surrounding hills. I was aware of starting new on a piece of ground, my own bit of land in the West. By now I had come to understand that the plains country here was not unlike the area in eastern Oregon where my father and grandfather had the ranch. I felt that in a transferred sort of way, I was regaining some part of my family's loss. I took nothing for granted. I did not think that this was something that was due to me. It was something I worked for, that I was able to work for because of my education.

In my first autumn on the place, 1984, I shot a coyote and had the pelt mounted as a rug for a wall hanging, as a reminder of how original the land was when I came. In the next few years, on my own land, I would hunt whitetail deer, mule deer, geese, pheasants, doves, and cottontail rabbits.

In the spring of 1985, I bought my first horse.

My girlfriend and I had gone with the college outing club to Havasu Canyon, and on the fourteen-mile hike down in and back up, I had become fond of the donkeys I saw. I told a fellow instructor, who was very knowledgeable about hunting, horses, and pack animals, about my interest. He told me I should consider a horse that I could pack with and also ride, a mountain horse. He offered to help me find one in the upcoming horse sales. After looking at many horses one day, when I was about to ask him what he would do, he said, "Fer God's sake, don't ask me what I would do." He had talked to another fellow about a horse that he, my friend had. I asked him about it. He told me it looked like a setup, but it wasn't. He showed me the horse and let me ride it, and we made a deal. I paid $500 for my first horse, Sonny Boy, with the proceeds from a series of talks I gave for the Wyoming Council for the Humanities.

I continued to write in a variety of genres. In 1985, I placed in the Wyoming Writers contest in poetry and in fiction (second place in each), and I began my long association with that organization. I also won second place in the Arizona Author's Association annual contest with an essay about growing up in poverty. I had a review published in *Western American Literature*, an essay on Zane Grey published in the *South Dakota Review*, and an essay on A.B. Guthrie, Jr., and Frederick Manfred published in the *North Dakota Quarterly*.

I felt that I was catching up in life and perhaps getting even in some respects. In the summer of that same year, having bought a used hardcover copy of *David Copperfield*, I sent it to the Orland library, with a letter of explanation about the copy I failed to return in 1966. I received a cordial letter from the librarian, who wrote, "I wish all our delinquent patrons had a conscience like yours." Seen through the telescope of time, that sentence means quite a bit to me.

Our college had a good re-entry program for older returning students, and as my students often wrote about their own lives and circumstances, I began to form an awareness of what it must have been like for my mother at the age of some of my students. I was older than she was at the time of her death, and I saw her as a young mother with several children, then a single mother, and a person with difficulties in managing her life.

In the spring of 1986, with the help of friends and the sustenance of beer, hamburgers, and hot dogs that are requisite for such work parties, I planted over six hundred trees on the property. I acquired them from the soil conservation program, along with plans for planting and maintenance. From that point, I became a planter and caretaker of trees, to go along with my other outdoor interests.

Bob rode back with me from California after Christmas

1986. We drove the black pickup and listened to Merle Haggard all the way. Bob stayed with me in the tour home, and we rode horses. I showed him my office and told him it was the fulfillment of my aspirations many years earlier. In his language, he said, that was pretty—good.

——

One evening as I was driving the black pickup home and turned off the highway by the leafless elms in the moonlight, I realized that I was about the same age as my father was when we lived in Grimes. I thought of how difficult it had been for him to raise us by himself. I was just reaching a point in my life when I thought I could take care of someone other than myself. I had told myself not to be hasty in marrying again, but I had thoughts. I wondered if I should be helping someone raise her children.

——

On winter mornings, diesel fumes hung in the air from the tractor clearing snow as I walked from the parking lot to the building that held my office. Time and again, the odor took me across miles and years to the orange orchards, and I thought about how thankful I was to have a professional job and not have to depend on the weather and endure the elements to make my living.

——

My teaching duties were becoming very heavy. I had five courses every semester, all of them with frequent writing assignments, with a total of more than a hundred students per term. I was worried about burnout. My girlfriend left to pursue a master's degree at Chadron State College, and I lived by myself in the trailer house on the prairie.

I felt that I needed to rejuvenate my career, so I went to speak with the new dean of instruction. The former dean had moved up to be the college president. The new dean considered my proposed ideas and approved of the one that entailed my studying more Spanish and becoming the Spanish instructor at our school.

In my seventh year at Eastern Wyoming College, at the age of thirty-nine, I took a semester off at my own expense and enrolled at the University of Wyoming.

I married for the second time. I had become enamored of a girl much younger than I, but as she had brothers my age and I had sisters her age, our relationship seemed feasible. She had been adopted, her father having been Anglo and her mother a combination of Pima and Papago. We went out for a year before we married in January of 1988, and we had a pleasant semester in a basement apartment in Laramie.

I studied Spanish and taught two sections of English. UW did not inspire me as much as I had hoped, as I found it to be better than Chico State but not up to the level of the UC schools I had known. Nevertheless, I learned a great deal in Spanish.

During spring break, we went to Mexico. We stayed in Nuevo Casas Grandes and came into Ciudad Juárez from the south. I knew where I was, from twenty-five years earlier. I found Mi Ranchito, where we had stayed in 1962. We met indigenous people, begging, and I had the illusion that I was seeing the same people I had seen earlier. It made for a good essay about poverty that later won a small award.

Back in Laramie, I received a call at my office on campus informing me that I had won a Wyoming Arts Council fellowship for four short stories I submitted, two of them based on my experiences in field work. By now I had published quite a few stories, articles, and reviews, and I had placed a few times in the Wyoming Writers contest and in the contest in Arizona. The fellowship raised me a little higher. I thought that no matter what came later, at least at this point in time, someone somewhere believed that I deserved this recognition.

———

One weekend when we went to Torrington, I met the tour home on the highway. It looked much larger. I flagged down the driver, and he told me it had been repossessed. Now I had an obligation to help my ex-girlfriend straighten out her credit, to the chagrin of my present wife.

Back in Torrington for the summer, we lived in a friend's basement apartment. I earned a little on a research grant with the Humanities Council, and I continued working on a novel I had begun in Laramie. I finished the first draft in handwriting on my fortieth birthday.

———

As a Spanish instructor, I had fewer papers to grade, but I spent a great deal of time improving my command of Spanish. I saw that I had never been as proficient in Spanish as I thought I was, and I began to be aware of how much complexity there is to even a simple language like Spanish.

———

We moved into a rented house for several months, and we made plans to build a house. Sandy and Bob, who both worked from one job to the next and did not have stable domestic situations, agreed to come and do the work.

We built the house in the summer and fall of 1989. Sandy and Bob fought, Sandy and my wife fought, and my wife and I fought. In October, she and I went to California for my sister Carmen's wedding, but we still all found time to hunt antelope, deer, and elk. I shot a cow elk in the Snowy Range, and Sandy and Bob and I lifted it into the bed of my black pickup.

———

The differences between my wife and me became more apparent, and we divorced in the summer of 1990. The change left me more submerged in debt than ever. I fell into a hopeless relationship with a woman who was yet to be divorced, and I entered a prolonged period of solitude worse than the one I had spent in town.

———

Also in 1990, my brother David moved to Spain. He had met a woman there in his travels, an Andalusian girl, as she called herself, named Mary Carmen. She had moved to California. They had married and had two children (Elizabeth and Alexander, named after our parents and grandparents), and now they were going to live in Spain.

In the same year, my sister Carmen moved with her husband, Steve, to New Jersey.

———

In the spring of 1991, the time came for the twenty-five-year reunion of the CSF Sealbearers. My distressed personal situation and my heavy teaching load kept me from going. I sent a letter to be read, encouraging students to do their best and to remember where they came from. I felt very poor about missing an event so significant to my education and to that of the new Sealbearers. I made all the class reunions in the summers, and when I went to the reunion that summer, I saw Mr. Penner, the CSF advisor. I apologized for my absence, and he said that was okay. I could go to the fifty-year event.

———

My teaching duties, my writing, and my outdoor work on the ranchito kept me so busy that I deferred for years my desire to go to France. I compromised in 1992 and went to Spain. I had a wonderful visit with David and his family and also with my sister Irene, who had gone to Granada to study and now lived there, close to David. They took me to see many great sights; my favorites were a prehistoric cave and some modern inhabited caves with living spaces built on in front.

———

In one conversation with Irene, I received encouragement to seek a wife in Mexico. For the next three years, I made several trips there—some with groups of my students, and some in a 1983 AMC Eagle that Bob had fixed up for me.

———

The dean of instruction who had become president, and who had inspired employee loyalty for years, retired in 1990. The new president had smiles and laughter until the fall of 1992, when it became known that he did not have the Ph.D. he had claimed. To deflect the issue, he made caustic remarks to a newspaper reporter about the director of the adult re-entry program. Many of us among the faculty and professional staff were appalled and signed a petition of protest. Others were reluctant to express disapproval, and some employees supported the president, saying that he was the boss and it was not their place to criticize. The board of trustees stuck with him and his brazen declaration that he had not lied and that it was all a misunderstanding. I felt that he had betrayed all of us and our mission to uphold academic integrity and to help people become educated. After another year, he went away. Resentment and divisiveness lingered, and I was glad that I was one who had protested and who had helped blow his cover. Out of this episode, I became more aware of political manipulation, having seen it up close, and I had an awakening of civic conscience, of concerning myself with what was best for the majority of people rather than for my own interests.

———

For the first several years in the country, I picked wild plums and chokecherries into regular pails. I had left my picket bucket behind when I moved here. I asked my stepmother if she could find me one or two. She sent me three in a large cardboard box, along with a pair of rusted-up orange clippers. Now I had a real picking bucket to pick chokecherries from bushes I had planted. The sun was hot on the back of my neck, and the straps of the bucket cut into my shoulders. It was as if I was in the old country in earlier days.

———

During my period alone, I took the advice of a literary agent and dared to write a conventional western novel, which had been a guarded ambition of mine since my time at UCLA. After a few rejections, I was almost overwhelmed when I had it accepted at Walker and Company, a hardcover publisher in New York. After more than fifteen years of having short stories, articles, reviews, and poems published, I had a book with my name on the cover. *One-Eyed Cowboy Wild* came out in March of 1994.

This major event was like earning a degree. I don't know how many times I heard someone say, of education, that it was something no one could take away. I often wondered why anyone would want to, but I saw the truth of the cliché. The same was true of having a book published. It added to who I was.

———

The hubbub of interviews and book signings had died down, and I was out of author copies, when I went to Saltillo, Coahuila, to study Spanish in a small private institute. I received a sabbatical for the fall semester but conducted my course of study in the summer. I came home after Labor Day, hugged my horse, and went to work on my second novel.

———

At the end of the year, I went to Chihuahua to meet more in a series of women I had met in the same way my father had met Carmen. Online dating was not yet developed, so I found listings through a magazine ad.

In December of 1994, I met Rocío Pérez, a person with a college education who worked as an auditor for the state of Chihuahua. She had a little boy, Dimitri, who became my son. Rocío and I married in El Paso in July of 1995, and we had our reception in Ciudad Juárez.

———

As I became acquainted with Rocío's family, I told stories about my first trip to Mexico. I told how I had met Pancho Villa's wife. Oh, yes, my new friends told me, that was a place where everyone went. All of the things now were in the Museum of the Revolution, which was only a few blocks away from the house the family had on La Avenida 20 de Noviembre (named for the day of the revolution). So one day I went by myself to see the museum.

It was a large, old-fashioned, two-story building with rooms all looking inward to a courtyard. (I understand from recent reading that it was a house owned by Villa, but I do believe that our visit in 1962 was to a smaller building with fewer items on exhibit, and residents of the city have told me as well that the earlier collection was in her home at a different location.) Not very far in from the entrance sat the Dodge. The bullet holes were on the same side as I remembered them. I remarked to one of the uniformed attendants that I had seen the car many years earlier and that it was a 1919 Dodge. No, said the attendant, it was a 1922. (The general was assassinated in 1923.) I went on, going into one room and another, seeing many different saddles and weapons and uniforms and other artifacts of life from that era.

When I finished my tour of the rooms, I lingered on the ground floor not far from the Dodge, and I saw something I had overlooked when I first went in. It was a room dedicated to Luz Corral, the general's wife. It was made up like living quarters, with a bed and other furniture, clothing, and the like. On the wall hung a picture of the lady in black and white. I did not recognize her. But I felt an affinity with her as I stood there at the doorway with the plexiglass partition keeping me out where I belonged. I think it would be sentimental to say that I felt her spirit, but I felt something, some kind of presence, based on my memory of having met her.

On a second visit, a couple of years later, I visited the museum again. I saw the same things, and I paused again at the doorway to the woman's room. I felt as before a kind of solemnity in the presence of the effects of a person I had met.

My mother-in-law told me that in the times of the revolution, most of that neighborhood, which rises up on the north side of the original city, was a bare hillside where the soldiers camped when they were in town. She told me that in all of the towns and cities, the women and girls fled, went into hiding, whenever the soldiers were on the way. The revolutionaries were well-known for being ruthless, not only with their adversaries but with women.

Others, including my professor in Saltillo, told me, and I have read, that the general himself was merciless with his enemies, had contempt for the gringos he killed, and mocked General John J. Pershing and President Woodrow Wilson.

I have since read that Doña Luz, in her later life, was a great defender and apologist of the general. She also knew that he had many wives, and she was known to raise some of his children by other women. She had to have known how women and girls fled from him and his troops. She had to have known how cruel he was with his enemies, even if she did not hear the story about how he sent back empty American uniforms with the taunting legend, "Here are the husks; send me more tamales."

I have also read a few accounts of other Americans who, like my father and me, visited Mrs. Villa. Their accounts are similar to mine, as they saw the same artifacts and had the same pleasant visit. (They also report that the Dodge was a 1919 model.)

Perhaps it is sentimental of me, as I recall standing by her doorway and thinking about the life of this woman who lived in the shadow of such a notorious and controversial figure, to imagine that she was no fool. But I believe she must have been a realist. She had to have known the bad things and to have made peace with them so that she could live her life with her husband and then by herself from the general's death in 1923 until her own in 1981. I do not think she was just making a living, taking money from American tourists and promulgating the general's fame. She was a polite, modest woman, as so many of the people in her country are, and I believe she met her guests with sincerity and good will. I know that in this one instance, she put her arm around a young American boy and left an imprint on his life.

————

Sandy had been living in Cheyenne with a companion named Vicki after we built the house. He came up for a few years in a row to hunt deer and antelope, and sometimes we met in Cheyenne to hunt elk. On one occasion, he and a friend met me at a service station where I was towing a horse trailer with Sunny Boy. Sandy smiled as if to say, that's John.

By 1994, his work took him to Nebraska and Kansas. His

next move took him to Bozeman, Montana. When Rocío had her immigration papers complete and came with Dimitri to live with me, we were into 1997.

One day I took her to a bookstore in Scottsbluff. I knew my second novel was supposed to come out in paperback reprint, but I had not seen the cover. I knew the HarperCollins logo, however, and I pointed to a book on the rack. This publisher, I said in Spanish. Then I saw that the book was my own *Twin Rivers*.

We went to visit Sandy and Vicki not long after my third novel, *Wild Rose of Ruby Canyon*, came out in 1997, and I did a book signing in Bozeman. Sandy had attended a signing in Cheyenne when my first novel came out, and he was proud on my behalf.

He had also had medical advice in Cheyenne that he should quit drinking. He told me that he tried it for a while and decided he did not want to be someone's patient. In Bozeman, he was working as always, but he had all of his old habits of smoking, drinking, and smoking pot.

In two consecutive years, I was recognized by Wyoming Writers. In 1999, I received an award for dedicated encouragement of other writers, and in 2000, I received the organization's highest honor for dedicated service to the organization. I appreciated this recognition and was glad to be of help to a community beyond my students.

By this time in my years at Eastern Wyoming College, I had developed a more explicit sense of being useful to my students and in more ways than in helping them learn the subject matter, which was still foremost. I became aware of helping them become better students, often in small ways of having them follow specific instructions. To help them become better consumers and citizens, sometimes it was a matter of incorporating details of world history and geography into sample sentences, and sometimes the effort was more direct, as in analyzing logical fallacies.

In my own life, I no longer wrote out a bill of sale for a lesser amount in order to help someone pay less sales tax, and I declined the favor if I was buying a vehicle. I was a functioning member of society, perhaps a late arrival in some ways along the journey.

Rocío did not adjust right away to life in the U.S. We separated a couple of times, and I went to my thirty-five-year class reunion by myself in 2001. To my great surprise, Tommie showed up with her brother, who had been in my class and who had bought the suits overseas. She and I had a good visit. I had not seen her since I had dropped into a bar in Willows a few years earlier to buy some beer to go, and she was waiting on customers. She and I had a good visit at the reunion. She had been married a few times, twice to Walt, and now she was separated from her current husband.

During a period when I lived by myself, I took a course in autobiographical writing and made the effort to correspond people from Colusa, Half Moon Bay, Gridley, and Orland. I also located my one-time stepbrother Fred and was able to find and meet my sister Jackie and her husband. She was living in Woodland, where Sandy's kids were now grown up.

Bob called in January of 2003 and said Sandy was in the hospital. Bob and his girlfriend's son were driving from California. We agreed that I would fly to Billings, and they would take me to Bozeman.

Bob and I went out to buy a computer so that Sandy would have a way to bid jobs and undertake a new phase in business. He came home from the hospital as we were setting up the computer. He showed little interest, and we were dismayed when we heard him crack a beer in the kitchen.

———

Rocío and Dimitri moved back to the ranchito in June. The Western Writers of America convention was in Helena that year, so we stopped in Bozeman on the way up. Sandy was not at home, but we found him at the bar. He looked like hell, with broken marks on his pale face, a swelling abdomen, and thin arms. I felt a great sense of sadness and waste as we went on our way.

On the return trip, we stopped in Bozeman, where we were to have a reunion with Bob and David. We had an outdoor barbecue, complete with beer, and we had several pictures taken. I was sure it was the last time we would all be together, but Sandy acted as if nothing had changed from twenty or thirty years earlier. We told stories, including the one about the streets of Bakersfield.

Bob and David and I met at a bar afterwards to say the things we couldn't say earlier, and I moped in the car the next day as Rocío drove us home through Yellowstone.

———

Sandy hung on longer than we expected. In June of the next year, I drove up to Bozeman (in the 1988 AMC Eagle station wagon that Bob had fixed me up with) and took Sandy to California to see his kids. All the way there and back, he acted as if everything was normal. At one point he said, "It's good of you to give me a ride like this, John." For a long time, I would be put out that he didn't square with me and admit what his life had come to, but in the end I concluded that it was his way of being stoic and not letting his problems weigh on others, even though they did.

––––––

We had a family reunion at Bob's place in Placerville in August. David and his family came from Spain. Grandma Carmen and several members of her family came from Willows. My sisters came with their kids. Chuck and Anne's four daughters showed up. We spoke in oblique references to Sandy, and we called him on the phone. Rocío, Dimitri, and I drove home in a 1997 GMC Sierra pickup that Bob had helped me buy from one of his automotive customers.

––––––

In October, not long after his fifty-seventh birthday, Sandy was in the hospital again. Bob and I were calling each other. Bob knew when I had classes, so he waited until I was out of my eleven o'clock Spanish class to call me and tell me that Sandy had died at a little after ten. The medical attendant said he had died a peaceful death. No funeral was planned. I called Vicki, and she told me how she had kissed him goodbye. He was a good brother. We had a lot of good times together, from our early days up until the many hunting and camping excursions. In a memorial I wrote for him, I observed that he never complained.

––––––

Bob and I had already arranged for him to go hunting. In a snowbound camper in the Snowy Range, where I had camped with Sandy and with Sonny Boy, we drank a bottle of whiskey, for all the good it did us.

Sober, we agreed that we did not know how much more time we would have together, and we needed to take every opportunity. Money was always an obstacle, but I was paying my way out of debt, and I could afford plane fare and a hunting permit for my brother.

———

My black pickup was wearing out. It was on its third engine, a good one, but the cab and front fenders were worn and rusted. When school let out in May of 2005, I drove it to California and left it at Bob's shop. We went to a few salvage yards without luck, and we settled upon a 1974 Chevrolet in Bob's own inventory for our donor. The cab would go onto my pickup, and the rear half would become a box trailer.

Bob brought the pickup and trailer to Wyoming in time for elk season the next year. We took the horses to a place where Dimitri and I had taken them in the summer. We saw no elk, but we had the adventure.

———

I was awarded my second Wyoming Arts Council Fellowship, this time for autobiographical non-fiction, in the fall of 2007.

The next week, Bob came to hunt for the fourth year in a row. Again we went to a place where Dimitri and I had taken the horses in the summer, this time near the North Platte River in the Snowy Range. Bob and I threw smooth rocks to break the ice at the edge of the river, where Dimitri and I had learned the way across. Bob and I rode through the cold water to the wilderness area on the other side. We saw no elk, but again we had the time together.

———

My novel *Raven Springs* was a finalist for the Western Writers of America Spur Award in 2008. Rocío and I had bought the shell of a small house next to her family's farm and ranch headquarters in a small village in the highlands of Chihuahua, and we spent some time working on it.

———

I found myself in the hospital on the opening day of hunting season that year after being thrown from a horse and suffering some serious internal injuries. Rocío was my angel, staying with me at the hospital. I missed two weeks of work and made a slow recovery.

At about the same time, Bob had what was later determined to be a small stroke. Neither of us would have been able to go to the mountains that year.

———

Bob had some legal problems early in 2009, and I helped him with a lawyer. Later that year, I visited him and read him a story I had written about a death in a peach orchard. It was published in a magazine called *Hardboiled*. I said that in reality, nothing that dramatic ever happened in the fields and labor camps, and he said the potential was always there.

In between these events with Bob, my novel *Trouble at the Redstone* won the Spur Award. Rocío, Dimitri, and the poodle went with me to Oklahoma City to receive the award. I was sixty years old, doing well as a writer, and managing my academic career with effort and dedication. I had developed four textbooks or course manuals for use in my own classes, and I had efficient plans for all my courses.

———

In May of 2010, while Rocío's mother was visiting, my great pal Casey Fortune, who had kept me in horses for the past fifteen years, sent me the gift of a large, dark donkey. I called him Pierre and became good friends with him.

In June, I received the Spur Award for my short story "At the End of the Orchard" and for my novel *Stranger in Thunder Basin*. For a short while, I was on top of the small world of western writers.

My good fortune was counterbalanced when a horse threw me. As I did when the dark horse threw me two years earlier, I got back on. This time, the horse threw me again, and I broke my ankle.

While I was hobbling around, Rocío and I bought an empty lot in South Torrington, an unincorporated and sometimes casual neighborhood. My income was better than it had been, thanks to my diligence when new tracks opened up on the salary schedule and to my writing, although my paperback publisher closed the western line a month after I won the Spur in that category.

———

In the spring of 2011, I bought a forty-acre parcel in the northernmost part of our county, near the base of the Rawhide Buttes. Rocío was in Mexico, and Dimitri and I went to look at it. I lost no time in clearing it with her and making an offer. In the summer, Dimitri and I leveled a site for a small building, and I engaged Charlie, a friend and former student with whom I had built a garage on our home property in 2005, to put up a utility building that would serve as a cabin.

On the evening before opening day, I unhooked the wire gate at dusk. I felt wonder, almost magic, at having such a property. It was as if I was adding to what I had reclaimed from the past. Forty-acre parcels are often called ranchettes, and I did not want to think that I had a ranch. But it was and has been a source of great satisfaction to me.

The next morning, I hunted a very nice buck antelope on my property.

————

Rocío and I were married in the church on December 12, 2011, the day of la Virgen de Guadalupe, a most revered figure among the Mexican people.

————

Bob continued to struggle after his legal problems were resolved, and I helped him when he asked. Over a period of time, I convinced him to move to Wyoming. At least he would not have to worry about a place to stay or a place to run his business.

He moved his tools and equipment to our place in November of 2012. We considered options and decided to build on the lot that Rocío and I had bought in South Torrington. We conferred, and Bob drew up a plan for a building where he could live, have his graphics business, and do auto repair.

I helped on weekends and on other time off from school. We hired a series of helpers, but Bob did a large share of the work and oversaw everything. By April, he was moved in.

————

Bob fixed up a flatbed trailer, and we hauled a few round bales of hay from the parcel in the north. The 1997 GMC was showing signs of age, so Bob found me a 1993 GMC with an extended cab, full bed, and five-speed transmission. He put a new engine in it, and we had good wheels to go camping and hunting.

I shot a five-point bull elk in the Snowy Range in October of 2013. Bob did not hunt, but he went with me. He helped me as I skinned the animal on the ground, and he helped a fellow who offered to bring horses. I quartered and trimmed the carcass, and they loaded the packhorses. I told the fellow I would dedicate a book to him, and I did. *Death in Cantera.*

———

The next year, Rocío and I bought another and larger lot in South Torrington. Dimitri and I spent the summer clearing it of chicken coops, pig sties, calf pens, a mobile home and its rotting room addition, and piles and piles of junk. I planted the first of many fruit trees.

———

Bob and Dimitri and I cleared out a basement house on the big lot, and we built a three-car garage where the mobile home (almost a twin of the tour home I had lived in) had stood. This was in 2015.

Bob and I took the horses to a friend's ranch in the Laramie Range south of Douglas. On the owner's advice, we left the horses in the corral and hunted the wind-packed snow dunes on foot. We saw a wondrous herd of about two hundred elk way out of range, crossing a set of bluffs and disappearing into a gorge.

———

I went to Orland for the annual CSF banquet in the spring of 2016. Three of my classmates attended as well. In my brief comments, I told how Mr. Penner had assured me I could come to the fifty-year anniversary, and the time had passed just as people said it did.

———

I often stopped at the shop on the way home from work. One day Bob and I were standing in the sunlight as he smoked a cigarette. I said, "Whichever of us goes first, the other one is going to have a hell of a hard time." He looked square at me and said, "That's for damn sure."

———

Bob was always ready to help me on any project, large or small. He took the lead in mounting the elk horns on a plaque to be hung in the tavern I had in the detached garage. He also rebuilt the frame of a camp trailer, and we mounted a slide-in camper and a utility box on it. We took it to the mountains during elk season and found it worth our effort.

———

In the spring of 2017, Rocío and I bought eighty acres of wheat strips with an agreement with the adjacent large wheat farm to continue farming it on shares. In subsequent years, our parcel would offer us opportunities for antelope and whitetail deer, plus wonderful views of a broad landscape and other wildlife.

———

In the early summer, I went to Llano, Texas, to collaborate with W.C. Jameson on a CD of Western songs. We had worked on the plan off and on for more than ten years. Now we had twelve good songs of which I had written the lyrics, and Jameson had a good working arrangement with a studio. He showed me great hospitality, and we worked well on the songs. *In a Large and Lonesome Land* would be released the next year.

———

In the fall of 2017, Rocío's brother Gus came to stay and to help me work on the properties. He and Bob worked well together and poured the concrete for two utility buildings on the big lot. At the house, they poured concrete for a sixteen-by-sixteen tack and garden shed. The three of us built the building, finishing all but the last touches on Thanksgiving Day. We had a beer or two by the wood-burning stove in my tavern.

The next day, Gus and I took tools to Bob's shop at his graphics business, now in town, and left tools at the lot. Bob was happy and looking forward to moving on to other projects.

The following day, at around noon, I saw Bob's car parked where he lived rather than at his business. It gave me pause. I went home and asked Dimitri to bear me company, as I had a premonition.

Bob had had a stroke. The ambulance came, and he went to the hospital. He was transferred to a hospital in Denver, where we visited him, and then he was transferred to a hospice in Wheat Ridge, in the Denver area.

Rocío and I went to the hospice. My sister Carmen arrived from North Carolina, and Bob's daughter, Michelle, arrived from Washington. David and Irene came on the same plane, having met in Madrid. David's son, Alexander, followed. Jackie and her husband drove from Nevada.

Bob improved, and it looked as if he might be able to go to a nursing home. I spoke with two former students at a care facility in Torrington, and we were making arrangements when Bob took a turn for the worse.

David and Alexander had been staying in Bob's room, sleeping in chairs, for four days until they had to take a flight back to Spain. David said his goodbyes, and he and Alexander left in a taxi. Bob went on his journey while they were on their way to the airport.

It was December 8, 2017. Bob was sixty-seven. He left a void with all of us.

My first song credit came out on a CD by the up-and-coming western artist Carol Markstrom. Micki Fuhrman had collaborated with me to turn my poem "Rangeland Lament" into a song, and she had done a powerful demo. The new release was a significant source of happiness at a time of sorrow.

———

On Memorial Day weekend of 2018, we had a memorial for Bob and a small, belated memorial for Sandy at our place in the country. Carmen, Steve, and their sons came, as did Irene and her husband, Tom; Michelle and her son, Zach; and Jackie and her husband, Dan. We had cookouts, singing, some sadness, and a strengthening of the family spirit. We planted trees for Sandy and Bob.

———

I had passed my thirty-year mark at the college, receiving a grandmotherly candy jar on a wooden base, and I had passed my thirty-five-year mark, receiving a wrist watch (which I did not wear). Each year, I told my young colleague that I was good for three years more, something like the reverse of my three-year plan at the beginning of my time at the college.

I did not want to give up my career. It meant too much to me. It had given me a stable life, a sense of worth, and a position of respect. It had allowed me to fulfill the promises and restore the losses of my childhood. I was still doing my work with efficiency and clarity. I do not remember a day when I wished I did not have to go to work.

On more than one spring morning, when I went out of the house on my way to town, I heard a pheasant rooster beat his wings, and I saw him on my fence brace as he crowed. On sunny days, as my students did their daily writing, I gazed out a window and saw horses grazing where the cows had grazed when I first came. On a winter morning, I saw deer by the service entrance of the fine arts auditorium.

———

In August of 2018, I came back from an overnight stay at the cabin and learned that my sister Suzi had died at some undetermined time in her house, where she lived with her dogs. She was seventy-six years old. I had not seen her for forty years, but I had spoken with her on the phone many times, and I always thought I would see her again.

———

In 2019, I was honored, with a classmate, by the Orland Alumni Association. We were co-alumni of the year. At my presentation, I gave thanks to the states of California and Wyoming and to our great system of public education.

Later that year, I received the Spur Award again, this time for a long poem entitled "Prairie Center," about an area I had come to know through hunting and through the hospitality of great friends who have a ranch there.

———

Between these two honors in 2019, I was saddened by the death of my beloved donkey, Pierre, who had been with me for almost nine years. I had buried two horses on my place, and now I undertook the task of digging another large grave.

———

By now I was thirty-eight years into my time at Eastern Wyoming College. I felt eyes upon me. I hoped to make it to forty, though I still did not want to give it up.

———

Rocío and I were at Casey Fortune's ranch in South Dakota in June of 2020, trading for another in a long series of horses, when I learned that my long-ish story "Leaving the Lariat Trail," about a young man who wants to go straight, had won the Western Fictioneers Peacemaker award for Best Western Short Story. My story "Return to Laurel" was a finalist for the Peacemaker as well as for the Spur.

Later that year, in anticipation of losing my office and all that it meant to me, I began work on an office building on the lot where we had utility buildings and fruit trees. My friend and expert carpenter, Charlie, who had built the garage with my help in 2005, the cabin in 2011, a smaller utility building next to the cabin in 2019, and a bale blind in early 2020, drew up the plans. I helped when I could. Charlie and I did everything but the concrete work, the carpets, and some of the plumbing. He did some very nice work on the wooden doors, the trim, and the bookshelves, plus some closet door handles made of antler.

———

At school, I was receiving hints that it was time. After attrition and loss of revenue during the COVID pandemic, the board and administration offered a small incentive for long-term employees. I had talked to myself about it in journal form for a few years, and I was resolved. I wrote my letter on my birthday and, as I wrote to a friend from graduate school, I signed it with a trembling hand.

I worked for weeks at getting rid of papers and books, but I had an enormous amount to move. My new office needed a few finishing touches, but I had a place to stack the fifty-some boxes.

I did not feel that very many people were sad to see me go

—my two immediate colleagues and perhaps a librarian. I had a checklist and a vacancy date.

I had been in the same office for thirty-six years, the office that had been my dream when I walked the city streets. It represented all that I was indebted to and all that I had achieved. I arranged to have the items on the list signed off and my keys handed in so that I could take one last look, grab my briefcase, and close the door behind me.

I drove out of the parking lot and down the hill with an empty feeling that was going to last for a while. But I had an office where I could land, and I had my place in the country and my comforting wife. By some standards, at least, I had run the game out just right. I had made it to an even forty years, had left on my own terms, and had come out on top.

———

Less than a month later, I learned that my novel *Great Lonesome* had won the Western Fictioneers Peacemaker Award for Best Western Novel. When I received the plaque, I found the phrase very gratifying.

———

It took me a long time to work through Bob's effects. I had sold the graphics business and his vehicles in the first six months, but all the automotive tools and parts, plus tools and materials for several other lines of work, weighed on me. Everything was to go to Michelle, and I felt that I owed it to her and to Bob's hovering spirit to get the most money I could.

I spent sieges in which I went through all his personal papers and all the relics from the many businesses he had had. Carmen and Steve and Irene came to see me in recognition for my giving up my career, and they supported me in the decision to have an auction. I had sold tools here and there, but I had not made much of a dent.

It took me several more months to set up an auction and to organize all the items. In the process of going through Bob's keepsakes, I found the program for the Frontier Days Rodeo we had gone to when we were building the house. At some point around 2004, at Bob's place in California, I had mentioned Lane Frost. Bob said, "The guy they made the movie about? We were there that day." I remembered we had gone to the rodeo, but I had suppressed the bull riding incident, as I did not like to focus on those catastrophes. Bob said, "We went to the bar that night, and we heard he had died." Back home, I checked all of my old receipts and checks, and it looked as if that might have been the day we went. Now I confirmed it. Lane Frost was in the bull riding on that program, July 30, 1989.

The auctioneer was an old bull rider and horseman, and I gave the program to him as a gift from Bob. He accepted it as a treasure.

The sale itself was demoralizing. Items that Bob had worked for all his life went away for a tenth or twentieth of their value. I had to take care of all the leftovers. But my big obligation to my brother came to a close.

Rocío and I went to Chicago to see Dimitri receive his master's degree in urban planning and design. We came down with COVID or something like it, and we recovered as the days grew warmer. My time at the college was now a year in the past.

Charlie and I built another garage at our place so that we could store a tractor or an ATV, machines to help me live in the country as I faced growing older.

Rocío and I sold the shop and business location that Bob

and I built. We bought a tractor, a UTV, and a lot in the small town of Yoder. It had a tour home similar to the other two I had known. It was still livable, so we sold it.

After constant encouragement from David (including a comment that we might not have many more chances to travel together) and many study sessions at my new office, I packed my clothes, a French dictionary, and a magnifying glass. In the first week of April in 2023, Rocío and I went to Spain. Irene and Tom visited for Easter at David's house near Granada. From there, David and I traveled in his car to the north of Spain. Near our friend José's home town in the Basque country, we crossed into France with no border, no signs, no fanfare. A dream of mine for more than fifty years was realized.

We stayed in medieval villages and saw castles and cave dwellings. David had traveled in France over the years, and he was functional in those situations where the people did not jump ahead of us and speak English. In spite of my preparation, I choked up in my first attempts to speak French. Over several days, however, I had a few successful conversations in a bakery, a grocery store, a bookstore, a marketplace, and a couple of restaurants.

At David's house, he showed me many of his projects and his collection of family photos. We spoke of a million things and had as many laughs. When it was time to go, we looked forward to the next trip.

At O'Hare Airport on the way back, I sat next to a family of people from India. The mother was giving a little boy a drink from a bottle of water. By nature, I am reserved with strangers, but I said to the boy, *"Pani pio."* The mother smiled and said,

"Do you speak Urdu?" I told her that many years ago, I had worked with a man from India and had learned a few phrases. I said, "That phrase is pretty universal." "Oh, yes," she said. I felt as if I had vindicated myself on one more small thing from the past.

A little more than three years have passed since I finished my work at the college. I have written five western novels, several short stories, a few novellas, a few poems, and the bulk of this current manuscript. I continue to do court interpreting, which I began in 1995. In warm weather, after doing my work outside, I sit in the shade of the house my brothers and I built, and I enjoy the company of the trees, bushes, and flowers I have planted. In cold weather, I go to the garage where I have my tavern and wood-burning stove, where Bob and I drank our last beer together. I burn wood that I gather by hand, practicing one of many manual chores that I have kept up all along, often with the idea that I never knew when I would have to go back to that kind of work and that I was never too good to do it.

In the past year, I loaded and unloaded several trailer loads of manure by hand, spaded my large garden plot and a few other areas, pulled and mowed massive amounts of weeds, cut firewood, picked many boxes of apples with my picking bucket and a ladder I ordered from Laura's family's business, replaced the gateposts on my horse corral, hunted my deer on foot and processed it, climbed the big ridge in the elk country, and rode my horse. I shovel snow for an hour or two whenever we have a snowfall. I can do just about any work or exercise I ever did, just not as much of it.

I am ready to write another story about a young man going straight or a person trying to do what is right, and I think about where I want to go on my next trip to practice French. I have another donkey, and I would like to take him on a pack trip with my horse.

Rocío, my wife, continues to be my angel. She looks after me, and she supports me and encourages me in everything I do. We speak Spanish on a regular basis, and our home-grown onions, garlic, and red and green chiles contribute to great Mexican food any time we want it.

I drive the 1993 GMC with the engine Bob put into it, and when I need to or want to, I drive the 1977 black Chevrolet with the cab and front clip, as they say in the salvage yards, that Bob put on it. I recall the last time he and I went through a salvage yard, a month or so before his stroke. I said it was just like old times, going back to our youth.

Somewhere in the world of dreams, in an older corrugated metal building that I own (all of the ones we have built are of flat, ribbed metal), is a 1950 Chevrolet that needs a little work. Bob and I will get to it when we can find the time.

In the daylight, the long procession of old cars has receded farther into the past, along with wooden orchard ladders, labor camps, auto courts, and two-dollar hotel rooms.

Many of my friends along the way have fallen by the side— Robert, Walt, the pal who dropped his ladder next to mine in the pear orchard, Tommie, the valedictorian, my friend from graduate school who became a judge in Alaska, a fellow writer with whom I exchanged critiques and cynical humor for twenty-five years, and the two faculty members and the dean of instruction (later president) who met me at the airport in Scottsbluff.

On the bright side, Laura and I have remained friends, writing each other on our birthdays. She lives with her spouse, and she has adopted a young man in Tanzania and has supported him through his education. I still have friends from high school, graduate school, and Eastern Wyoming College, plus a great many friends I have made in the world of writing.

From time to time, at an odd moment, I expect Sandy and Bob to show up in an old pickup or Blazer, each of them smoking a cigarette and drinking a beer, getting out to take a leak in my driveway. But I know I am the only one left who was in the car that day when we saw someone take the "For Rent" sign out of the window.

Sometimes it seems as if most of life is packed up and put away, but sometimes it is all alive as always, a continuum as in God's eye, where my father is always kneeling and squinting against cigarette smoke as he trims stakes for the tomato plants in the garden, where Sandy is always standing in the convertible and throwing a wine bottle at a billboard, where Bob is always raising his head beneath a car hood after getting an engine to run, where David is always drawing a perfect picture of Grandpa, and where I am always waiting for the ice cream to take out to the old Ford station wagon where the four straw hats are stacked.

A LOOK AT
DARK PRAIRIE

In a town where indifference and disbelief cloud the pursuit of justice, one cowboy vows to right their wrongs.

Taking up work at the Little Six Ranch in Winsome, Dunbar finds himself immersed in the dealings of Tut Whipple, a prominent water project developer. What begins as a simple inquiry into stolen beef soon spirals into something far darker with the disappearance of Annie Mora.

As Dunbar delves deeper into the young girl's disappearance, he becomes embroiled in the intricacies of Whipple's schemes and the mystery surrounding a recently constructed dam and reservoir. With each step closer to the truth, he faces off against increasing dangers.

But in a land where ruthless men hold sway, Dunbar welcomes a showdown on the dark prairie.

Second place recipient of the esteemed 2014 Will Rogers Medallion Award for Western fiction, Dark Prairie *is an original tale of intrigue, betrayal, and courage set against the backdrop of a frontier town on the brink of transformation.*

AVAILABLE NOW

ACKNOWLEDGMENTS

Some of the incidents and details in this work may have appeared in different form in essays, personal experience pieces, short stories, novellas, and novels that appeared in my name. Several of those works won awards. I express my thanks to all the editors and judges who recognized my work and gave me encouragement.

I would also like to thank Julie from Colusa and Carla from Gridley, friends who were kind to me in my youth and who helped me recover some information and impressions when I went poking around in the past.

ABOUT THE AUTHOR

John D. Nesbitt is the author of more than forty books, including traditional Westerns, crossover Western mysteries, contemporary Western fiction, retro/noir fiction, nonfiction, and poetry. He has won the Western Writers of America Spur Award four times—twice for paperback novel, once for short story, and once for poem. He has won the Western Fictioneers Peacemaker Award twice—once for novel and once for short story. He has been a finalist for the Spur Award twice, the Peacemaker seven times, and the Will Rogers Medallion Award eight times. He has also received two creative writing fellowships with the Wyoming Arts Council—once for fiction, once for nonfiction—and he has won the fiction award four times with the Wyoming State Historical Society. Recent works include *Summer's Lease* and *Riders of the Skull*. New work is forthcoming with Wolfpack Publishing. Visit his website at www.johndnesbitt.com.

www.ingramcontent.com/pod-product-compliance
Lightning Source LLC
Chambersburg PA
CBHW010856090426
42737CB00020B/3389